A SILOAM WOMAN, HER INFANT ON HER BACK AND PRODUCE ON HER HEAD

THE PEOPLE OF PALESTINE

AN ENLARGED EDITION OF
"THE PEASANTRY OF PALESTINE, LIFE,
MANNERS AND CUSTOMS OF THE VILLAGE"

BY
ELIHU GRANT
PROFESSOR OF BIBLICAL LITERATURE IN HAVERFORD COLLEGE

ILLUSTRATED

Wipf & Stock
PUBLISHERS
Eugene, Oregon

Wipf and Stock Publishers
199 W 8th Ave, Suite 3
Eugene, OR 97401

The People of Palestine
An Enlarged Edition of The Peasantry of Palestine, Life, Manners and Customs of the Village
By Grant, Elihu
ISBN: 1-59752-272-4
Publication date 6/21/2005
Previously published by J. B. Lippincott Company, 1921

TO THE MEMORY OF

HINCKLEY GILBERT MITCHELL

PREFACE TO SECOND EDITION

We thought that Palestine had passed into ancient history, but it has been a centre of modern events. No country in the world has a more continuously interesting and profitable story. Its present population is made of sturdy and able people. Three great religions call it Holy Land. It presents to view three distinct types of human society, the desert nomad who dwells in the tented encampment, the peasant villager who reminds us in so many ways of the people of the Bible, and the more foreign looking and mingled folk of the large cities.

We have picked the village life as most suggestive of the quaint customs of the past. It has been gratifying to have those who know this life best, including villagers themselves, praise the accuracy and sympathy of the descriptions.

The volume has not been compiled from books, but drawn from life. An additional chapter seeks to sum present conditions.

Life has changed even in the East but much remained in Palestine, especially under the Turkish régime, that is suggestive of Bible Times. We trust that we have provided here a cross-section of a most interesting period. We hope for even more, that the reader with dramatic imagination may be able to fill the places and figures of the biblical past with life.

E. G.

Haverford, Pa.,
February 24, 1921.

A few words that are pretty well fixed in popular usage, as Beirut, Jaffa, Jerusalem, etc., are not changed in spelling, but for most Arabic words the following alphabet has been used in transliteration:

—	r	gh	y
b	z	f	a
t	s	ḳ	u
th	sh	k	i
j	ṣ	l	â
ḥ	ḍ	m	û
kh	ṭ	n	î
d	ḍh or ẓ	h	
dh		w	

The use of y final and of ô as aids to pronunciation will be of obvious import. When a foreign word occurs in the book for the first time it is put in italics.

CONTENTS

CHAPTER I

Introductory. Remarks on the country of Western Palestine: historical, topographical and geological; distances, levels, rock composition, hills, valleys, caves, soil, etc. The waters: rivers, lakes, the watershed, the Shephelah, ponds, springs, cisterns, reservoirs and pools. The seasons: wet and dry, the rainfall, sun, drought, the weather according to the months, effect on health and on food supply, harvest. The winds. Flora: trees and flowers. Fauna: wild animals, birds. Scenery: appearance of cities and villages in Palestine. Sites, buildings, gardens, roads, paths, wilderness, agricultural matters, ripening fruit, vineyards, care of the soil, walls, watch-towers, terraces, orchards, olives, figs, pomegranates, etc. Page 11.

CHAPTER II

General characteristics of the population of Palestine. The Bedawîn or nomads. The village and its people. Moslems and Christians: their distribution, their mutual relations. Description of the peasant man and the peasant woman. Page 43.

CHAPTER III

Village Life. Introductory. The tribe: how constituted, its fellowship and significance. The family within the tribe. Importance of a strong family. Marriage in family and tribe: marriage settlement, qualities of a good wife, customs and ceremonies preliminary to marriage, wedding festivities and the celebration. The status of the new wife. An anomalous state of affairs. A disappointed lover. Children: boyhood and girlhood, importance of sons, birth, announcing the newlyborn, naming the child. The midwife, care of babies, attention to children in health and in sickness, clothing, growing up, play, amusements and work, training. Family and personal names. Page 51.

CHAPTER IV

Village Life. The houses of the peasants: structure, arrangement, conveniences, utensils and furnishings. Foods: their preparation and storing, eating customs. Costumes; male attire, female attire. Household industry: division of labor between members, women's work, house, oven, field and wilderness. Health data: poverty and superstition as foes to health, treatment of the sick, common ailments, diseases, hospitals and medical assistance. The dumb and the blind. Treatment of the insane, the leprous. Death, mourning, burial, graves. The cholera and its ravages in Palestine in 1902, attendant evils, famine and quarantines. Page 75.

CHAPTER V

Village Life. Religion. The religious basis of the peasant life. Country shrines venerated by the peasantry, saints, tombs, lamps, ruined churches, mosks, reverence for patriarchs and prophets, sacred trees. Superstitions concerning localities, minor superstitions, hair, doorways, food, evil eye. Prayer of women. Fatalism. Moslem prayer. Neby Mûsâ procession. Ramaḍân, Bairam. Eastern and Western Churches, organization, priesthood. Fasts, feasts, proselyting. The Samaritans and their Passover. Page 110.

CHAPTER VI

Village Life. Business. The Palestine peasant as a worker. Farming the first business of the village. The transition from the life of the nomad to the life of the peasant. Fellaḥîn. Land holdings and titles. Farming rights. Crops and sowing, work animals and their management, care of the standing crops, tares, mists, simultaneous reapings, harvest-time, threshing and cleaning. Grape season, vineyard districts, use of the fruit, raisins, export trade in raisins, care of vineyards, watch-towers in vineyards and orchards. The olive crop and its care. Flocks of sheep and goats, the young, varieties, the shepherd. The wool business and kindred industries, spinning and weaving. Undeveloped agricultural possibilities. The village market, shops, stores, bargaining and trade customs, measures and weights, currency, accounts, money-lending, village crier, the go-between, the shaykhs in business capacity. Transport and travel in the country, roads and vehicles. Stone and building trades, the materials and the tools. Miscellaneous trades, peasants in the city for business or for hire, dealers in antiquities and their ways. Page 130.

CHAPTER VII

Village Life. Social privileges and customs. The elements that contribute to these, kinship, religious association, party traditions, proximity. Predominance of kinship as a factor. The influence of religion as a factor. Diversions of the peasant, conversation and the amenities, calling and calls. Greetings, salutations, colloquial address, business talk and discussion. Guest-house and its uses, coffee-making, food for guests. A roofing-bee. Play, games, celebrations. Hunting. Gipsies. Quarrels as an anti-social and social factor. Revenge, etc. Page 158.

CONTENTS

CHAPTER VIII

Village Life. Intellectual matters. The state of learning, revival, services of the press in the Levant. Education, schools, missionary influence. Languages heard in the country, native and foreign. The peasant's pride in his mother tongue. The Arabic language, its beauty and symmetry, literature, dialects, idioms, colloquialisms, exclamatory remarks, gestures, curses, proverbs. Page 170.

CHAPTER IX

Village life in the concrete. Description of actual villages, Râm Allâh and el-Bîreh. Page 187.

CHAPTER X

Village life in the concrete, continued, with some village environs. Eṭ-Ṭîreh, Khullet el-'Adas, 'Ayn 'Arîk, Kefr Shiyân, 'Ayn Ṣôba, Baytîn, Khurbet el-Moḳâṭîr, Dayr Dîwân, eṭ-Ṭayyibeh, Jifnâ, 'Ayn Sînyâ, Bîr ez-Zayt, 'Âbûd, Mukhmâs. Page 213.

CHAPTER XI

The village in its external relations. Attitude of villagers to the city and city people, now and formerly. Administration of the village from the city. The peasant and the government, taxes, private and official settlement of disputes. Postal service, native and foreign, telegraph. Passage of news and rumor. Travel, hindrances, quarantines, coastwise shipping, railway travel, peasant travel, pilgrimage travel, Russian pilgrims and the peasantry, other European pilgrim parties, tourists, traveling passes, transference of parcels, baggage, money, banking, consular service, the desire of the natives to emigrate. Page 225.

CHAPTER XII

Recent events. Effects of the revolution. Syrians and the World War. Syrian ability. Schools and education. The new administration; certain functions and methods. Archæological interests. The Arabian problem. Arabia and its people, social customs, politics, poets, prophet and religion. Page 242.

ILLUSTRATIONS

PAGE

A Siloam Woman, Her Infant on Her Back and Produce on Her Head .... *Frontispiece*

River Auja of Jaffa 20

Donkey at the Threshing Floor With a Load of Wheat 28

Wild Anemones From Wady El-Kelb 32

A Vineyard at Râm Allâh 36

Râm Allâh Man and a Basket of Olives 38

Stretch of Olive Trees on Road to Ayn Sînyâ 38

A Bedawy House 42

Bedawy Drinking 42

Peasants on Way to Market With Produce 44

Bedawin Horseman 44

Woman's Work 48

Bringing Home the Bridal Trousseau 54

Girls at Play Carrying Headloads of Grass in Imitation of the Women 54

Washing a Child 58

A Swaddled Infant 58

Three Kinds of Houses—Mud, Dry-Stone, Stone-and-Mortar 68

Household Utensils 76

Bread-Making Utensils 82

In a Dooryard. Women Cleaning Wheat 94

On Top of an Oven. Women Sifting Wheat 94

Pottery 114

On the Way to Jerusalem. For the Neby Musa Procession. 126

A Neby Musa Contingent Arriving Within the Jaffa Gate, Jerusalem 126

Farming Implements 130

A Sower 132

Children Gleaning 132

Threshing 140

A Threshing Scene in the Old Pool at Bethel 140

1. Hand Spinning 2. Reeling 3. Straightening Threads For Loom 142

Various Articles Made of Skin: Bottles, Bags, Pouches and Buckets 150

A Market Scene: Peasantry Near David's Tower, Jerusalem 154

ILLUSTRATIONS

Women at thf Spring 164
Fountain at Nazareth 164
A House-Roofing Bee (Et Tayyibeh) 172
A Râm Allâh Matron at Her own door 187
Camel Carrying a Rope Net Filled With Clay Jars 194
Râm Allâh, as Entered by the Sinuous, Walled Lane From the East 194
Little Girls of the Village 196
The Village of Râm Allâh and Outlying Vineyards 204
El-Bireh (From the South) 212
Vineyards and Stone Watch Towers 220
Peasant Plowing 220
Primitive Rug Weaving (Bedawin) 230
Straw Mat and Basket Making: Jifna Woman 230

The PEASANTRY of
PALESTINE

CHAPTER I

INTRODUCTORY. THE COUNTRY OF WESTERN PALESTINE. GENERAL FEATURES

THIS little book will make no attempt to tell all that could be said of its subject, but we hope that its selection of things to tell will be gratifying to you. Our wish is that not many of its pages may be condemned as dry, but that most of them may have interest and refreshment. If sometime when you are tired you can sit down and be pleased with some of these pages, here or there, you will know a little of how the trudging peasant of the village feels as, going over hill after hill, from each top he gazes off towards the west and sees the evening mists thickening and looking like good, cool mountains in the sea. It is pleasant to see the face of the native light up as he catches sight of the clouds heavy with blessings of moisture. Perhaps fierce sirocco days have followed one another for some time, longer than usual. Such days are usually looked for in trios at least, but often they hold for a longer time. Their peculiarly enervating heat is very trying, and when they have passed one welcomes eagerly an evening that brings the heavy mist. This announces that the succession of hot days is broken and that some days of respite are coming. The welcome moisture blesses the vineyards, the fig orchards, the tomatoes, squashes and melons, and it is sure to bring out ejaculations of blessing from the fervent peasant, praising the Father of all, whose favoring mercy he feels.

Look out on a morning early and you will see the mists[1] scudding, drifting, veiling and dissevering like masses of gauze, like streamers of truant hair. Perhaps some near mountain may be cut off from the little hill half-way down by a moat filled with billowing fog. Soon the sun cuts it and scatters it away and the hot, dry day sets in. The roads and rocks are powdered with lime dust, the somber morning tones on the hills are touched with whitening brightness. Here and there is the dusty gray of an olive-orchard or the bright green of vineyards. Overhead, the brightest blue is set with one yellow gem of fire that creeps up and up until noon, and then the toiling peasantry, who have watched this timepiece of the heavens, sit down in the nearest shade to eat their food and chat. That done, they roll over for the luxury of a nap and forget a hot, dry hour in a healthy doze. The click of the chisel in the quarry ceases, the hoe is cast aside, the driver is lying on his face, fast asleep, while the donkey nibbles and rolls his load-sore back deliciously in the dust. The camel sits like a salamander, apparently minding no change of weather. Little birds pant for breath. All is very still and hot.

But work-time comes again before the heat goes, and the workmen half sit up, looking around, perhaps playfully tossing a stick or clod on the head of a lazier comrade. The work-saddles are roped on the backs of the animals. The camel, long habituated to complaining, whether made to kneel or rise again, utters grating gutturals from his long throat. He is the Oriental striker, objecting, vocally, at least, to every new demand upon him. Well waked, the country-side begins to be busy again and work goes on until sundown. As the afternoon slips into the evening you will see traveling peasants hastening to make their villages. The hills are touched with pinks and purples that shade into dark blue. The gray owl calls, the foxes reconnoiter the fields, the village

[1] Hosea 13: 3.

dogs bark, lights straggle out from the settlements. One may hear the song of a watcher in a vineyard or the bang of his musket as he shoots at a dog or fox meddling with the vines. As we hastened one evening through a village two hours distance from our own, the people, sitting about the doors and in the alleys, seemed astonished and urged us to stop overnight, not understanding our preference to travel on in the growing dusk. But we went on, passing possible sites for Ai, then Bethel and Beeroth, and so to our own Râm Allâh. The way was precarious and stony, with only the starlight to help us, and the evening was chilly.

We might call Palestine, even the western part of it, which is more familiar to us, a world in little, so much has been packed into this little space between the Jordan and the Mediterranean. Sometimes it has been a kingdom and sometimes kingdoms. As a province or provinces it has acknowledged masters on the south, east, north and west.

Far back in time the country was the range of numerous unruly tribes. To-day it contains several districts within the Asiatic holdings of the Turkish Empire. As one looks inland from the Mediterranean on the Judean country, first comes the straight unindented coast line of sand, then a fertile strip of land parallel to it in which the orange and the grains flourish. Next comes the secondary ridge of Judean hills; then its primary ridge of mountains. These latter are thirty-five miles from the sea and three fifths of a mile above its level. Now, as we stand on the mountain range, we have only twenty miles between us and the country of the Dead Sea, but a rapid fall in levels which, in so short a distance, makes the sand-hills seem to drop down and away from us in a precipitous stairway to one of the lowest spots on earth, the basin in which the Jordan River and the Dead Sea lie, the so-called Ghôr. This depression is a quarter of a mile below sea-level and hence three quarters of a mile below the high country in the neighborhood of Jerusalem.

Western Palestine is a limestone country that is, geologically speaking, new. Faulting, erosion and earthquake as well have been hard at work in comparatively recent geological times to make a most diversified surface in a land of short distances. Its rocks are peppered with nodules of flint. The weather wear on the country rocks of some districts allows the flint nodules to drop out, thus leaving a peculiar worm-eaten look in the stones and cliffs. In other localities the cherty material runs in ribbon-like bands within the limestone. The lime rock is often beautified by geode-like recesses of lime crystal, and the slabs of lamellar stone so much used for flooring, window-seats and roofing are frequently penciled with exquisite dendritic markings. Often the face of cleavage between blocks of building material is glazed with a native pink. There are a few houses in the villages whose external walls are constructed of regular blocks so arranged as to alternate in a manner resembling checkerwork of pink and white squares.

One thought that may occur to an American or European as he looks at the numerous hills and mountains up and down the middle and back of Western Palestine is that never before has he had such a fine opportunity to see the shapes of hills and valleys. For at home he seldom sees the whole, real shape of a hill or a mountain, so covered is it with trees or smaller growth. But here there is very little clothing on the hills. Their knobs and shoulders, cliffs and ribs, are almost as naked of trees as the blue skies above them. The rock layers stand out at the worn edges very plainly. Some hills are banded round and round horizontally with successive layers of rock. Others are made up of layers slightly inclined, and some look like giant clam-shells set down on the land. In yet other hills the twistings and heavings have given the sedimentary layers a vertical position up and down over the mountains, as if they had been tipped over. These bands of rock are usually of limestone interspersed with chunks of chert. Ordinarily the tops of the hills assume a long, sloping, rounded shape because of the soft nature of the rock and the wearing power of the deluging rains.

All around the highland country of Western Palestine are mellow plains and fertile valleys. Up and down the western border between the highlands and the Mediterranean is the Maritime Plain, from eight to fifteen miles wide. Along the eastern edge is the great depression of the Ghôr, the low fertile basin that separates Western from Eastern Palestine and provides a bed for the plunging current of the Jordan and a sink for the Dead Sea. These two fertile strips are barely connected toward the north by an arm of the Ghôr, formerly called the Valley of Jezreel, that reaches to the site of ancient Jezreel, and a succession of plains formerly called the Plain of Esdraelon, that touch the Maritime Plain around the nose of Carmel. The highland country is pierced by many a cut called, in the language of the country, *wâd*, or *wâdy*, the equivalent ordinarily of our *valley*, though the climate of Palestine is such as to make it almost always the case that a wâdy is a brook in the rainy weather of winter and a dry gully during the rest of the year.[1] Some of these wâdys are of considerable breadth and offer arable lands; others are narrow, deep gorges. Into some of these gorges the débris from the hillsides has tumbled so as to make it impossible to use the valley bed as a road even in dry weather.

Many of the passes mentioned in the literature of Palestine are really highland paths. Valleys must often be avoided as impassable during the winter rains and as stiflingly hot in summer. Invading armies would seldom risk using narrow valleys for their approach, as they would be easily assailable from the hillsides.

[1] 1 Kings 17:7; Job 6:15, 17.

The limestone is full of holes and caves varying in size from a pocket to a palace. The caves may be near the surface or far in the secret places of the deep-chested mountains. They make reservoirs for the catching of the rain from the surface and hold it through the long dry season, giving some of it in springs [1] and probably losing floods of it in lower and lower caverns. Sometimes the caves are like small rooms,[2] let into the sides of the cliffs, as at 'Ayn Fâra in the Wâdy Fâra, a few hours northeast of Jerusalem, where there is a suite of four connecting rooms in the side wall of the valley, thirty feet above the path. In front of the rooms is a narrow ledge overhanging the path, and up through this natural platform is a manhole which offers the one way of access from below. All up and down this wâdy are caves, some having been improved, probably for purposes of hermit dwelling. In Wâdy es-Suwaynîṭ, that is, the valley of Michmash, there are a good many such cliff dwellings [3] which seem to be approachable only by a rope let down from the top of the precipice above. All through the wild gorges of the country one is apt to come upon these caves with signs of use in some previous age by troglodytes and hermits. When possible they are now used as goat-pens, and thus offer unclean but dry quarters to any one caught in a rain. At the cave near Kharayṭûn the entrance is difficult to reach, up in the side of a precipitous mountain. It is a narrow passage leading to a large, high, vaulted room, a sort of natural cathedral, with a large side chamber. Thence one may go through a low, tortuous passage to other smaller rooms as far as most of the adventurous care to go, the natives say to Hebron, but the guide-books, something over five hundred feet. About Jeba', east of er-Râm, the ground sounds hollow under foot because of caves to which one may descend, in some

[1] Psalm 104 : 10. [2] 1 Kings 18 : 4; 19 : 9, 13; Judges 6 : 2.
[3] 1 Sam. 13 : 5, 6; 14: 11, 22.

cases by cut stairs, to find that the caves have been enlarged and cemented. About two thirds of the way from el-Bîreh to Baytîn, on the left of the path, is a cave which has been made to do service as a catch-basin for the water from the spring above. The mouth of the spring has been enlarged artificially and connected by a rock-cut channel with the cave. This channel has little grooves branching from it and there seem to be here the conveniences of an ancient laundering or fulling place. In the cave are two supporting columns cut from the rock. The interior is well adorned to-day with a pretty growth of delicate maidenhair ferns.

There are many caves in the hillsides of what is called the Samson Country,[1] through which the railway from Jaffa to Jerusalem passes. In and about Jerusalem are caves the discussion of which does not belong here, though they can hardly have failed, in their long association with the history of that city, of having much significant connection with the political and religious history of the people of the country. Such are the caves about the Church of the Holy Sepulcher, the little one under the great rock beneath the Dome of the Rock, the artificially enlarged caves on the south side of the Valley of Hinnom, the huge cave of Jeremiah, north of the city, under the hill where the Moslems have a cemetery, not to mention its counterpart across the road and under the city, called Solomon's Quarry or the Cotton Grotto.

Near the village of Ḳubâb, but nearer the tiny village of Abu Shûsheh, is a large cave now used as a sheep and goat pen. It is called by the neighboring Moslems Noah's Cave. The top of it has evidently at some time fallen in, thus diminishing its size, but giving it an immense mouth, quite conspicuous all about the neighboring country to the north. The peasantry, in their double desire to account for it and also to say something against the Jews, tell this story about

[1] Judges 13-15.

the cave. They say that Noah was making war against the Jews who, being hard pressed, ran into this cave for shelter. Thereupon Noah brought up his heavy guns and bombarded the cave with such effect as to crush in the top, which fell on the Jews, killing them all.

In connection with caves the peasants tell certain stories of hyenas. To the peasant any story that has to do with these creatures is gruesome. The hyena, they say, will accost a lone pedestrian, rub up against him and cast a spell over him until, in a dazed way, the man follows the animal to its cave, where the hyena will despatch him. The tale is continued to describe how the hyena is captured. They say that a man strips himself naked and crawls into the cave of the hyena, carrying one end of a rope which is held by his companions outside. Once inside, his condition deceives the hyena, as does also a cajoling tone which he uses until the creature, quite unsuspecting, begins to fawn and roll over. The man at once secures a leg of the hyena with his rope, whereupon the men outside draw out the beast and kill it with their clubs.

New graves are usually loaded with heavy stones and watched at night to prevent the hyenas from exhuming the dead bodies.

As the rock of the country is of a quickly dissolving kind, the torrential force of the winter rains greatly facilitates soil-making. The ground is strewn with loose stones, in some places so thickly that the soil cannot be seen a few rods away. Soil is carried rapidly about, so that where there are no terraces or pockets to catch it the shelving rock is soon denuded and the only deep earth is found in the valleys or hollow plains.

The Jordan and the 'Aujâ (Crooked) are the two largest rivers of Palestine; Ḥûleh (Merom), Tiberias (Galilee) and Baḥret Lût (the Dead Sea), its three lakes. There are many streams, brooks and winter ponds that disappear with the rainy season. In a few deep-cut beds, where strong springs supply the brooks, water flows in a current all the year.

The watershed of Western Palestine is considerably nearer to the Jordan than to the Mediterranean, being about thirty-five or forty miles from the Sea, but scarcely more than twenty miles on the average from the river. The valley courses of the streams generally take a southeasterly direction from the watershed to the Jordan basin, and a northwesterly direction towards the Mediterranean Sea. Those on the east are narrower and more precipitous, since they have on that side of the country the shorter distance and the more remarkable fall in levels.

Fertility and population have generally favored the western side of the watershed, with some notable exceptions. This western slope is flanked by the low-lying hills of the Shephelah and comes gradually down to the Maritime Plain. The hills and plain on this side have very great historical interest and have formed the bridge of the civilizations to the north and to the south of Palestine. At the present time, when travel comes by sea from the Western world, this country is a threshold to the shrines and ancient sites of Syria and the East.

The only ponds in the country are the winter ponds called by the native name, *balû'a*. These are formed by the winter rains. They stand for about five months in low places, and then disappear until the next rainy season.[1] Robinson, in 1838, passed by one of these on his way from el-Bîreh to Jifnâ. As his journey that way was on June 13, the pond was then dry. But this same pond may now be seen every winter and spring full of water. The new carriage road cuts the eastern end of it at a point a little over a mile north of el-Bîreh. Another of these ponds may be seen just under the village of Baytûnyeh, towards Râm Allâh. Were it not for such short-lived ponds many of the country people would

[1] Isa. 35: 7; 41: 18; 42: 15.

have little idea of any body of water larger than a rain-water cistern. The Dead Sea may be seen from the high hills to the east of these ponds and the Mediterranean from those to the west, but only a small proportion of the peasantry ever get to see either one of them. A distant view gives the unexperienced no adequate notion of their size. People living in Jaffa, on the sea, have been known to poke fun at the upland folk and bewilder them with yarns about the sea. One story that they impose on the credulous countryman is that every night, at dark, a cover is put over the sea, as one would cover over a jar of water, or a bowl of dough. One man, on reaching Jaffa late in the afternoon for his first visit, hastened down to the beach in order to see the water before the cover should be put on for the night. Perhaps the best known winter ponds are in the extensive *sunken meadows* of the Plain of Esdraelon, athwart the way from Jenîn to Nazareth.

The springs of Palestine are its eyes, as the Arabs put it, and when they are sparkling with life the whole face of the country lights up with a wholesome expression.[1] In places where the springs are remote from the present settlements, and now used only for the flocks or by travelers, there are often to be seen remains of former buildings. Sometimes villas or even villages may be traced; old aqueducts also, and ruined reservoirs, showing how great pains were once taken to utilize the water supply. At 'Ayn Fâra is a copious supply of water forming one of the few perennial brooks. In its deeper pools the herdsmen water and wash their flocks.[2] There is a very feeble attempt at gardening in the vicinity, but for the most part the precious treasure flows away unused. The valley sides show ancient masonry belonging to more thrifty times. On the hill 'Aṭâra, a mile south of el-Bîreh, are ruined reservoirs to which the waters of the spring now called 'Ayn en-Nuṣbeh were carried by stone

[1] *Cf.* Joshua 15: 19.

[2] Song 4: 2; 6: 6.

RIVER AUJA NORTH OF JAFFA

conduits, of which only small pieces remain. So may similar indications be seen at 'Ayn Ṣôba, at 'Ayn Jeriyût, 'Ayn Kefrîyeh, all of which are west of Râm Allâh. Present-day villages are often a considerable distance from the spring on which they depend for drinking water. Many large places are provided with but one spring. Nazareth and Jerusalem are thus limited to one good spring each. Around the Sea of Galilee and the Dead Sea are warm, even hot, springs once much prized as watering-places. They are generally sulphurous in character. Those at Tiberias, on the Sea of Galilee, are used now as baths.

Of wells Palestine has but few. Some of those mentioned in the Bible still remain, though not all are in use.[1] It comes more naturally to the mind of an Oriental to devote the labor and expense that it would take to dig a well to the construction of something in which to catch a portion of the rainfall. It is quite essential to the prosperity of Palestine that its water resources be husbanded through the long dry season.[2] As has been suggested, there is plenty of evidence that formerly this was done in a very painstaking manner, but at the present time far less care is given to this very important matter. Numerous cisterns and reservoirs were made to catch rain-water and the overflow of the fountains. The large number of these ancient devices for saving water, in contrast with the few made and used in these days, offers one basis for a comparison of the condition of the country in old and new Palestine. Rain-water was caught in cemented pits not very unlike huge pear-shaped bottles. Such water was used for all household purposes where spring water failed; also for watering the animals. It was drawn up as from a well. Occasionally these old cemented cisterns are still in use. But all through the country there are vast numbers of them that are no longer used. All about Jerusalem, especially north of the city, among the

[1] John 4: 6. [2] *Cf.* Eccles. 2: 6.

olives, they may be seen; also about the district of Râm Allâh, at Teḳûʻa and at Jânyeh.

The overflow of springs was provided for by more pretentious structures, — the great rectangular box pools built of solid masonry. The most noteworthy of these reservoirs are the so-called Pools of Solomon, three in number, south of Bethlehem, by the road that leads to Hebron. These three immense reservoirs, each of which, when full, would float a battleship, have a combined capacity of over forty million gallons. Formerly stone aqueducts conveyed the waters to Jerusalem. Remains of these are still to be seen. The water is conveyed now through iron pipes, fully eight miles, to the city. Jerusalem itself has the famous Pool of Siloam,[1] the Sultan's Pool and the Pool of Mâmilla. The last one mentioned feeds a large reservoir within the city walls, sometimes called the Patriarch's Pool and sometimes Hezekiah's Pool.[2] At Bethel (Baytîn) the spring is surrounded by an old reservoir larger than the Pool of Mâmilla. It is now dry and its bottom is used as a threshing-floor. And so all about the country are found the remains of costly works designed for the saving and proper use of the water supply. With such means of irrigation the productiveness of the country must have been much greater than at the present day.

Sometimes, in speaking of the seasons in Palestine, we say summer and winter,[3] and sometimes we mention the four seasons. Perhaps if we should say wet season and dry season it would be less misleading, but even then one would have to bear in mind that the wet season is not a time of general downpour but simply the season in which the rains of the year come.

The wet season, or winter,[4] as it is more generally called, ought to provide, for the welfare of the country, from twenty-five to thirty inches of rainfall in the highlands. Sometimes

[1] John 9: 7. [2] 2 Kings 20: 20. [3] Gen. 8: 22. [4] Song 2: 11.

it is as low as sixteen inches, and it occasionally exceeds thirty-five or even forty inches. Roughly speaking, the wet season claims the five months, November to March. In a very wet winter, perhaps, the rains will reach over a period of nearly six months, but, on the other hand, the rainy period may shrink to four. The most frequent and heavy falls of rain in an ordinary season are looked for near the beginning and at the close of the wet season. Many pleasant days,[1] and even some entire weeks of rainless weather, may be expected during this wet season. Now and then there may be a winter during which the water will be glazed over in the puddles a few times, or there may be several falls of snow.[2] Driving, raw, chilling rains and winds may prevail for a week at a time, or longer, and be less easy to bear than the stronger cold of a more northerly climate.[3]

The dry season is more in keeping with its name throughout its control of nearly seven months, although rain in May has been experienced and a *slip* in one of the summer months is not unknown. At the end of September or at the beginning of October a slight shower is expected. One scarcely expects rain, however, until well into November. Despite the very hot days in the dry summer season, the nights in the Palestine highlands are generally cool. The Syrian sun is a synonym for piercing, intense heat, and foreigners are more apt to be thoughtless of its power than to overdo caution. During the midsummer months it is hard to take photographs except very early or very late, or with very slow-acting lenses and plates. Then, too, the poorest light for distant views may be in summer, when the intense heat fills the air with a haze. Those who have seen the dead, brown look that comes on a district of country which has suffered an unusual period of drought may partly imagine the appearance of Palestine after a six months' absence of

[1] 2 Sam. 23: 4. [2] 2 Sam. 23: 20. [3] Matt. 24: 20; Mark 13: 18.

rain unrelieved except for the night-mists that may prevail during some of that time.

After the drought the peasant, like the country, is pantingly ready for the first rains of the autumn. He never hesitates to choose between rain and sunshine. It is always the former. Even if rain comes in destructive abundance he has only to think of the terrors of a scanty rainfall to repress all complaints. As we say in a complimentary way to a guest, " You have brought pleasant weather," so the Syrian will say, " Your foot is green," that is, " Your coming is accompanied by the benedictions of rain." Rains usually begin with an appearance of reluctance,[1] but sometime in November or December they ought to come down heavily for most of a fortnight. Sometimes there are several weeks of delightfully balmy weather between the drenching rains. During an unusually dry winter, when the rainfall is below twenty inches, much of the winter will be pleasant, at the expense of the crops and of the general welfare. At such times the price of wheat goes up and the scantily supplied cisterns give no promise of holding out through the succeeding summer. Springs dry down until the best of them offer but a tiny stream, and hours must be spent at some of the fountains to fill a few jars. Much of January is apt to be rainy. February is strange and fickle, and because it is especially trying to the vital forces of the aged and weak is called Old Woman's Month. We remember a very pleasant February, but such are rare. Honest March is pretty much its boisterous self even in Palestine. April is sunny and a charming month for a journey. If the latter rains have been delayed they may come even in April, though that is late. But the needed rain has been known to come as late as middle May, with unusually cold weather. Then the peasants deemed such weather portentous.[2] The latter rains — how familiar a phrase to the ears of many who may not

[1] *Cf.* 1 Kings 18: 43–45. [2] *Cf.* Prov. 26: 1.

know just why they are so called![1] The downpour of November or December washed out the ground, made the heat flee, brought back health to the succulent plants, hastened the ripening of the oranges and did pretty well for the cisterns, but this latter rain is the key of the situation. If it does not come, wheat may sell at famine prices and all the pains of a drought take hold of the land.[2] But if it only will come, then wealth and comfort and a healthy summer.[3]

Harvest begins in the springtime. May brings the yellow heads on the grain, and it must be gathered or soon the summer will be ended and the harvest past.[4] The grain on the hills is a few weeks later than that in the valleys and plains. A little donkey coming in from the hill terraces with a back-load of sheaves looks very porcupiny. The reaper grasps the stalks of wheat or barley with one hand and cuts a long straw with the sickle in the other hand. If he is hungry he starts a little fire and holds some of the wheat heads over it until well parched, and then, rubbing off the husks between his palms, he has a feast of the *new corn of the land.* Thus treated, new wheat is called *frîky* (rubbed).

During the time of ripening wheat one may see in the fields, close to the ground, the heavy green leaves and yellow, shiny apples of the mandrake.[5] The natives say that if one eats the seeds of the fruit they will make him crazy. The pulp has a pleasant, sweetish flavor and an agreeable smell.[6]

The only dreadful wind in Palestine is the east wind,[7] because it blows from the inland desert and brings excessive heat. The Arabic word for *east* is *sherḳ*, and so for east wind

[1] *Cf.* Deut. 11: 14; Job 29: 23; Prov. 16: 15; Jer. 3: 3; 5: 24; Hosea 6: 3; Joel 2: 23; Zech. 10: 1; James 5: 7.

[2] Amos 4: 7. [3] *Cf.* Psalm 65: 9–13. [4] Jer. 8: 20. [5] Gen. 30: 14.

[6] Song 7: 13.

[7] Jer. 18: 17; Ezek. 17: 10; 19: 12; Hosea 13: 15; Jonah 4: 8.

the Arab says *Sherḳ-iyeh.* From this we get, by corruption, our word sirocco (or sherokkoh), which has come to mean simply a hot, enervating blast from any direction. To the Arab it is that wearing east wind whose coming can be felt in the early morning before a breath of air seems stirring. There is a certain chemical effect on the nervous system of those who are particularly sensitive to the blighting touch of the Sherḳîyeh. Sometimes this wind goes away suddenly after a short day, but almost always its coming means that it will run three days at least, and often more. There is a similar wind in Egypt known to residents of Cairo as the Khumsûn (fifty), from the likelihood that it will remain fifty days. Such an unbroken period of hot winds must be exceedingly rare in Palestine, though in the early autumn of 1902 there was an almost continuous Sherḳîyeh for five weeks. The east wind of winter is usually as disagreeably cold as its relative in summer is hot and suffocating. The only good thing that I ever knew the summer sirocco to do was to cure quickly the raisin grapes spread on the ground in September.

The west wind prevails a generous share of the time and brings mists and coolness from the sea during the summer. In the rainy season a northwest wind brings rain.[1] The showers are often presaged by high winds from the west and north.

September, with its trying siroccos, is often hotter than May. The pomegranates ripen in this month. In the country districts it is very hard to get goats' milk from this time onward for several months. The flocks are too far distant, having been driven away to find pasture and water, and a little later on the milk is all needed for the young. During these days, too, it is not thought good to weaken the goats by milking them any more than is quite necessary. In the cities milk is always to be had.

[1] Prov. 25: 23.

The Greek Feast of the Cross, about the end of September, is looked forward to as marking the date for an early shower which may be sufficiently strong to cleanse the roofs. After that the rain may come in a month, or it may wait two. The people notice a period of general unhealthiness just preceding the autumn rains. Their advent usually puts an end to it, bringing healthier conditions. Sometime along in the autumn there is often noticed a warm spell of weather which the natives call *Ṣayf Ṣaghîr*, or *Ṣayf Rummân*, that is, *Little Summer*, or *Pomegranate Summer*.

The cement in the paved roofs cracks under the fierce heat of summer and the early showers help to discover the bad places which must be patched before the heavy winter rains. In the case of earth-covered roofs the first shower ought to be followed by a good rolling, the owners going over and over them with stone rollers rigged with wooden handles that creak out upon the clear air after the rain as they work in the sockets. From the peculiar noise thus made the Râm Allâh people have a local name of *zukzâkeh* for the wooden handles of these stone rollers. In the northern part of the country the name *nâ'uṣ* is given to the roller handles for a similar reason. The roofs of rolled earth can be kept very tight. The covering of such roofs is made by mixing sandy soil with clay and with the finest grade of chaff, called *mûṣ*, from the threshing-floor. On old earth roofs patches of grass[1] grow, and even grain has been seen springing up in such places.

The Syrian peasant divides trees into classes by pairs. There are those that are good to sit under and those that are not. Then there are those that yield food and those that do not. Finally there are those that are holy, and therefore cannot be cut for charcoal or fuel, and those that are not thus tabooed.

The fig-tree is a very useful food producer and is much

[1] Psalm 129: 6.

cultivated. As elsewhere mentioned, the irritating effect of the juices of the broken fig branch or leaf makes it less desirable as a shade tree, but because of its dense shade it must be resorted to in hot weather. The olive-tree gives rather a thin shade. The carob-tree is a fine shade-giver. The pine is a favorite in this respect, though few pines are left. The needly cypress shades only its own central mast. One might as well snuggle up to one's own shadow for protection as to expect it from a cypress. Pomegranate, lemon and orange-trees, when large enough, afford shade, but they are often in low, miasmatic places. The apple-tree does not do well except in parts of northern Syria, as at Zebedâny, near Damascus. Some fine pear-trees are to be seen above Bîr ez-Zayt, though as a rule they are as difficult to cultivate as apple-trees. At 'Ayn Sînyâ are flourishing mulberry-trees of great size. The opinion is held that the mulberry and the silk culture usually associated with it would thrive peculiarly well in Palestine. Mount Tabor is thinly studded with trees except on the southeast side. Mount Carmel also has yet some remains of its one-time forest. The oak is found in a number of varieties, but is a great temptation to the charcoal burner, as it affords the most desirable coal. The *zinzilakt* is a favorite for shade. The best substitute for a shade tree in the land is a large rock, the cool side of which helps one to forget the burning glare of the noon sun.[1]

We shall have to call winter the season of rain, flowers and travel. Rain ushers in the winter and also closes it. To the middle and latter part of that season is due the bursting of the blossoms and a push that sends flowers scattering into the first months of the dry season.[2] Travel might find a better time than much of the winter, but then it is cool and if it rains, why, that is the way of the country, and this explanation often suffices.

On the flowers of the country Dr. Post's book offers a

[1] Isa. 32: 2. [2] Song 2: 12.

DONKEY AT THE THRESHING FLOOR WITH A LOAD OF WHEAT

mine of information for those skilled enough in the elements of botany to make use of it. The little booklets of pressed specimens offered for sale, when fresh, give an excellent idea of the variety of wild-flower life in Palestine. Mrs. Hannah Zeller, a daughter of former Bishop Gobat of Jerusalem, and the wife of the late Rev. John Zeller of Nazareth and Jerusalem, has been most successful in reproducing in color many of the flowers of Palestine. Mrs. Zeller's book of color plates, published some years ago, is now hard to secure. She still has the originals and an even larger collection which awaits a publisher. Until some such publication in color is attempted it will be difficult to describe in writing the unusual splendor and variety of Palestine's wild flowers.

The flower season really begins in what we should call midautumn with the little lavender-colored crocus called by the natives the *serâj el-ghûleh* or *the lamp of the ghoul.* A better name for it would be *serâj esh-shugâ'* which would mean *the lamp of courage,* as it thrusts its dainty head up through the calcined earth, scarcely waiting for a drop of moisture. After this brave little color-bearer of Flora's troop there follow the narcissus, heavily sweet, and the cyclamen, clinging with its ample bulb in rocky cracks as well as nestling in moist beds. But of all the flowers the general favorite is the wild anemone, especially in its rarer varieties, white, pink, salmon, blue and purple. The most common is the red anemone, which is seen everywhere and sometimes measures four or five inches across. Near Dayr Dîwân we once rode through an orchard where the ground was covered with a cloud of these red ones, so voluptuous, so prodigally spread in a carpet of crimson beauty that one almost held one's breath at the charming scene. The red ranunculus, which comes later, is almost as large, but it looks thick and heavy in comparison, and the flaunting red poppy, which comes still later, looks weak and characterless beside the anemone. Even the wild red tulip suffers beside it. The colors of the anemone other than red are more rare, but usually come earlier. About Jaffa they appear shortly after Christmas. White ones and some of delicate shades are found between there and the river 'Aujâ. White ones abound near Jifnâ, and are found east of Ḳubâb and east of Sejed station. Purple, pink and blue ones are plentiful in Wâdy el-Kelb and the Khullet el-'Adas near Râm Allâh. The large red ranunculus mentioned is found in large patches between Jericho and the Dead Sea in early February. Considerably later there is an acre-patch east of Dayr Dîwân near the cliff descent towards eṭ-Ṭayyibeh. The red tulip is rarer and follows soon. The red poppy is very abundant. It has the delicacy of crêpe. It is scarcely welcome as it betokens the close of the flower season. But one may for some time yet gather flowers that blaze forth as brilliantly in middle spring as do the autumn flowers in America: the adonis, gorse, flax, mustard, bachelor's button, anise, vetch, everlasting, wild mignonette and geranium. In the vineyards, about pruning time, the ground is covered with a rich purple glow. The sweet-scented gorse abounds in the valleys towards Ṭayyibeh. The vetches come in many colors, and there are scores of other scarcely noticed little blossoms.

When the season has been especially rainy, as may occur about every fifth or sixth year, the valleys such as 'Ayn Fâra will be knee-deep with the abundant flowering herbs and weeds. The scented jasmine and the tall waving reeds over the watercourse will add their charm to this favored spot. Later, yellow thistles abound.

One of the oddities of the flower family is the black lily of the calla order, which the natives call *calf (leg) of the negro.*

In the moist, shady caves, and sometimes in old cisterns, masses of maidenhair fern grow in the cool shelter throughout the year.

On the shores of Tiberias (Galilee) oleanders and blue thistles are seen in May.

In speaking of the wild animals of Palestine one is almost led to include the dog and the cat. They are, however, on the edge of domesticity and may fairly be omitted. Wolves, hyenas, jackals and foxes are the troublesome wild beasts. The last two are often about vineyards seeking to feed on the grapes.[1] The jackal cry at night is very mournful and sure to start up the barking of the dogs, who are themselves often grape thieves.

The beautiful little gazels are started up in the wilderness and go bounding off like thistle-down in a breeze, turning every now and then, however, to look with wonder at the traveler. Once, near eṭ-Ṭayyibeh we saw four together, and once, east of Jebaʿ, we saw a herd of nine gazels.

Among the smaller creatures met with are the mole-rat, the big horny-headed lizard, called by the natives *ḥirdhôn,* the ordinary lizard about the color of the gray-brown rocks among which it speeds, the little green lizard that darts about, and the pallid gecko, climbing on house-walls. The beautiful and odd chameleon must also be mentioned. Snakes are not commonly seen by the traveler. Scorpions, black beetles, mosquitoes, fleas and a diabolical little sand-fly, called by the natives *ḥisḥis,* are among the less agreeable creatures noticed.

At Haifa, in the house of the Spanish vice-consul, we saw the skin of a crocodile caught in the river Zerḳâ in 1902. They spoke also of one which had been caught fourteen years before in the same waters.

One of the showiest birds of Palestine is the stork, which is mostly white, but has black wings, a red bill and red legs. Its eyes, too, have a border of the latter color. The natives call it *abu saʿd.* Flocks of them may be seen frequently. Now and then a solitary bird is seen in a wheat-field. Crows with gray bodies and black wings are plentiful. Ravens, vultures, hawks and sparrows are common. Twice I saw

[1] Song 2: 15.

the capture of a sparrow by a hawk. Once, after having started his victim from a flock, the hawk dashed after him and caught him in a small tree but six feet from my head. It was done with such terrific quickness as to surprise the spectator out of all action. Gray owls (bûmeh), partridges (shunnar), wild pigeons (ḥamâm) and quails (furri) are seen. It seemed quite appropriate to see doves on the shores of Galilee. On the surface of the same lake water-fowls were observed. At Jericho we saw the robin redbreast; in the gorge at Mâr Sâbâ, the grackle. Starlings in clouds haunt the wheat-fields in harvest. Meadow-larks, crested, are very common. Goldfinches, bulbuls, thrushes and wagtails are also noticed.

The scenery of Western Palestine lacks the charm that woods and water provide. Yet one grows to like it. The early and late parts of the day are best for the most pleasing effects. Then the views out across the vineyards and off on the hills are very restful. The rolling coast plain backed by the distant hills of the Judean highlands makes a pleasing prospect, especially when decked with the herbage that follows the rains. Quiet tastes are satisfied with such pastoral scenes as those in the valley at Lubban or in the plain of Makhna. Excellent distant views are afforded from the hills near Nazareth, from which are seen the rich plains of Esdraelon, Haifa, Mount Carmel and the Mediterranean. The Sea of Galilee is delightfully satisfying. From Tabor one gets a glorious sight of Hermon, snow-white, whence the natives call it Jebel esh-Shaykh (Old Man Mountain). The views from Mount Carmel of sea and coast-line and much of the interior, the glimpse of the Mediterranean from the hill of Samaria and the sweeping prospect from Gerizim are all good. An easily attained and little known view-point is Jebel Ṭawîl (Long Mountain) east of el-Bîreh. From here of a late afternoon the country lies open in sharp, clear lines throughout the central region. Jerusalem is seen lying due

WILD ANEMONES FROM WADY EL-KELB

south in beautiful silhouette; the Mount of Olives is a little east of it. The Dead Sea is southeast, eṭ-Ṭayyibeh north of east, Bethel (Baytîn) northeast, Gibeon southwest, near which is Neby Samwîl. Near at hand, to the south, are el-Bîreh and Râm Allâh. Only one thing is lacking in this view; that is the Mediterranean Sea. But this can be seen, as well as Jaffa, Ramleh and Ludd from Râm Allâh. The mountain east of the Jordan is plainly visible from all the high points up and down the middle of the country. Other good view-points are Neby Samwîl, Jeba', Mukhmâs, the hills about Jerusalem, especially from the tower on the Mount of Olives and from Herodium. Heroic scenery may be found in the so-called Samson Country through which the railroad from Jaffa to Jerusalem runs, in the Mukhmâs Valley, the Wâdy Ḳelt and gorges around Mâr Sâbâ. Crag, ravine, precipice and cave make such places memorable.

The approach to cities and villages is as characteristic as any other aspect of them. There is a look from afar peculiar to the settlements of different countries. As seen from a distance American settlements are chiefly noticeable for the chimneys, the sharp spires of churches, the long, monotonous lines of factory buildings and mills and often the pointed shape of house roofs. Add to these enormous bridges, miles of railroad yards and cars, a nimbus of smoke and you have the elements from which to make a view of any good-sized town. For the smaller, sweeter, country places you must subtract some of the above features and substitute some woodsy and meadowy effects. In Syria the contrasts with our more familiar scenes are plain to us in the distant view of its cities and villages. Instead of the triangular shape is the square look of the buildings. Instead of chimneys and spires are the huge domes resting on square substructures, and the pencil-like minarets rising up among them. The distant view of Jerusalem is one of the most pleasing in the entire country. It has been one of the standard charms of

Palestine, delighting warrior, poet and pilgrim, and more lately student, missionary and tourist. There she sits with her feet in deep valleys, her royal waist girdled with the crenelated wall and her head crowned with the altar sites of ancient time. There are about her the things that charm the poetic sense, — age, chivalry, religion. Not even eternal Rome can be so rich in these and so equally possessed of them all.

Though it is not always the case, yet the greater number of Syrian cities and villages seek hilly sites.[1] The ports cannot always do this, though Jaffa does. Damascus spreads out over a low flat area. Ramleh and Ludd, being plain dwellers, must live in lowlands. But defense is very commonly sought by settling on the sides or top of a hill and building the houses close together, if not one above another, as if in steps.

Garden plots and vineyards are fenced in with hastily-constructed walls of the loose stone picked up on the inside.[2] Between these curving walls run sinuous lanes[3] into the villages from the paths and roads outside.

It would be very easy to make a pocket-edition of a book of all the roads in the country, no matter how small the pocket. Some roads are planned for, taxed for and looked for a great many years before the semblance of road-making begins. But never mind that; Orientals enjoy a road in prospect and in retrospect much longer than in fact. Where the government does put through a road it is usually good traveling. The highlands afford the best of road-making materials and, if often enough repaired, no better roads could be asked for. Many carriageways are over favoring bits of country where the frequent passing has marked out the only road. The Romans were the greatest road-makers in Palestine. The remains of their work may even now be seen in various places. Many of their old roads are indicated

[1] Matt. 5: 14. [2] Isa. 5: 2. [3] Num. 22: 24.

on the best maps. Roman roads at this day of decay do not, as a rule, offer easy travel. The washings of a millennium or two of rain have made them of the corduroy order.

Of paths one may make as many as one pleases in a country where no barbed wire and few walls prevent. The permanency of the old well-worn paths[1] is very noticeable, the best one always leading to a village or to a spring. There is such a thing as the tyranny of the path. It is very evident where railroads rule, and even in a country where the travel must be on the backs of animals, the little bridle-paths impose on one and, taking advantage of the inertia of human mentality, mark out one's way with arbitrary exclusiveness. When one's time is limited to just a sufficient number of days to allow one to see all the more notable places in the country, it is scarcely to be expected that one will sacrifice the surety of seeing a noted place for the chance of stumbling on a place of less popular interest. The paths and time required for seeing most places are almost as clearly indicated as any schedule of trips in countries possessed of time-tables. This accounts for the fact that, although thousands of travelers pass over the beaten paths, and scores of students go over the rarer paths, not one in the twenty or the thousand is likely to get off the paths.

One of the bits of country thus scantily known to foreigners is northern Judea, especially to the northwest of Jerusalem. Most travelers passing through it on the way to Jerusalem are in haste to reach the city, and once there, the fact that any place is a few hours farther distant than a day's trip would allow forbids easy investigation.

One does not have to go far to reach the wilderness.[2] It is any uncultivated place. It is the pasture for flocks,[3] the wild of rocks and short, thorny bushes. The thorns[4] are gathered every other year to build fires in the lime-kilns, where the abundant lime-rock of the country is burned.

[1] Jer. 6: 16. [2] Psalm 107: 4–7. [3] Ezek. 34: 14. [4] Isa. 33: 12.

When the men gather them for the lime-kilns the thorns are piled in great heaps with heavy stones on them to hold them down. When needed the heap is pierced with a long pole and carried over the shoulder as on a huge pitchfork. During the late winter and in spring only may one see green fields in anything like a Western sense. The Plain of el-Makhna presents a very lovely prospect from the height above it. Something like a small prairie effect is had in the Maritime and Esdraelon plains. Pasture privilege is commonly had anywhere if the land be not under actual cultivation. In the uplands the custom of leaving great tracts idle in alternate years[1] in lieu of dressing the ground permits wide pasturage. As the dry season advances the herdsmen seek the deep valleys with their flocks. There is little opportunity for new trees or shrubs to survive this universal browsing. So it comes about that, except where orchards are set out or scraps of ancient woods remain, trees are seldom seen.

Summer is the time of fierce heat, and yet through it all the grape-vines keep green and the luscious clusters grow larger and ripen under their heavy armor-plate of leaves. The peasants enjoy the tart taste of green fruit. Half-grown grapes are sometimes eaten with salt on them. Green almonds are eaten in the same way. Often it is hard to get ripe peaches, melons and other fruits because of the tendency of the peasants to pick them before they are ripe. But the time of the ripe grapes is the glad time of the year. Instead of saying "August" the peasants often use the expression "In grapes." It is a season by itself to them. The vineyard owners build summer booths among the vines and sleep there through the season. In large vineyards it is common to employ a black man, perhaps a Moroccan, as a watcher. The Syrian peasant stands in peculiar awe of the black stranger. The watchers are provided with shotguns, for

[1] Jer. 4: 3; Hosea 10: 12.

A VINEYARD AT RÂM ALLÂH

foxes and dogs like to eat grapes. All fruit must be guarded against thievishly disposed neighbors. One who knows his vineyard watches the progress of the choicest clusters, having covered some of them early to keep them from drying and to allow them to develop unplucked. Should any grapes be stolen he quickly notices the loss. He sets a thin row of fine stones along the top of his wall in such a way that a night marauder must necessarily rattle them down and thus awaken him. One of the heartless bits of meanness that a hostile peasant can perpetrate in order to pay a grudge is to cut the vine stocks of his enemy's vineyard. Since it takes three years for a new vineyard to bear, such an act is a serious damage.

The finest grapes within reach of Jerusalem are those from Hebron and Râm Allâh. Large white clusters similar to the Malaga grapes are the favorites, though purple grapes are also grown. At Râm Allâh the vines lie flat on the ground. The vine is pruned back to leave three joints on every small branch that is spared in the rigorous treatment.[1] At Jifnâ the vines may be seen trained on stakes. At Zaḥleh, in the Lebanon, the growers have a way of propping up the main vine a few inches above the ground, so that a vineyard has the look of waves of green. In Jerusalem some of the grapes at the Greek Hospital and at the White Fathers' near St. Stephen's Gate are raised on arbors, and the clusters are covered with little bags. Thus protected the grapes ripen slowly and are enjoyed until late in the season. Vast quantities of fresh grapes are consumed as an article of daily food during August, September and October. The price, when cheap, is a cent a pound, and it gradually creeps up to the fancy price of six cents a pound late in the season. Grapes have been provided from the country vineyards as late as the first of December.

Trees need considerable soil, but the grape-vine will thrive

[1] *Cf.* John 15.

with very little and will penetrate with its rootlets all the fissures of the lime-rock for yards about. Then, too, the luscious bunches lying on a pebbled ground do better than those on clear soil. Most of the grass and wild, weedy growth of the country is bulbous and clings in scanty soil, gathering as in a reservoir all the available moisture.

When the crop demands clear ground the native farmer piles the stones into walls, watch-towers or a huge heap in a less fertile spot of the field.[1] It is often a problem to find room for the waste stones. They may be tossed out into the roads and paths. A stranger says, "I don't see why these people don't clear these paths of stone; surely it would pay." But the farmers prefer stones in the paths to stones in the garden patch. With their bare feet, or on their donkeys, they are able by a lifetime of practise to pick their way over such paths. Moreover, peasants are not nervous in Palestine. Stones always furnish a handy weapon,[2] or a reminder on the heels of a slow donkey. In going about through the country one often sees piles of little stones set up one on another. Sometimes these little piles are meant for scarecrows; sometimes they are used to mark a boundary; but there is a wider and more constant use for such loosely built little columns. They are set up in sight of holy spots. Apparently they are not only set up in the vicinity of shrines, *wilys*, etc., but also in places whence a distant view may be had of some holy place, as Jerusalem, which the natives call "el-Ḳuds esh-Sharîf" (The Noble Holy) or, for short, el-Ḳuds, which is practically equivalent to our expression "The Holy City."[3] These little columnar piles may also be met in sight of the hill or mount called Neby Samwîl, which we usually identify with the Mizpeh of Samuel.[4]

The terrace is a thing of great utility to the hill farmer of Palestine. To the traveler it is a thing of beauty as it climbs

[1] Isa. 5:2. [2] 1 Sam. 30:6; 1 Kings 12:18; 2 Kings 3:25; *cf.* Matt. 23:37; John 8:59; 10:31. [3] *Cf.* Matt. 4:5; 27:53. [4] 1 Sam. 7:5.

RÂM ALLÂH MAN AND A BASKET OF OLIVES

STRETCH OF OLIVE TREES ON ROAD TO AYN SÎNYÂ

the hills with its artistically irregular breaks in what would be otherwise a rather monotonous slope. But with terraces and some water the earth is caught and filled with many possibilities of fruit and vegetables. A hill well terraced and well watered looks like a hanging garden. Much of the farming in Judea is on the sides of hills. The little iron-shod wooden plow is run scratching along the terraces. Sometimes one of the oxen will be on a lower level than the other. To go forward without slipping down the hillside is not easy. What cannot be plowed is dug up with the pickax, and wheat or barley will find lodgment in every pocket of soil. As all the reaping is done by hand it offers no especial difficulty, and the monotony of which some people complain on prairie land is never experienced on such a pitched-roof farm. Even where the made terrace is allowed to decay there are many natural terraces where the horizontal layers outcrop from the hillsides. Were the country well kept up, all these terraces would be guarded artificially, for in time a natural terrace loses its protecting edge and the soil and rain come down cascading over the hill stairs until the bed of the stream is reached.

Of food trees the olive is probably the most valuable. It takes ten or fifteen years to bring it to the state of bearing much fruit, but it may go on bearing heavy crops for a century. The oil is freely used in cooking, for salads, for lighting and for anointing. A hard-pressed peasant will occasionally yield to the temptation to cut down some of his olive-trees, selling the finest pieces of wood to the makers of the olive-wood articles[1] which are prized by tourists, and disposing of the rest as fire-wood.[2] A hundredweight of such fire-wood sells for from twelve to twenty-five cents, according to the season and the market, the city price being considerably higher than the country price. A good olive-orchard is a sure source of income, unless the taxes are too

[1] 1 Kings 6: 23, 31–33. [2] Matt. 7: 19.

harshly and arbitrarily imposed. The cutting them down is a real calamity to the country, but it is done only too frequently in a poor year to avoid taxes. The trunk of an aged olive-tree attains a great girth and a gnarled, knobby look. Sometimes a large part of one of these huge trunks will be quite hollowed out by decay, in which case the peasants often fill up the cavities with a core of stones. The tree goes on bearing with chief dependence on the state of the bark for its healthy condition. The heavy crops and light crops follow each other in somewhat the same relation as the apple crops in our New England country. Women and children gather up those olive berries that fall to the ground early in the season. Whenever it is desired to gather the crop of a tree or orchard the men beat the branches with very long light poles and the women and the children pick up the fallen fruit from the ground. Of course this is a poor way to gather the best olives, but inasmuch as the chief use of the olive in Palestine is to express the oil, it makes less difference. The berries do not ordinarily grow to the larger sizes so often seen in our markets. Perhaps one of the very handsomest stretches of olive-orchards in the East is at what is called the Ṣaḥrâ, near Beirut, between that city and Shwayfât. Other smaller but excellent orchards are to be seen between Bethlehem and Bayt Jâlâ, at Mâr Elyâs, Bîr ez-Zayt and to the south of eṭ-Ṭayyibeh.

The fig in Judea ripens in August and its fruit may be had for several months, as new fruit keeps maturing. There are several varieties of this valuable tree. A few ripe figs are often found as early as June and are luxuries.[1] The natives sometimes hasten the ripening of a few early figs by touching the ends with honey. The natives declare that the fig-tree will not thrive near houses but will become wormy. The action of the milk of fig branches and leaves on the tissues of the eyes, lips and mouth is very disagreeable,

[1] Isa. 28: 4.

A BEDAWY HOUSE

BEDAWY DRINKING

sometimes making them very sore. The eyes of children in the fig season are often very repulsive. For this reason the people prefer other shade, if obtainable, than that of fig-trees. Most fig-trees are small, about the size of an ordinary plum-tree, but the large green varieties may grow to a considerable size. When small fig-trees have sent up two pliable trunk-shoots these are usually twisted together to strengthen each other. They look like a suggestion of that ugly taste in architecture that delighted in twisted columns. The appearance of the branches of a leafless fig-tree is not unlike that of the horse-chestnut in winter time. Large quantities of the black figs and some of the white figs are dried in the orchards, being spread out on the ground under the strong sun-rays.

The pomegranate-tree looks more like an unkempt shrub. The beautiful red bell-like blossoms are very attractive. Lemons and oranges grown for profit are often small trees. The sour marmalade orange grows into a larger, statelier tree.

At Urṭâs, near Solomon's Pools, the largest and most beautifully colored apricots grow. Peaches, plums, quinces and almonds are plentiful, and the cherry, mulberry and walnut thrive.

Concerning trees about the shrines and wilys and all the so-called sacred trees there will be a more appropriate place to speak later on.

In a land where fruit grows and flourishes one may have far less fruit than in some fruitless city in a colder climate but favored with ample facilities for transportation. Right here within a few miles of the finest orange groves in the land, near the vineyards, under the olive and fig-trees, with peaches, pomegranates, apricots and plums, we probably find shorter seasons for each than is the case in some Anglo-Saxon city of the middle temperatures. Here fruit will be much cheaper while it lasts, and some fruits, which must be found near the trees, if enjoyed at all, such as the fig, will be available nowhere else as here. The peach, plum, orange, apricot and grape go to the London, Liverpool, New York, Chicago and Boston markets from the place producing the earliest crops, and the trains and steamships continue bringing from various markets as the season shifts from one garden spot to another. But right here, under this particular orange-tree or by this grape-vine, we usually wait for the ripening of the local crop, knowing that lack of carrying facilities forbids us eating from a tree that yields earlier fruit some hundred miles away, or from a tree that yields when our tree is bare. And so while people who never saw an orange-tree may buy oranges ten months in the year, we who have an orange-tree in sight may have to be content with the orange season of our district. But they will be cheap while they last. Fifty cents is a very ordinary price for a hundred of the best oranges, and one dollar a hundred is pretty dear.

The large raised map of Palestine in fibrous plaster, over seven feet by four, published by the Palestine Exploration Fund, London, and the smaller one help in the study of the physical features of the country.

An excellent small Relief Map of Palestine is edited by Ernest D. Burton and published by the Atlas Relief Map Co., Chicago.

READING LIST

WILSON, C. T.: "Peasant Life in the Holy Land." (Dutton.)

VAN LENNEP: "Bible Lands. (Harper, 1875.)

SMITH, G. A.: "Historical Geography of the Holy Land."

HUNTINGTON, ELLSWORTH: "Palestine and Its Transformation."

The Annual of the American School of Oriental Research in Jerusalem, 1919–20.

BELL, GERTRUDE L.: "The Desert and the Sown."

SEE ARTS. on Crocodiles in the Pal. Expl. Fund Quarterly, 1920 (p. 167), 1921 (p. 19). (Gray and Masterman.)

Stereoscopic Views of Palestine by Underwood and Underwood, and lantern slides sold by the Palestine Exploration Fund.

(The statement on page 13, line 20, needs change in the light of recent history.)

CHAPTER II

THE PEOPLE OF PALESTINE

THE population of Palestine is divided into three parts, desert, village and city. The desert population is the original Arab stock of pastoral nomads.[1] The village population is the agricultural society of the country, and the cities are the meeting places of these two with the population of other countries. The Bedawy population of the desert is the subject of much praise on the part of all writers. All who speak of the Bedawîn use a certain tone of respect, even though occasion is taken to poke fun at them for their rude ways as viewed by the dwellers in towns. The religion of the Bedawîn is a simplified Islâm, or, as it may perhaps be styled, a Moslemized simplicity. The encampment and the march, herding and the raid, mark the features of a roving life over some thousands of square miles of wild land. The different tribes have their general boundaries in the great Syrian and Arabian deserts in about the same way that the North American Indian once kept within certain regions of the continent according to nations.

The cities and villages of Palestine, so far as appearance is concerned, vary in size merely. The houses of a small village are oftentimes just as closely packed as the buildings in a city, so that a village will look like a fragment knocked off a city. With us Westerners a village may have as much land area as some cities, only the dwellings will be far apart, the difference being in comparative density as well as in size. In Palestine the density is about the same and the difference is in the area. This compactness of the village became a fashion in times of insecurity, when feuds between

[1] *Cf.* Job 1: 1–3.

villages led to raids and reprisals. The village was built as solidly as possible on rising ground. In the middle of the core of original houses was the chief's house, with a lofty roof from which watch could be kept of all the surrounding country and approaches.[1] If you wish to trace the growth of a village, inquire for the *burj*, and probably you will be directed to the highest spot in the village, at least to the highest house, around which the early village clustered. If this be on top of a hill, as is frequently the case, the growing village creeps down the slopes, the roof of one house being the dooryard of the house above it, until the effect of a pyramidal structure of children's building-blocks results. In troublesome times a watcher on the *burj* of the village could warn his fellows working in the outlying fields of the approach of an enemy by the firing of a musket or by a shrill cry. All fled to the nest on the height, and a successful attack was difficult against the heavy stone houses and narrow lanes of the village.

Just as among the cities there are those mostly or altogether Moslem and others mostly or altogether Christian, so with the villages. While the Moslem population greatly outnumbers the Christian, yet there is a very considerable Christian population. Râm Allâh, Bayt Jâlâ, eṭ-Ṭayyibeh and Jifnâ are Christian villages. In Bîr ez-Zayt, 'Ayn 'Arîk and 'Âbûd the Christians exceed the Moslems. In el-Bîreh and Ludd the Christians are comparatively few. A Christian village is known from afar by its more prosperous look, and the Christian quarters of a mixed village are also distinguishable by the same favorable marks.

Christian villages have powerful ecclesiastical establishments behind them which work energetically to secure rights for their constituents. Church life in the country is political life, and church dignitaries are adepts in politics. The wealth and cleverness of the church are employed to hold

[1] 2 Kings 9: 17.

PEASANTS ON WAY TO MARKET WITH PRODUCE

BEDAWÎN HORSEMAN

fast all traditions and all concessions which favor the Communion and to hinder excessive injustice from overtaking the members. There results a firm bond of union between the native membership and the ecclesiastical establishment. The Communion is a religious nation, as it were.

The Christian native is not subject to army service, as only Moslems are thus eligible. This disability works to the industrial advantage of the Christians, who pay an extra tax or tribute in lieu of service. Centuries of this condition of things have developed the industrial abilities of the Christian population in spite of discriminations against them in the courts and in administration. A kind of religious status is now recognized in the relations between the Moslem and the Christian peasants. The Moslem stands hard by his faith and the Christian of the Greek Orthodox Church will scorn the thought that Christ and the Bible may be for Moslems.

Religious sects in the East remind one of volcanic islands; they are either ablaze with the fierce fires of an eruption or else they are overlaid with the ashes of an extinct fire. Between crazy fanaticism and cold inanition there are no warm impulses of unselfish evangelism.

The Semitic peasant has always been a conservative. In many ways he is to-day much like what the Canaanite occupier of the land must have been. Each wave of conquest or shower of civilization has left its effect, but underneath the Palestine peasant is a primitive Semite. Until within a few score years religion of one sort or another has usually come to him at the point of the sword. He has often adopted the veneer of a new faith in order to escape death. So it was when Joshua and the Hebrew host swept into the land, Bedawy fashion; so when Maccabean, Roman, Moslem, Crusader, and Moslem again took control. The Palestine peasant has worshiped the Baalim, Yahweh, Moloch, the God of Israel, the Son of God, the God of Islâm. All the time he has kept a certain core of Semitic custom and superstition, a sort of basic religion that has been much the same all through these changes. But it is ofttimes impossible to distinguish between a survival of the old and a reversion or degeneration.

The native Christian is a shrewd business man. He is courteous even to self-effacement. He can work hard, bargain shrewdly, save much, take disappointment and persist. He loves his family dearly. He is humorous, philosophic, a voluble fellow, non-secretive. He respects the Western style of education, largely perhaps because it seems to lift people into an easy life. Ease and grace are Eastern ideals of superiority.

If the Moslem and the Christian could be put on the same political footing and justice done to each impartially in court practise and taxation, I firmly believe that they would draw together, that Palestine would in time be a country with a people and that it would be well equipped from among its own with men of ability, competent to do its political and social work.

In general it may be said that where the Palestine peasant has not come into relationship with the tourist business in any form, and where he is some little distance from any city, he is naturally simple in his tastes and requirements, interested in novelty, sociable, hospitable, fun-loving, hard-working, though not steady in effort.

A lone walker on the road will often sing. Whistling is almost unknown. Peasants make a twenty-mile journey on foot with considerable ease, and half that distance is done very commonly. Distances are always reckoned by them in hours or days, never in miles. They often walk behind their laden animals. Sometimes it is a donkey, bearing the plow and seed-bag or loaded with fagots, grain, sheaves, dried figs or grapes, according to the season. Or it may be a camel similarly laded or carrying stone; or a mule. Seldom are horses used, except by a village shaykh or a city official on the highway. When groups of peasants are on the road there is much talk, often laughter, horse-play, joking, chaffing; sometimes bickering and quarreling.

The peasant stands in awe of learning, especially of learning in the Arabic language. He is sensitive to ridicule, and therefore loath to make such a change in customs as would bring it on him. He is eager in discussion, inquisitive, strong in memory and at imitating, but slow to adopt strange ways not tested by the conditions of life to which he is accustomed. You seldom or never find him nervous, fretful or discontented. He never questions the wisdom of Providence. He seldom mentions weather probabilities. He, like his Old Testament countryman, refers all things to a First Cause. Divine cause or permission is prominent in his explanation of any phenomena.

The personal appearance of the villagers and the look of their houses vary with the country level at which they live. In the plains and lowlands, where thatch and earth are more commonly used in building, there is a population noticeably different from the dwellers in the stone villages in the highlands. The inhabitants lower down are darker and smaller than the hill villagers. These latter are often of good size and development and, especially among the Christians, are frequently of lighter color. It is not very uncommon to see sandy complexions among them.[1] The women and girls in the best villages are often handsome. The men are lithe of body and finely formed. Both men and women are usually supple, slow-motioned, strong. They have dark, expressive eyes, neutral mouths, medium foreheads, heavy features with curving lines, browned skins and black hair. Fair complexions are admired, especially the so-called *wheat-colored* complexion (*ḳumḥeh*). Eyes are distinguished by the epithets *'asaliyeh* (honey-colored), *koḥli* (kohl-colored), *ghuzlaniyeh* (gazel-like) and so on.

[1] 1 Sam. 16: 12; Song 5: 10.

Different villages and their inhabitants get reputations for doing one or another kind of work especially well. Or they are distinguished according to disposition, as harsh and fanatical, or as courteous and reasonable. Some villages get a name for dulness and others for sharpness. The villagers are known about the country by slight variation in dress, by differing casts of countenance and peculiarities of speech.[1]

We must not magnify too much the differences between civilizations and peoples, or between this people of whom we speak and our own people. The difference is often but quantitative. They emphasize some qualities which we possess, though in quieter color or in less distinctive marking. Oftentimes the differences would not be apparent except that, as we have passed rapidly from place to place, our eyes have synchronized phenomena of different stages of culture. We see really among these strangers many practises and notions of our own distant forebears.

Western people are so in the habit of pitying all the women of Asia that they will probably go on doing so until the end of time in spite of the facts. To our Western idea woman in the East is a pitiable, miserable abstraction. The Turkish harem, the Indian child-widow and the deformed Chinese foot stand for all Asia to many of us. There is probably a large, free area of life open to thousands of the women of Asia that does not seem cramped by comparison with the total civilization of which they are a part. The Bedawy woman would not change places with any of us, and the village peasant woman of Palestine enjoys life fully as well as the male villagers. She is not supposed to enter the field marked out by custom for male members of society, nor will the field she occupies be intruded upon by them. She shares with the man a preference for male children. Her position in this regard is only an exaggeration of the condition that prevails in all modern society. She, like her brothers and

[1] Matt. 26: 73.

WOMAN'S WORK

1. At the Cistern. 2. In the Market. 3. Bringing Brush.

sisters the world over, is influenced by customs to which she yields obedience a little more gracefully than do many of us. She goes about her work cheerfully if she is well. Too often she is not well, and in a few years drudging toil and frequent childbearing age her. Like her sisters in other countries, she is sometimes tidy and sometimes not. She loves her children. Whether she loves her husband or not is not easy to discover, but she pays him proper respect and, if kind, she probably cherishes real esteem for him. The marriage was probably not of her choosing, and very likely not of his. Marriage is a state entered into dutifully by all sons and daughters. It builds the tribe or great family which is at bottom the object of a Syrian's greatest devotion next to himself, and often before himself.

If you awake in the early hours of morning you will hear the monotonous rumble of the stone mills, telling that the day's work for the women has begun. When the spring is very small or low, and it takes a long time to fill a jar, the women and young girls will sometimes go out before it is light to get the first turn at the trickling stream. Long journeys are made into the waste places to secure headloads of brush or grass-fodder. A woman usually wears a dark blue crash dress while at work. Her legs and feet are bare; perhaps she carries a rough pair of shoes such as the men wear, but they are for the briers and stones outside the village. Should she put them on within the village the other women would laugh at her and call her proud or citified.

Unmarried women are very scarce among the peasantry. Marriage usually comes at an early age for girls. One of the owners of a house that we had to hire for the work of the new boys' training school had as wife such a mere slip of a girl that we were curious to know her age. She couldn't tell us how old she was, but said that she had been married five years. A companion with her ventured the guess that her age was thirteen years. The little wife seemed happy and was the only peasant wife I ever saw receiving any affectionate attentions from her husband. She was a pretty girl and seemed to be a pet in the family. She had her own little ways of enjoying her little life. One day, when some much poorer women from el-Bîreh were toiling on the house which her husband's family was building, bringing stone and mortar on their heads, Mrs. Thirteen-years put on her best dress of blue with some Bethlehem needlework on the breast, adorned her fingers with the rings of cheap nickel and glass, commonly worn, and taking a piece of embroidery, stood thus, plying her needle genteelly, where the other women were toiling at their severer task. Many were the glances they threw at her, but when they looked her eyes were on her handiwork.

Several statements on page 45 *f.*, especially the one on army service, need modification now. See Chapter XII. The classical work in English on the modern life of the Bedawin is Charles M. Doughty's Arabia Deserta which has recently come out in a new and expensive edition.

CHAPTER III

FAMILY LIFE

When our sons shall be as plants grown up in their youth,
And our daughters as corner-stones hewn after the fashion of a palace;
When our garners are full, affording all manner of store,
And our sheep bring forth thousands and ten thousands in our fields;
When our oxen are well laden;
When there is no breaking in, and no going forth,
And no outcry in our streets:
Happy is the people that is in such a case;
Yea, happy is the people whose God is Jehovah.

Psalm 144: 12–15.

THE above bit of ancient expression would describe the ideal of happiness of a village people in Palestine to-day.

In a village there may be few or many tribes. In a village tribe there may be scores of families. The tribe is a great family and goes by the Arabic name *Dâr* (court or house). In el-Bîreh, for instance, there are four tribes among its eight hundred Moslems and one tribe of Christians numbering less than a hundred. The Moslem tribes are *Dâr Ṭawîl, Dâr Ḳurân, Dâr Hamayil* and *Dâr 'Abid.* The Christian tribe goes by the name *Rafîdya,* because originally the members came from a village of that name, near Nâblus. *Dâr Ṭawîl* is by far the most influential and supplies two of the three shaykhs of the village recognized by the general government. The other shaykh comes from *Dâr Ḳurân.* These three shaykhs are the intermediaries between the general government and the village. Sometimes the tribe will become so large as to have subordinate divisions within it. In Râm Allâh there are five original tribes, the Ḥadadeh, the Dâr Ibrahîm, the Dâr Jurjus, the Ḥasâsineh and the Shaḳara. But the tribe of Ḥadadeh is nearly the equal in numbers of the other four, and has been divided into four sub-tribes, the Sharaḳa, the Dâr Awâd, the Dâr Yûsuf and the Dâr Abu Jaghab. The result is that there are practically eight tribes in the village. The four branches of the Ḥadadeh feel a kinship and importance from their common source and present size. The other four tribes go by the common designation of the Hamayil.

Birth is the usual mode of entering a tribe, but outsiders are sometimes admitted. A man from another part of Syria had occasion to live in one of the large Christian villages of Palestine and wished to be counted as a citizen there. He decided to join a certain tribe in that village. As much as he was permitted, he fellowshiped with that tribe, went to their guest-house occasionally and contributed to expenses by sharing in their provision of food for visiting strangers and soldiers. He then had the government at Jerusalem change his *kushan* or paper of residence and citizenship so that it should now declare him a resident of such and such a village. When he had spoken to the elders of the tribe that he sought to join, and they in turn to the members of the tribe, he was admitted to membership with them by common consent. Thenceforth he paid his military tribute through the chief men of this tribe. The elders mentioned are the heads of families and are called the *ukhtiyarîyeh*. They are the tribal chiefs and representatives.

Ordinarily friendship is confined to this tribal relationship, and marriage is usually restricted to its limits. As an Arabic proverb expresses it, " I am against my cousin, but my cousin and I are against the world." People outside this tribal family are strangers and possible foes.[1] If, contrary to what they expect of outsiders, we should show ourselves kindly disposed to them by continual helpful acts, very likely they might set up a hypothetical relationship

[1] Deut. 14: 21; 15: 3; 23: 20; *cf.* Matt. 5: 44–46.

between themselves and us, at least in conversation, in order to gloss over the anomaly.

Closer yet is the relationship within the immediate family. As long as the size of the family permits, it occupies the one house, or extensions of it, but if it is prosperous and growing, new households are set up and by such a process the tribe develops. Where friendship is practically confined to the family and tribe the importance of family membership and numerous family connections will be appreciated.[1] The larger and more influential one's family, the more secure are its fortunes.[2] And influence depends on the number of the men.

A Moslem was killed and it was several months before his slayers were detected and brought to punishment. The family of the deceased was large and worked together to ferret out the secret. A smaller family might never have been able to accomplish the object. Outsiders or the government would have made no such persistent effort.[3]

Marriages in the country are usually with some kindred family.[4] Marrying outside one's tribe is comparatively rare. Marriage is the one important subject among parents of boys and girls. Girls are sometimes married as early as seven years. They are betrothed at much tenderer ages. A mother brought a little child in arms to one of the village day-schools and urged its acceptance, doubtless to have relief from the care of it for a part of the day. The child was a girl, and the teacher of the girls' school refused to take her, exclaiming, "Why, she's a mere baby. We cannot teach her to read now." The mother argued and finally said, "If you don't take her now she will be betrothed soon." The introduction of school privileges into the country, for girls as well as for boys, has resulted, in many cases, in lengthening the childhood of those who otherwise

[1] Psalm 127: 3–5. [2] Gen. 24: 60. [3] *Cf.* Deut. 21: 1–9.
[4] Gen. 24: 3–4; 28: 2; Num. 36: 8–11.

would have been betrothed and married early in life. Parents are generally unwilling to allow a younger daughter to be married before an elder daughter.[1]

A marriage settlement in money is expected from the bridegroom and paid to the father of the bride. Parents often attempt to avoid cash payments by an exchange of brothers and sisters. A family with a boy and a girl make overtures to an eligible family having a girl and a boy, and the young people are paired off at more advantageous terms all round than would be the case if the families were strangers, that is, if they were out of tribal relations with each other. Sometimes, of course, this matter of exchange causes people of very different ages to be joined, but then the years heal that, and the theory is that if the bride is considerably younger than the groom the husband as he comes to old age will have a comparatively strong and able housekeeper and caretaker in his wife.

The usual wedding payment to the father of the bride is about two hundred twenty-five dollars in this village. From this sum the father may make his daughter such presents as he pleases of jewels and head-coins. The wedding costume of the bride is the gift of the groom's family.

Where a widowed woman is remarried, the marriage portion paid her father is less than in the case of a first marriage, and she is apt to receive a larger share of it in presents from her father, since she cannot, in this case, be made to marry except by her own consent.

To get the business of marriage settled at the earliest date and in the most advantageous way possible is the aim of guardians and parents. The wife will have done her part well if she bears children, mostly boys,[2] sees that no unnecessary losses of money or food occur in the house and holds her tongue. If she fails in any of these points she may dim

[1] Gen. 29: 26. [2] Gen. 29: 34; 30: 20.

BRINGING HOME THE BRIDAL TROUSSEAU

GIRLS AT PLAY. CARRYING HEADLOADS OF GRASS IN IMITATION OF THE WOMEN

the felicities of the married state, that is, of her husband and his father and brothers.

There are three occasions preceding the actual marriage of the man and woman on which public celebration is made. The first is the engagement. This is arranged between the fathers of the young people. The initiative is taken by the father of the young man working through friends, who approach the father of the girl and make a proposition of betrothal. If all is favorable the bargain may be bound by money paid to the father of the young woman. A betrothal party is arranged for friends of both the contracting young people at the home of the prospective bride. The young man prepares a feast for the invited guests, a sheep is killed, a priest may be present and the betrothal made public. The agreement is but a little less strong than the marriage contract itself.[1] The second public manifestation is the purchase by the groom of the marriage outfit of garments, including the bridal trousseau, and the procession that carries the articles home. The bridegroom's party goes to some large near-by village or the nearest city for these purchases. One day we were apprised of such a trousseau party by shouting and the firing of arms, and later a procession of women went by on their way to their own village, carrying with them the bundle of wedding garments. One of their village chiefs was with them. At another time a group returning from Jerusalem on a similar errand was met by a crowd of women on the outskirts of the village and accompanied into it with singing and dancing. This time the women had a stick dressed up with the bridal costume. There was the red striped dress and gay jacket on a cross-stick frame to hold out the sleeves. There were also a girdle, the heavy coin head-dress and three small mirrors, one on each arm and one on the breast. The Bethlehem costume is very commonly used for gala occasions by peo-

[1] *Cf.* Deut. 22: 23, 24.

ple of other sections, as it is one of the showiest costumes of the country. The bridegroom is expected to provide wedding garments for relatives of the bride, though they in turn may be expected to return a wedding gift of equal value to him. The third celebration may last two or three days. Towards the close of it the wedding itself takes place.

We went one Saturday evening to see the jollification that preceded a wedding to be solemnized the next day. Outside the house of the groom there were two lines of young men, their number varying from forty to sixty as they shifted places, some dropping out and others falling into line from time to time. These two lines were facing each other and a bright brush fire was blazing in the middle. As more men crowded in to participate a line was formed at one end, thus making a third side of a parallelogram. The men on either side were singing back and forth to each other, in antiphonal fashion, while they kept up a sort of swaying dance in line called the *mil'ab*. By pressing their shoulders, neighbor to neighbor, the line moved as one mass. The left foot was made the base of movement for each singer. The right foot was swayed and then lifted high and forward until the whole body swung forward in a sweeping bow or duck. The hands were also keeping time, rubbing up and down the forearms from the elbows to the finger-tips, the head meanwhile swaying from side to side, all to the native peasant singing of the same simple tune over and over again. Certain fixed verses were made the basis and were finished out with impromptu verses for the occasion. Some of these were, "We are glad to see your faces." "We have come to you; if it were not for love we should not be here." "Love is sweet." "We hope for good large dishes." "Did you see any Bedawîn coming up from the East?" "Such and such (naming them) villages will help you against the enemy." "Fear not, delicate young women, our young men will protect you," and so on, passing compliments, singing the praises of love and acknowledging its power in bringing them together, or mingling snatches of war sentiment, anticipation of generous servings of the wedding-feast and assurances of alliance, friendship, defense and security in the strength and equipment of their young men. The bridegroom mingled joyfully with the others, sometimes performing in the line and sometimes replenishing the brush fire. All around, on the roofs of the neighboring houses, in the darkness that was black by contrast with the brilliant fire, the women of the tribe were seated. Every now and then, at any seeming lull in the excitement, some woman would set up the peculiar trilling cry called the *zaghârût* or *zaghârît*, at which the men would fairly leap into a renewal of the dance and song. Pistols and muskets were shot off occasionally. Although this was all taking place in a Christian village, a good number of Moslem youths from a neighboring village came over to join in the fun. They had brought two sheep which had been slaughtered and were now simmering in immense kettles for a feast. The father of the groom acted as an overseer of the gayeties and was trying, apparently, to curb the zeal of those who had firearms to discharge.

On the wedding-day in a Christian village the bride and groom with their attendant friends form two parties and approach the church from different quarters. If obtainable, horses are provided for the bride and groom to ride on and she is completely covered over with a mantle,[1] a feather being stuck in the top of it over her head. Inside the church the bridal party, consisting of groom, bride, best man, bridesmaid, the mothers and some other relatives, stand in the middle of the church facing the altar. The groom stands at the bride's right hand; she is heavily veiled. Guests and spectators, in the case of the wedding mentioned above, filled the church on either side of the bridal party and a large

[1] *Cf.* Gen. 24: 65.

concourse filled the yard outside. Four priests and a censer boy entered the church. Tapers were provided for those guests nearest the young people, while candles were given to the bride and groom. These were lighted. The censer was swung. The ritual, hymns and Scripture were read or intoned, partly in Arabic and partly in Greek. The head priest, who was a Greek by blood, read the Greek portions, while his assistants, natives of the village, read the Arabic parts. Rings which had been touched on the head and lips of bride and groom were placed on their hands and afterwards changed about. Wreaths of artificial flowers were placed on their heads. The book to which most respect had been shown, the Bible, was brought down between them, dividing their joined fingers. Then, headed by the priests, the bridal party marched around in a circling course with all the attendant relatives. Some old women, following closely behind the bride and groom, caught at their robes and, joining them, went through the motions of sewing them with threadless needles. After this the final pronouncement was made by the head priest and the ceremony was over. Immediately the best man grabbed the groom in a sort of ecstasy of congratulation and lifted him into the air twice, and would have done so a third time had not the priest interfered, probably thinking that these demonstrations were out of place in the church. A gun was fired outside the church as soon as it was known that the ceremony was complete. After some hearty felicitations the party moved off in procession with priests and guests.

The groom, with the men, went to the guest-room[1] of the tribe, where they enjoyed conversation, coffee and cigarettes. The bride and her party of women went to the home of the groom. As she was about to enter the house a water-jar was placed on her head and her hand was assisted to plaster a piece of bread-dough on the jamb of the doorway.

[1] Matt. 9: 15.

WASHING A CHILD

A SWADDLED INFANT

These signs were in token of good housewifely qualities. After the bride had been seated for some time inside the house her women friends were granted their entreaty and she allowed them to uncover her face. Then she consented to exhibit her jewelry,[1] silver bracelets, bangles, head-coins, ear-jewels, etc. She seemed very sad, as is expected when a young girl leaves her mother, and quite exhausted. Her hands and nails were stained with ḥennâ. It is said that the hands, wrists and lower limbs are always stained thus on the night before the wedding. Outside the house five kettles filled with mutton were set on stones over wood fires. They were seething and bubbling, getting into readiness for the wedding-feast in the evening.[2]

At the guest-house assembly, where the groom and his men friends are gathered, some one calls out the names of those who have given money presents to the bridegroom and the amount in each case.

If there are reasons for a less public wedding celebration than usual, the ceremony is performed on a week-day. Such is the case when some near relative has died recently, where haste is desired, or where the man or the woman has been married previously.

One Sunday we saw a double wedding celebration. But one was in the Greek Orthodox Church and the other was in the United Greek Church, which is papal in allegiance. The contracting families were so closely related as to allow of but one of the marriages planned between them, according to Greek Church law. But as each family had a son and daughter to marry off to the daughter and son of the other family and considered their own interests in the matter as of more importance than church law, one bridal party was sent to one church and one to the other.

The party of one of the bridegrooms was provided with sword dancers, and as they reached any open place of suffi-

[1] Isa. 61: 10; Jer. 2: 32. [2] Gen. 29: 22.

cient size, as at the street corners, a space was cleared and a dancer with a short curved sword in one hand and a waving cloth in the other, went through the graceful movements, leaping and crouching.

AN INTRODUCTION TO A WEDDING-SONG

This bride is clothed with silk from Damascus:
Her hair is perfumed sweetly.

When the bridegroom goes to greet her,
Goes to press on her forehead the golden coin,[1]

He finds her as a fragrant branch;
Praise be unto God.

O comrades, when I saw her,
Three silver rings were on her little finger.

Foolish one! did I not tell thee " heed her "?
This good girl bears the key of relief.

THE BRIDE'S GOOD-BYE TO HER FAMILY[2]

O mother mine, fill for me my pillows;
I left the house without a farewell to my friends.

O mother mine, fill them for me;
I left the house without a thought for my gospels.

O one possessed of rosy cheeks,
Thou'rt worth of gold a deal.

May God shield those who reared thee;
Never a day did'st thou go out alone.

O one possessed of rosy cheeks,
Thou'rt worth of gold a closet full.

May God shield those who trained thee;
Not a day didst thou go out angry.

---

[1] In the evening of the wedding-day when the bridegroom is allowed a glimpse of his wife's face before he goes to join his friends in the merrymaking, he presses a gold coin on her forehead. It is his gift, and falls into her lap.

[2] The two songs on this page are from eṭ-Ṭayyibeh.

Thou art a branch of willow, my daughter,
Thou art a branch of willow, thou.

On thy strands thou puttest the coins,
Dangling the coins from thy head.

Thou'rt a branch of riḥân,[1] O daughter,
A branch of riḥân art thou.

On the braids thou puttest silver dollars,
On the braids the coins, O thou!

Do not go from my house, my pet,
Thou who repairest my house in its borders.

Thou wentest forth from my house, O pet,
And there wast none other like thee.

Going out of the house of the good to the house of a prince,
Wearing anklets on her feet and dressed in a robe of silk.

Going from the house of the good to that of a prince,
Anklets on her feet and dressed in a silken robe.

WHEN THE BRIDEGROOM TAKES PART IN THE PROCESSION[2]

Where is the bridegroom, where? Let us amuse him.
May he be preserved for us and long life to his brother.

The procession went along; in front was dancing.
O prince, with gold are the guns of the youths glistening.

Going down to the procession like a prince;
I wish thee in the prophet's keeping.

O mounted bridegroom, no one is like thee to me.
Thou art as a ring of silver placed on my breast.

O bridegroom, riding, as an apple art thou;
Go to thine own before I snatch thee as the wind.

O bridegroom, riding, as a lemon art thou;
Go to thine own before I snatch thee with my eyes.

[1] A fragrant herb. [2] From eṭ-Ṭayyibeh.

SONG BEFORE THE BRIDEGROOM[1]

Be happy, cousin, at sight of thee fled my trouble;
Be happy, owner of the ṭarbûsh, be jealous of our wealth.

Be happy, thou with the ample drawers, and jealous of our gold.
" O uncle," said Ghâlyeh, the costly bride,

" I'll marry none but the Bedawy with his tilted head-dress;
The one who at noonday threshes in the face of the Arabs."[2]

Cut and be cut, O pomegranate, the water flows in the orchard.
She came to the garden which is full of pomegranates.

SONG BEFORE THE BRIDE[3]

Come out, O pet, O jewel mine, costly;
Tell us the precious price thy father asked.

We have walked from country to country
And we have found maidens costly.

We have asked for the girl from her father,
Her father who is as rich as Aleppo.

We have walked from street to street,
And have found many who were daughters of princes.

Ride on, O daughter of the Ḥadâdîyeh,[4]
Thy worth in gold is two hundred hundred.

Tighten the saddle for her, O father, tighten it;
Count out to her a hundred quarter riyals.

THE VOICES OF THE WOMEN IN HIGH TONES CALLING OUT ABOUT THE BRIDE[5]

Bend gracefully from side to side,
O thou who bendest as a palm in the mountains.

Thou art not bad to lower thy value,
But thou art like the well-bred horses, perfect.

Put thy sleeve over thy mouth, thou beauty, like thy mother;
The man is thy uncle, he will make and enlarge thy sleeve.

[1] From Râm Allâh. [2] *Cf.* Judges 6:11. [3] From Râm Allâh. [4] Means a woman who is a member of the tribe of Ḥadâd. [5] From eṭ-Ṭayyibeh.

Thy garment, O choice one, two did cut it,
And more than a fortnight did seven tailors make it.

If love were not like fleet horses,
Love and I should be separated as day from night.

WHEN THE BRIDE ENTERS THE HOUSE OF THE GROOM[1]

Sprinkle the cushions with roses and ḥennâ;
Let the bridegroom rejoice and be refreshed.

Sprinkle the cushions with roses and perfume;
Let the bridegroom sit on the cushion with his dear one.

O pair of gazels, how you are marked with ḥennâ!
May you two rejoice each other.

By marriage the wife becomes a member of her husband's family. She assists her mother-in-law in the household duties. One of the reasons given for some of the very early marriages is that the young woman may be trained into a suitable wife for the son by his mother.

It is counted an affliction[2] if the new wife is not a mother in due time, and it is a joyous occasion when a male child is born. There are many parents who love their girl babies tenderly, but they are almost sure to be partial to boys, and the majority of parents are greatly disappointed if boys do not make up the larger part of the children.

One day I stumbled into a house where an anomalous condition of things existed for a Christian village. On coming away I learned that the man was a bigamist. He was reputed to have become rich through thieving, and his fine house was childless. What did he do but bring home another wife! The laws of his country were not against such a practise, but the law of his church, with the sentiment and practise of his fellow villagers, was sternly against it. He defied all, even though he was cut off from communion. He became an object of reproach and abhorrence to the pious

[1] From eṭ-Ṭayyibeh. [2] Gen. 15:2.

and the superstitious of the whole village, who looked for terrible consequences. A long time afterwards, some mention of this man having occurred in conversation, I learned that he was without any children by his second wife also, and that his childlessness was considered by the villagers as a token of the wrath of God. Although rich, his lot was considered miserable by the neighbors. He was said to be worth about fifteen thousand dollars. He was accused of having made a business of stealing wedding finery from festive and sleepy bridal parties.

Disappointed lovers are not unknown among the peasantry. One young man of a prominent family fell in love with the daughter of the owner of a fig orchard next to his father's orchard. For some reason, possibly the fact that they belonged to different tribes (though of the same village), the father of the girl was unwilling that these two young people should marry each other. He gave his daughter in marriage to another youth, a member of her own tribe. The disappointed young man has never been consoled, refuses to marry any other or even to enter into the social affairs of his own family. He lives, a recluse, at some distance from his village in one of the valleys. The villagers think that in time he may become a priest.

Boyhood and girlhood are shorter in Palestine than in America, but often merry. Stories illustrating the preference for boys among Oriental parents are plentiful, but no one who examines the society of the Orient will fail to find that it could not well be otherwise without very great changes. Boys increase the size, force, wealth and importance of the family. When they marry they bring home their wives and the children perpetuate the house of the father. Should the husband die, the wife and her boy children may be assisted by her husband's relatives, the boys certainly. Should the mother of the boys marry again, the boys go from her to be brought up by her former husband's family. Boys increase the house, girls decrease it. The earnings of the father and the sons go to provide a substantial family dwelling and to defend the house against adverse circumstances. Girls are sure to marry and, although they bring in a money payment to their fathers, yet in every other respect they are a disadvantage, as they go to strengthen another house, not the house where they were fed and reared. But there is not an iron-clad observance of an inhuman rule here as some seem to imagine. All customs strange to our Western ideas may surely be supposed to be grounded in very human causes and to be very natural after all. Many parents are very fond of their girls. Relations through the mother's family and through sisters are often highly esteemed.

One evening two fatherless little girls belonging to a Moslem tribe in el-Bîreh were going home from Râm Allâh and were caught in a heavy hail and thunder-storm just behind our house. Knowing that they would be endangered we went out to bring them into the house until the storm should pass. We found them very frightened and cowering in the poor defense of a wall. They were soon quite happy after we had dried and fed them.

But, just as in any other country, there were anxious mother-hearts a mile away in el-Bîreh, and soon those mothers were out in the storm, having enlisted two men and two boys in their eager search for the little girls. Their terror was changed to keen pleasure when they found the children safely sheltered from harm.

As the demands of the tribal life become less imperative, following the improvement of social and general governmental conditions, the customs of the people approach more nearly those of other nations.

At the time of the baby's birth one of the neighboring women goes with the good news to the father. For her welcome news she may receive a gift from him. The father also provides fruit and other dainties for those who come to congratulate him on the birth of a child. All this happens in case the child is a boy. Quieter times ensue on the birth of a little girl. The father and mother are known after the birth of the first son as the father of so and so and the mother of so and so. For instance, Abu Fâris and Umm Fâris are the new titles and practically the names of the father and mother of the boy Fâris. The child adds its father's first name after its own. Simon Bar Jona (Simon, Son of Jona) was the style of name among the ancient Jews. In modern times the Arab omits the word *son* in common usage, thus making the name simply Simon Jona.

The midwife attends to the dressing of the baby. She rubs the little body with salt and oil and swaddles it tightly. This woman attendant comes every day for forty days to cleanse and wrap the child. Woe betide the mother or any other meddler who interferes with the wrapping and other peculiar functions of the midwife, who is very jealous of the dignity of her profession. She is mistress of her department and brooks no interference.

The Christian baby is ordinarily baptized after the fortieth day. The occasion is celebrated with a dinner. Babies are not weaned early. Some are nursed for two years, while the last baby may be weaned only after it is four or five years old. Dainties are brought to sweeten the little gums and cause the weaning child to forget its mother's milk.[1]

One day we stepped into a near neighbor's to see a new-born boy. He was fast asleep, wound and dressed in his tight little wraps, and lying on one of those circular straw mats of the kind used to cover the wooden bread bowl. The mat in this case was put on top of a round shallow straw basket such as the peasant woman uses to carry wheat. The whole was about six inches high. The mother lay on a pallet on the floor beside it. Considerable interest was felt

[1] Psalm 131: 2.

in the health of this baby boy. There were three girl children in the family, no boys, two other boy babies having died. Their death illustrated the saying, "Killed with kindness." Being boys they received more attention, that is to say, more pampering, than they would have received had they been girls. This consisted in heeding their every wish in the matter of food, which was especially harmful in times of sickness.

Children are the rulers of most houses in the country villages. They exceed in number and dirtiness. If they are well they run in and out in all kinds of weather, barefooted, bareheaded. If they are unwell, not overmuch attention is paid to them at first except to bring them extras to eat. If they become dangerously ill, all the medical help within reach is summoned in a frenzy of helplessness. If they recover, their convalescence is retarded by the same excessive generosity that seeks to stuff them with whatever edibles they may call for. An ordinary country parent is simply unable to resist the crying demands of a sick child, and scarcely of a well one. The more ignorant parents are fond of encouraging the precocity of their children, even teaching them to utter baby curses against the members of their families, and laughing and patting the little swearers in encouragement.

The poorer children are seldom bothered with more than one garment, unless it be a skull-cap. If the parents are more prosperous a little cloth cap embroidered, and with a few bangles or blue beads sewed on the front, is provided. As they grow older the children may gain a jacket over the little shirt. The little girls may have a row of coins on their head-dresses and a little shawl or sash about them. On festivals the little girl may be allowed to wear her mother's holiday jacket or shawl. The shawl has to be folded several times for the girl's use. The Bethlehem jacket, so commonly sought for festivals, is never meant to be an exact fit for any one. Its beauty is in its surface, embroidered with yellow, red and green silk.

The little girls begin very early to bring water in a jar on the head, first beginning with a tiny jar which they steady by the hands, and progressing until able to carry the heavy full-sized jar without the touch of a hand, yes, even to carry such a jar, weighing thirty pounds, tilted forward on the head. Of such a one, having a strong muscular neck, and swinging forward gracefully and easily, the others may say as they point, " See, she is strong, she can carry her jar tipped like the comb of a cock."

When very little, boys and girls play together in the streets and around the ovens, sometimes even on the roofs. By the time they are six years old they are very apt to separate and play with their own kind and to differ a little in their choice of games. The older girls in the families have to care for the little children a great deal, and have to carry and amuse them. Boys and girls are soon able to help in the vineyards, or in picking up olives, or gathering grass and brush, or carrying things for older members of the family.

The receipt for making men and women in Palestine is the same as elsewhere: Take boys and girls and give them a few years of responsibility and you have men and women. The result of these few years of responsibility is to take away the freedom of play and innocency and to add the reserve of work and insight.

The following story is sometimes told to children to warn them against foolish pride and to inculcate obedience to fathers.

A young tiger who had heard about the ability of men, though he had never seen one, felt so eager in his strength to have a combat that he expressed to his father a wish to go out and find a man and have a fight with him. The father tiger advised against such an undertaking, saying, "Even I who am older and stronger than you should not

THREE KINDS OF HOUSES—MUD, DRY-STONE, STONE-AND-MORTAR

think of seeking a fight with a man, for I could not prevail against him." But the proud young tiger, not heeding his father's advice, went to seek a man. He journeyed until he came to a road much frequented by travelers and lay down under a tree to await a foe. While waiting there he noticed a camel running down the road, although loaded heavily. The camel was running away from his master. The young, inexperienced tiger got up and said to the camel, "Are you a man?" The camel answered hastily, "I am not a man, but I am running away from a man, because he loads such heavy burdens on me." The young tiger thought to himself, "How strong must the man be if he causes so much distress and fear in this great creature." Next a horse passed, and the tiger thought, "Maybe this is the man," but received a negative reply to his question as he had from the camel. Then there came along a weak little donkey, loaded with wood and driven by a man. The tiger asked his question of the man, "Are you a man?" "Yes," the man answered. Then the young tiger said, "I have come to have a fight with you." "All right," replied the man, "but I am not quite ready now. May I tie you with my rope to the tree until I can come back?" The tiger allowed the man to tie him, which the man did very securely, and then cut a strong, thick club from the tree, with which he beat the young tiger cruelly. The tiger cried out in pain, "Oh, please let me go; I'll never try to fight with a man again." Then the man let him go and the young tiger went to his father and told his experience.

A bit of current fiction regarding Asiatics is that the children are chronically unhappy. Moslem children are the especial victims of this Christian species of prevarication. To such people "children playing in the streets of Jerusalem" belong to the good time coming and are the sign of fulfilled prophecy,[1] despite the probable fact that children have been

[1] Zech. 8: 5.

playing in Jerusalem's streets for some thousands of years, whether tourists have seen them or not. Doubtless, as the tourist appears in any street, playing ceases and small children flee or stand in mute amazement. The child will probably be happy again when the apparition vanishes. Along the tourists' route the children are too often taught to cry out for gifts (*bakshîsh*) and to show themselves at a disadvantage in order to excite pity. Moslem children sometimes curse or even attempt to stone travelers.

A matter of wonderment to us is the apparent immunity from harm with which children play on unprotected places, such as roofs and about empty pits and cisterns. Now and then we hear of some accident, but rarely. A neighbor's little girl, playing on the flat housetop, fell over into the street and died.[1]

One day I saw some little girls five or six years of age playing at carrying head bundles of grass in imitation of women. Boys make and play with slings (*miḳlâ'*) for throwing stones. When quarreling, the first impulse is for them to reach for a stone to throw. We noticed severe burns on some of the boys, near the wrist. Some of them made huge sores which roused our pitying concern. We found out that the wounds were self-inflicted, however, the superstitious scamps having a boyish notion that burning the wrist or forearm would insure for them greater accuracy in throwing. The boys play horse vigorously. They have a game played with pegs of wood very similar to our peggy, in which one strikes a double-pointed peg on one end with a stick and tries to gain ground with an opponent. Another game is played in a soft, spongy spot of ground with longer pegs sharpened on one end only. It is something like playing stick-knife. The object is so to drive the peg by a throw into the soft space in the ground as to dislodge an opponent's pegs, previously thrown, and made to stick in the same place.

[1] *Cf.* Deut. 22: 8.

A game among the boys, called *'alâm,* is very similar to the game of *roll to the bat.* The privileged player strikes a ball with a stick and drives it out into a field of other players. The boy who secures the ball tries to throw or roll it so as to hit a stone marker ('alâm) set up by the first player. The one thus aiming at the stone marker warns the others to stand aside and allow him to play by saying "*Dustûr,*" signifying, "By your leave."

The boys in our school played a game called *wolf.* A circle of boys joined hands and went dancing around while one outside the moving circle, called the wolf, kept trying to snatch one from the circle of boys who represented sheep. But whenever a boy in the dancing circle came anywhere near the hovering wolf he let fly his heels to prevent capture. As boy after boy was snatched successfully by the outside boy the circle grew smaller until but one was left, who was to be the wolf in the next game.

Boys play about the threshing-floor and are often in the vineyards and gardens. They play many games that are either the same or very similar to those played by boys elsewhere. Such are marbles, duck-on-the-rock, seesaw, swinging, blindman, leap-frog and hide-and-seek. In Râm Allâh there is a variation of this last game called *khurrak,* played by sides. There is a game called *ilkûrat* which might well be considered a primitive relative of golf.

There is as much difference between the training of the children of the better class of peasants and the poorer in Palestine as obtains in the differing grades of homes in other countries. Most youths come to exhibit a very admirable respect for their elders and their teachers. They are taught to kiss the hand of their father[1] or of any guest who is visiting him. They seldom interject their own conversation or ideas into the current of talk going on about them, but listen with keen though modest attention. They are proud

[1] *Cf.* Ex. 20: 12.

of the standing of the family in the respect of the neighborhood and eager to learn their part in the business of life.

One father, a shaykh in his village, on sending away a son to another village to attend school, was gruff in manner for some days before the boy's departure and treated the boy so unhandsomely that the mother protested and said that it was wrong to let the boy go away feeling badly. In explanation of his treatment of his son the father said, " Do you love the boy more than I do? I am acting so that he will not be homesick."

A boy was noticed who had a fiery temper. When in a passionate fit of anger he seemed to lose control of himself and wished to harm other boys, being restrained only by force. An experienced mother in the village who was related to the family explained the lad's disposition to sudden fits of anger by saying that when the child was very young the mother's milk was scanty and the baby had to be fed from the breasts of several different women to help out a little now and then, and that this variety of breasts for feeding accounted for the violent temper of the boy.

Few families, comparatively, have what we should call a family name. The nearest to it for the generality would be the name of the tribe to which the family belongs. The tribal name is not used except in a formal or legal designation. Generally a child bears two names, his own, or, as we should say, a Christian or first name, followed by the name of his father. Thus the child is given the personal name Yakûb (Jacob), and if his father's personal name is Ibrahîm (Abraham), he goes by the two names, Yakûb Ibrahîm, which is equivalent to saying, " This is Yakûb, the son of Ibrahîm." If Ibrahîm had a daughter, he might name her 'Azîzeh, and she would be 'Azîzeh Ibrahîm. Ibrahîm's own father's name may have been Dâûd (David), so Ibrahîm's full name would be Ibrahîm Dâûd, that is, Ibrahîm, the son of Dâûd. But more likely Ibrahîm's father's name was Yakûb, the same names being used often in a family with the omission of a generation, so that grandfather and grandson may have the same name.[1] In such a case the list of names would run:

(Grandfather)	Yakûb Ibrahîm.
(Father)	Ibrahîm Yakûb.
(Son)	Yakûb Ibrahîm.

If this boy should have a son he probably would be called Ibrahîm Yakûb. Sometimes one of these names, say Ibrahîm, is kept as a continuous family name, and so ordinary names become stiffened into family or house names. Occasionally the name thus taken may have been that of a mother rather than a father. There is the very pretty custom, already mentioned, that is quite general, of calling a man and his wife after the name of their first-born son. So in the above case the father would seldom be called Ibrahîm Yakûb, but Abu Yakûb, that is, father of (the little) Yakûb, and the mother, Umm Yakûb, the mother of Yakûb. Even though the child die the parents will be called henceforth by these designations, which are esteemed titles of honor. In other cases family names are derived from trades, as Ḥadâd, blacksmith; Bannâ, mason; Bustâny, gardener or orchard-keeper; Ḥajjâr, stone worker. Or, it may be from a former place of residence, as Rafîdya (a village near Nâblus). If a member of the family has been a priest the name of all the family and descendants is apt to be Khûry. Some family names are hard to interpret. One of the most frequently heard names in the Lebanon district is that of Ma'lûf. The word itself means a fatted sheep, but the history of the application of the name is obscure unless it was given to families possessing such animals. Another family name, possibly of modern origin, is Baṭâṭô, or Baṭâṭâ, the second form being the same as the word now used for the new vegetable, potato, which fact may explain the name, or it is possible that another significance attaches to the term.

[1] *Cf.* Luke 1: 61; 2 Sam. 2: 12, etc.

Some names are indicative of the religion to which the bearer belongs. 'Abd er-Raḥman, Muḥammad, Maḥmûd, Ḥasan, Zayd, would be understood as being Moslem names. A woman with the name Ḥâjar (Hagar) would be a Moslem. On the other hand, Ḥannâ (John) for a man (feminine, Ḥannâh), would be pretty sure to mark a Christian. Such masculine names as Khalîl, Mûsâ, Dîâb, 'Azîz, Ghânim and Farîd would not betray the religion of the bearer, nor such feminine names as Ḥelweh, Anîseh, Ḥabîbeh and Ṣabḥah.

Many of the above names and others are very significant when translated.[1] Miladeh means that the little girl bearing it was born at Christmas, which is known as the " Feast of the Birth " ('Aîd el-Mîlâd). Needless to say, this little girl was born in a Christian family. Tufâḥah, *apple,* makes a pretty feminine name. So also Farḥâ, *joy,* and Nijmeh, *star.* Not so pleasant are the names Tamâm, *complete,* and Kâfyeh, *enough,* which mean that girl babies are not welcome in the homes where such names are given.

Nicknames are often bestowed and often stick fast to individuals and families.[2] We knew a dumb man whose family went by the name Akhras, *dumb.* A trickster whose cleverness was really admired and honored by his fellows was dubbed esh-Shayṭân, *Satan.* No more enviable compliment can be paid a sharp business man than this same designation, Shayṭân. We knew a little girl who, in common with the family, shared the nickname that the villagers had given to her father, Ṣarṣûr (or Ṣurṣur), *cricket.*

Many customs and much lore of the people have been described from time to time during the past twenty-five years by Baldensperger in the Quarterly Statements of the Palestine Exploration Fund.

---

[1] Ruth 1: 20. [2] *Cf.* Ish-bosheth.

CHAPTER IV

HOME AFFAIRS

THE houses of the peasants show at a glance the grade of well-being in the different villages. There are many in the lowlands made of mud, or a worse material, with thatch and straw. But in the hills stone is so plentiful that even the poorest builder may use it. The low, hutlike, *skîfeh* cabin is made of loose stone piled up without mortar. The roof is constructed of boughs, on which clay and straw are laid to make it water-tight. The usual stone house is called, in contrast to the above, *ḥajjar-wa-tîn*, that is, stone and mortar, and is more or less substantial according to the hardness of the stone, the care in dressing the blocks and the proportion of lime in the mortar. The arch for the roof of such a house is usually so high as to be able to support itself by its own weight. The result, in the typical house, is a square box room with a lofty ceiling, the walls being unrelieved in most instances even by whitewash. But as this must serve in many cases for the family and also for such animals as are possessed, or for a living-room and a store cellar combined, an extra floor is put in, over most of the room, from four to six feet higher than the ground. This platformed portion may be supported by small stone arches and paved with beaten clay, or lime, or flat stones. From the door stone steps ascend to this living floor. In former times these steps were so constructed that any shot from a firearm sent through the wooden door would strike them and thus fail of reaching either the people on the platform above, or the animals sheltered underneath. Sometimes there is excavated under the house a cistern to which the rain-water from the roof is conducted. As the family prospers and outgrows the accommodations of a single room, others may be built at right angles on either side around a little court on which all the doors open. Still more rooms may be added above as a second story, with stairs leading up outside. By such a process of agglutination the house grows, looking like a miniature fort or castle, where father, brothers and sons with their families live in patriarchal unity. Rooms with inner connecting doors come as a later refinement of the more wealthy.

In summer-time a little shady booth of boughs may be made in the court or on the roof. Many of the peasants sleep out-of-doors fully half the year.

Within the house the floor of the living-room will be covered in part with straw mats. Grain and food-bins made of clay stand along one side. Large jars stand back against the wall or in corners. One jar is to hold spring water brought for drinking; another will hold olives; and a third, olive-oil. There are also wooden bread-bowls, straw covers, the stone flour-mill, some baskets, a clay brazier, copper cooking vessels whitened, sieves, a wooden chest or two, gaudily painted, utensils for grinding, roasting and cooking coffee, a clay fire-pot set in a fire-nook, and on pegs in the wall a brass-bound flint-lock and a water-bottle made from a goat's skin. A recess in the wall, across which a curtain is drawn, holds the bedding. At night the pallet bed is spread on the floor,[1] the chief covering being a quilt enclosed in a cotton case.

In a two-room house one room will be the kitchen and women's apartment and the other the place of entertainment, where the men chat and eat together. This extra room may have divan couches and perhaps an Oriental rug on the floor. Glass *nârjîlehs* (often pronounced *ârjîleh*) stand ready for the guests who smoke. This glass smoking-bottle and pipes, an outfit which foreigners sometimes call

[1] John 5: 8, 9.

HOUSEHOLD UTENSILS

1. Woman's wardrobe and treasure box. 2. Rough straw basket. 3. Wheat basket. 4. Vegetable basket. 5. Chair. 6. Groups of baskets. 8 and 9. On this shelf are coffee utensils, wooden spoons, a wooden lock and a gourd bottle. 11. A cooking vessel on top of a wooden cutting-board. 12. Bellows. 13. Wooden mortar and pestle for pounding coffee berries. 14. Short-handled broom. (From the Hartford Theological Seminary Collection.)

the hubble-bubble, is used by men and some women of the well-to-do classes. The common name for it among the peasants is *shîsheh*.

Below is a list of the utensils and furnishings commonly found in houses of Palestinian peasants.

Khâbyeh, a large store-bin made of clay.
Ṣandûḳ, a small box used by the women as a chest for clothing and personal treasures.
Ṭâḥûn, a stone mill for grinding wheat.
Môḳadeh, an earthen fire-pot.
Kânûn, a clay brazier on which charcoal is burned. Coffee is roasted and cooked over this brazier.
Jurun, a mortar.
Mahbâsh (*mahbâj*), the pestle.
Maḥmaṣeh, a rotary coffee-roaster of tin, turned by a handle.
Ibrîḳ, a small pitcher or pot.
Ḥaṣîreh, a straw mat for the floor.
Mikniseh, a short-handled broom.
Ḳuda' (or ḳudah), a large basket, wide and shallow.
Ḳuba', a tiny basket of the same shape.
Ṣînîyeh, a plain straw mat used as a tray or as a cover for the *bâṭeyeh*.
Ṭubuḳ,[1] a fancy straw mat used in the same way as the *ṣînîyeh*.
Hanâbeh, a small clay eating-dish.
Kirmîyeh, a trencher.
Bâṭeyeh, a dough-bowl (of wood).
Ṭôs, an earthen bowl.
Zibdîyeh, a larger bowl.
Ṭunjereh, a copper cooking vessel, whitened, sometimes used as a serving-dish.
Dist, a very large ṭunjereh for serving food to guests; also used as a pan in which to wash clothes.
Maftûlîyeh, a special dish for making *maftûl*, a paste that looks like buckshot. The dish has a perforated bottom like a colander.
Jarreh, a general name for a jar.
Ghuṭâh, a cover of a jar (a general name for a cover).
Mughṭâs, a dipper.
Ḍharf, a goat skin for fetching water.
'Aslîyeh, a slender jar.
Sifl, a jar for oil.

[1] *Cf.* Arabic Bible, Matt. 14: 8.

Sherbeh, a drinking jar.
Ghurbâl, a wheat sieve.
Minkhul (corrupted into *mûkhil*), a flour sieve made of hair.
Sirâj, a lamp.
Misrajeh, a lâmp shelf.
Khûṣeh, a knife.
Sikkîneh, a knife.
Finjân, a cup.
Mughrafeh, a ladle.
Mua'laḳah, a spoon.
Watad, a peg driven into the wall.
Ḳûseh, an alcove for stowaway.
Khurraḳeh, a poke-hole in the wall.
Firâsh, a bed.
Ilḥâf, a quilt.
Mukhaddeh (or *wasâdeh*), a pillow, often filled with *tibn*.

Wheat, the most important item of the well-to-do peasants' food, has been spoken of elsewhere. It offers a scheme for classification in welfare. Those on the level of wheat bread and those below that level in life form very readily distinguishable classes. Bread made of barley or of millet is used by the poorest people. The flour used for most of the wheat bread is of graham quality. A lump of dough is saved from the mixture for the next batch. This leaven [1] goes by the name *khamîreh*. After the early morning grindings the dough is mixed in a wooden bowl, the woman generally sitting outside her door on the ground. When the dough has been mixed the bowl is covered with a straw mat called the *ṣînîyeh*. When ready for baking, the whole, surmounted by a tiny little basket, *ḳuba'*, filled with dry flour for the hands when the loaves are formed, is carried on the woman's head to the nearest oven. One oven is shared by several neighboring families. The oven is within a stone hut, or cabin, not much unlike the *sḳîfeh*, or loose stone house, mentioned elsewhere. The woman may have to wait her turn at the oven, as other women may be baking before

[1] Matt. 13: 33.

her. She sits at one side and chats with the women and girls about her as she plies her needlework, sewing or embroidery. Being at work and unobserved, she generally has her head-shawl thrown one side. The oven is a domed pit. Inside the pit are little stones on which the cakes of bread are baked. The clay dome has a cover which may shut the baking bread within. The fire of grass[1], refuse from the olive presses, twigs or caked dung, is built outside the dome, and therefore does not come in contact with the interior when the oven is heated for baking. The cakes of bread are from a quarter to a half-inch thick and of the shape and size of a medium dessert plate. The hot stones give a hubbly surface to the loaves, and as the dough is not very stiff a delicious warm, spongy, graham bread results. The bread baked for sale in the shops is generally made of lighter flour and the loaves are smaller and sometimes thicker.

In buying wheat for *burghul* we sought the best grade of white wheat, paying three piasters a ruṭl for it, that is, about eleven cents for six and a quarter pounds. Burghul is prepared as a winter food. The wheat, after cleansing, is boiled until it is partly cooked. It is spread in the sun and dried and finally crushed in the hand-mill to the required fineness. The favorite size is about like broken rice. The chaff-like refuse is then blown off and, after another cleansing, the burghul is ready for a winter supply. Crushed wheat, called *jerîsheh,* may be prepared and used as a breakfast cereal would be with us. *Smîd* is the name given to the unground portions of wheat, called with us semolina, separated from the flour by the bolting-machine of a modern mill.

The lentil,[2] *'adas,* is considered by the native peasant a very nourishing food. The little seeds are reddish or brown and are shaped like tiny eyestones. When made into soup the taste is similar to that of dried peas. For the winter supply they are sifted, washed and given a treatment with

[1] Matt. 6: 30. [2] Gen. 25: 34.

olive-oil to prevent the attack of a little fly called *sûs*, which eats out the inside of the seeds, leaving only the shells.

Rice is consumed in large quantities, but, as it is an imported food, it is bought as needed. A sack weighing two hundred twenty-five pounds may sometimes be bought for five dollars. A brand called Japanese rice, harder and cleaner, supposed to swell better and absorb less *semen* in cooking, costs considerably more. In the markets one often sees rice which has been colored with a red powder. Pine-nuts from the cones of the *ṣnôber*-pine, which are very toothsome, are often cooked with rice.

The olive fruit as it comes from the tree is exceedingly puckery in flavor. For early eating the people put the berries into a strong brine, cracking them somewhat with stones to hasten the curing process. For late use the cracking of the berries is dispensed with and they are simply set away in the salt water. It takes several months to extract all the bitter taste of the whole berries and render them pleasant in flavor. The peasant much prefers ripe olives to green ones for eating. Most people who learn to eat ripe olives share in this preference for them. Usually the ripe olive is black, though some varieties are not so. They are very nourishing and full of oil, while green olives are a mere relish. Olive-oil is used very commonly as a food. The purest grade may be purchased as low as the rate of six cents a pound when bought by the jar. It is usually measured out in a heavy copper vessel shaped like a water jar of the *zarawîyeh* type, holding seven ruṭls, or about forty-four pounds, of oil. These copper jars are always very bright in color, as the action of olive-oil on copper is sufficient to keep it perfectly clean from corrosion. Those who make olive-oil have large cemented cisterns in which to store it, and as the cisterns are not cleaned very often, and the different grades are put in promiscuously, the flavor becomes disagreeable to the European palate, though the peasants do not mind if it acquires even a sting in taste. This defect in flavor is increased when the heaps of berries are left too long before pressing them. They become heated and more or less rancid, and acquire the sting which we think so unpleasant. But if one is painstaking, one will learn where and how to secure some of the first-grade oil which comes from the early berries and direct from the press. This early oil is often so delicate as scarcely to have any distinctive flavor. It is of a light greenish color.

Much of the inferior grades of oil is made into a soap very soft to the touch. The Mount Carmel soap is especially well liked. A great deal of soap is made in Nâblus.

As has been suggested, the grape is the choicest fruit of the country. With bread and grapes many hundreds are daily content. The native people do not wait until August, when the first ripe grapes are to be had, but enjoy eating green grapes, *ḥiṣrim,* with salt. Grape molasses, *dibs,* and grape marmalade and jam, *ṭoṭleh,* are prepared for winter by the more prosperous households.

Figs are next in general favor and are dried in large quantities for winter use.[1] Some are strung on strings, but most of them are pressed in bins. The black variety is preferred, as it is somewhat richer than the white and green kinds. Figs make a hearty food. Nothing more delicious in the line of fruit can be found than large, fresh figs with the morning dew yet on them. Fresh, ripe figs are often brought into the village in the little home-made, wheat-straw baskets, covered with the strong-smelling *marâmîyeh* leaves. The very early fruit that precedes the regular crop by two months is called *dâfûr* and is esteemed a luxury. A cooked dish of dried figs flavored with anise is called *khubayṣeh.*

This list of the most common staples for the peasants' use would not be complete without coffee, which, while it might appear more in the light of a luxury, is yet so essential in a re-

[1] 1 Sam. 30: 12.

spectable household as to be classed here with the necessities. It must be on hand for guests, whether afforded for daily use or not, and wherever men meet for business or ceremony coffee is expected. It is purchased in the raw berry at about eleven cents a pound for a good grade, and the preparation of it becomes a matter of personal accomplishment. Men often carry some coffee berries in their pockets for use at gatherings with their friends. In drinking coffee, one cup is frequently passed about among a company of men, being replenished for another drinker when one has had some. The beverage is drawn into the mouth with a noisy sip that both cools it, if hot, and testifies to the drinker's satisfaction with the quality. When done properly the business of coffee-making includes roasting on an iron spoon, pulverizing in a wooden mortar with a wooden pestle, and boiling in a tiny copper or tin pot from which it is poured into a handleless coffee-cup, *finjân*, of about the size of an egg.

To continue the list of foods. Tomatoes, though comparatively new to the country, have become a favorite vegetable. Tomatoes are a summer crop, and acres of them may be seen. A cooked tomato sauce is boiled down and then evaporated in the sun until of considerable density, when it is set away as a winter seasoning for soups, stews and rice. Sliced tomatoes are dried in the sun for preservation. The fresh tomato is enjoyed in salads. The price per pound is something less than one cent.

The seed pods of okra or gumbo, or, as the peasants call it, *bâmyeh*, are strung on twine and dried for the winter stores. It is cultivated in the plains near Ludd.

Many of the villages fail to cultivate garden vegetables in any considerable variety or quantity. They submit to a more monotonous diet than seems necessary. Other villages go into gardening extensively. They are villages with superior facilities for irrigating the crops. The vegetables are retailed in the less favored villages, or, more often, taken

BREAD-MAKING UTENSILS

1. Wheat bin. 2. Stone mill. 3. Fine sieve. 4. Wooden bread-bowls. 5. Straw mat used as a tray or as a bread-bowl cover. 6 and 7. Ovens made of clay, fire is to be built around the outside. 8. Metal cooking plate. 9. Tiny basket for dry flour. (From the Hartford Theological Seminary Collection.)

to the surer market of the nearest city. Squash, pumpkin, cabbage, cauliflower, lettuce, turnip, beet, parsnip, bean, pea, chick-pea, onion, garlic, leek, radish, mallow and eggplant are common varieties. Of the eggplant it is said that, since there are so many ways of preparing it, should a woman say to her husband, during the eggplant season, "I know not what to provide for dinner," he has a sufficient cause for divorcing her. Doubtless, if he were hungry and sensible at the same time, he would at least try the expedient of getting a dish of the savory vegetable before discharging the cook. But, on the other hand, one might quote the Arabic proverb, "Minds are lost with stomachs." There are two kinds of cucumber. The one like our own goes by the name *khîyâr*. The other, called *faḳûs*, is thinner, longer and fuzzy, and is eaten without peeling. The buds of the artichoke when boiled make a delicious dish. Potatoes are getting to be quite common now. Most of them are still imported, but probably more and more success will be met in raising a native crop.

A pleasant little story is told of how potatoes may have first come to Jerusalem. Sister Charlotte, a Kaiserswerth deaconess, was for fifty years in mission work in Jerusalem. At the time of her death in 1903 she was the revered head of the German Orphanage for girls in the city. When the Emperor Frederick, then Crown Prince, visited Jerusalem, he accepted an invitation to dine with Sister Charlotte and the other German sisters. He asked them what, of all things, they would like from Germany. They said that they thought potatoes would be their choice. Two barrels of potatoes were the result of this incident, and Sister Charlotte thought that these were the first potatoes in Jerusalem. It is to be regretted that this is not the place to go into a thorough appreciation of the work of these blessed women who, in hospital, school and other Christian service in the East have performed a most gracious ministry of Christian womanliness.

The milk of the flocks is made into butter, and that in turn is often cooked down into what we should call clarified butter, but which the Arabs call *semen*. It will keep a year and is much used in cooking, especially in preparing rice. There is a very pleasant, cooling preparation of milk called *leben*,[1] which is thick and has a slightly acid taste. It looks like junket. A little of it, when put into slightly warmed milk and set away in a warm place for a few hours, will make leben of the milk. The process is one of partial digestion and makes a wholesome food for invalids, particularly for those suffering from fevers. *Lebbeneh* is strained *leben* to which a little salt has been added. It is a sort of compromise between butter and cheese. A cream cheese, *jiben*, is made in square cakes averaging the size of a man's hand. These cakes are put away in brine for keeping and, when needed, are soaked in hot water. Many meals are made of wheat bread and cheese. Hard, dried leben, pressed into little balls, may be kept for months. It is then called *kishk*. When they are to be used the balls are cracked into little fragments and soaked in water.

Eggs, mutton and goat's meat are obtainable in most villages. For game, the gazel, pigeon, quail and partridge, as well as smaller birds, are shot and used by a few of the peasants. For those who live near the Sea of Tiberias (Galilee), the fish there found add to the variety.[2] In parts of Palestine locusts are eaten.[3] They are usually dried or roasted. A story and a proverb are mentioned concerning the vigor and spryness of these insects. A man who was in great haste and yet wished something to eat caught a locust and, holding it by the legs, roasted it over a fire. He didn't wait to do it very thoroughly before he put it in his mouth. Fearing that it would burn him he delayed shutting his teeth together on it. The moment he loosened the grasp of his fingers, therefore, away went the locust.

[1] Judges 4: 19; 5: 25. [2] Matt. 4: 18. [3] Matt. 3: 4.

Now for the proverb: "Âflat min jarâdeh," which means, " Better at escaping than a locust."

Baked dishes are not common among the peasantry. Boiling, roasting and frying are the common modes of preparing food. *Kibbeh* is a mixture of meat and burghul, bruised together in a mortar until it becomes a jellied mass, when it is pressed into pans, scored off into cakes and fried with semen. *Maḳlûbeh* is a preparation of rice and eggplant cooked in a deep dish, and, when served, turned out, upside down; whence the name, which means " turned over." *Keftah* is a meat cake fried in semen, not very different from Hamburg steak. *Mujedderah*, or *'aṣîdeh*, is a mixture of rice and lentils. Sometimes fried onion scraps are served with it.

A favorite vegetable called *kûsâ*, which looks like a cucumber and tastes like our summer squash, is often hollowed out, stuffed with meat and rice and boiled. Here is a combination of fruit, flesh and vegetable worth trying: A roll of tender grape-leaves stuffed with rice and meat and then boiled. It makes a little sausage-like affair of which a Scotch professor said that, if there were sausages in Paradise, they would be of this kind. The natives call all stuffed dishes of these sorts *maḥshy, stuffed.* A maḥshy made of eggplant is called *shaykh el-maḥshy*, the chief of the maḥshys. Kids, lambs and chickens also are stuffed. With some of these maḥshys, leben sauce is served and with others lemon-juice.

Salads of all kinds are enjoyed by the people. *Ḥumuṣ b'ṭeḥîneh* is made from dried chick-peas boiled, mashed with olive-oil and flavored with *ṭeḥîneh.* Ṭeḥîneh is a mixture of olive-oil, *serej* and some sour substance, either vinegar or lemon-juice.

Caraway, anise, thyme and mint are used as seasonings.

The common cooking fats are semen, olive-oil and *serej*, the latter being a rich cooking oil made from simsim seeds.

An out-of-door luxury is the new parched wheat,[1] called *frîḳy,* when immature heads are roasted, and *kalîyeh,* when ripe grain is roasted. The peculiar milk of a fresh goat or sheep, curdled a little, by being placed over the fire, and sweetened, is considered a dainty. Cooked sheep's brains are a delicacy and very nourishing.

The fruits of Palestine are many. The better known varieties are the grape, orange, lemon, apricot, plum, pomegranate, quince, citron, watermelon, cantaloup, date, mulberry and medlar. This last mentioned fruit is known by the Turkish name *akydunya,* literally, *the next world.* The cherry and peach find a congenial climate in the country. The apple and pear do not thrive so well in Palestine as in the neighborhood of Damascus. Of apricots there are several varieties. A large sweet kind, of which the seed pit has a taste similar to the almond nut, is called for that reason *lôzeh.* Another kind is called *klâby,* and yet another *mestkâwy.* Apricot leather is displayed in large sheets in the markets. From pomegranates, of which there are at least three flavors, sweet, medium and sour, and from lemons, drinks are prepared. Distilled orange-flower water is esteemed as a flavoring extract. A little of it in water is good for a sour stomach.

Of nuts there are the almond, pistachio and walnut. The almond is frequently eaten green, when the kernel is in a milky state and the whole nut with its shell is tender. Chestnuts and peanuts are imported. Melon and pumpkin seeds are eaten. Sesame, or simsim, seeds are sprinkled over cakes. Partially ripened chick-peas, roasted on the stems, are very much liked. *Mulabbas,* which simply means *covered,* generally refers to sugar-coated, roasted chick-peas. These roasted peas without the sugar are called *iḳdâmeh,* or *ḳaḍâmeh.*

Jellies are called ṭoṭleh. They are often served to guests,

[1] Josh. 5: 11; Ruth 2: 14.

in such cases being offered before the coffee, which must always be the last of any number of refreshments. A dish of jelly or jam, with several spoons and a tumbler of water, is passed around. Each guest takes a spoon and helps himself to a taste of jelly, then puts the soiled spoon into the vessel of water.

The people are very fond of honey. Many kinds of pastes, cakes and confections have honey as a prominent ingredient. Some of them seem very cloying to the unaccustomed Western taste. *Ḥelâweh* and *mulabbas* are the very common confections in the villages. The first looks like light-colored molasses candy and comes in bulk. It is used as a food with bread. It is made from the root of the simsim plant, the oil of which imparts to it its peculiar flavor. There is a local hit to the effect that " the people of Nâblus eat their sweets first." The word used to express satisfaction with a flavor is *zâky,* which is equal to our colloquialism, " it tastes fine," or the German, "grossartig." A rebuke of an inordinate appetite is apparent in the proverb, " Let a dog take a taste, but not a son of Adam [*i. e.,* a man]."

The list of foods should include some of the many varieties of edible wild growths.[1]

Khurfaysh is a plant with a little notched leaf having milk-white veins. The edible stalk that grows up from the center is very delicious and refreshing when tender.

Murrâr, a bitter herb, looks, during its early growth, a little like the dandelion. Later it develops a thorn.

Ḳurṣ 'anneh bears a small leaf suitable for salad.

Ḥumayḍeh has a leaf with red veins and a red back. It is used less commonly than the others.

Dhanbat faras (tail of a mare) looks like young onion leaves.

Ḥasak is used more especially for cows, and *ḥalîbet es-sukûl* is fed to the kids when milk is scarce. It yields, when

[1] *Cf.* 2 Kings 4: 39.

broken, a thick milky juice. The fruit of the cactus or prickly-pear is yellow, seedy and sweetish. For some reason or other the name for this plant, in Arabic, and the word for *patience* are the same, *ṣubr*. This cactus fruit is much esteemed. A story is told of a man with a prodigious appetite for it who was going along by the hedges of prickly-pear near Ludd and followed by some cows which ate up the peelings of the fruit as he dropped them. The story says that the cows had to stop eating the peelings before the man's appetite for the fruit had been fully gratified. This is only a sample of the many stories told about great eaters.

The carob-pod is chewed.[1] It has a flavor like that of sweetened chocolate. Green carob-pods may be cooked in a toothsome way with milk.

A receipt for making "Turkish Delight." The first essential is a perfectly clean cooking dish, as the secret of good Turkish Delight is to prevent burning or sticking. One-half pound of corn-starch, three pounds of sugar and ten cups of water are to be used. The corn-starch is to be dissolved in two cups of water and strained. The remaining eight cups of water, hot, and the sugar are to be made into a syrup. When the syrup is almost at the boiling point, clear with the white of an egg, skim off, add the juice of a half lemon and strain through a cloth. Pour the corn-starch solution into the hot syrup, stirring continually, and allowing the mixture to boil until very thick, an hour if necessary, stirring all the time to prevent sticking to the bottom. This constant stirring during the cooking is very important. Blanched almonds and the flavoring (generally *mistkâ* gum) are put in just before taking the dish from the fire. The whole is then poured into a large shallow tin into which fine sugar has been sifted. When the paste has cooled it may be scored and cut.

There is almost no drinking of alcoholic liquors among the peasantry. On the feast-days the convents offer *'araḳ*, a

[1] Luke 15: 16.

native grape brandy, to callers. The increasing influence of foreigners tends to an increase of drinking customs in the cities and the extension of such habits into the country villages. This influence comes through the foreign ecclesiastics in the convents, monasteries and patriarchates, business and travel, and sometimes the example of missionaries. Among Moslems the habit of using ardent liquors is supposed not to exist, but an aged official of wide experience told me that he knew of two hundred fifty Moslems in Jerusalem who were hard drinkers, and that the Turkish officials as a class were taking up the custom rapidly. Said a poor Moslem girl in Hebron despairingly of her brother, who had taken up with the drinking habit, " Why, my brother drinks like a Christian! " Of an inveterate and shameless toper the Arabs say that " he would drink from his shoe."

The custom among the country people is to eat out of a common dish.[1] If it contains rice the food is rolled into balls and put into the mouth with the fingers. The bread is held on the knee, as one sits in squatting posture, and bits are torn from it. With these bits of bread the food may be dipped up, especially if it be oil or leben. Portions of meat are taken with the fingers. A wooden spoon is sometimes used. When guests are eating, the women of the family are not present, but often eat in another place and use the remains of the men's feast. In the field the workers gather around the dish that has been brought from the village. They may be sitting in the broiling sun. It is customary to invite the passer-by to the repast.

The first meal of the day is not usually taken until the middle of the forenoon, and is a light one. The second one, at or after noon, may be heartier. The evening meal is the best. Meat is almost a luxury, the increase in its use denoting progress in prosperity.

Almost any discriminating person will decide for the native

[1] *Cf.* Matt. 26: 23.

peasant costume as more modest, graceful and artistic than the European styles. One feels disappointed and defrauded at sight of a villager togged in European trouserings. The village woman descends in the scale of attractiveness just so far as she submits to the fashion of Western dressmaking. Stockings are seldom worn by the country people when they are in vigorous health. At best the stocking is an unsanitary snare. Men generally wear the roomy shoe having buffalo rawhide from India for the soles and a red or brown goat-skin for the uppers. Women seldom wear shoes inside the village for fear of ridicule. When they are out in the rough places they wear the same kind of shoe as the men.

The fully dressed *fellâḥ* (peasant) has in his outfit the following articles:

Dîmâyeh, or *ḳumbâz,* a long dress or tunic.

Shirîhah, a girdle studded with the *razât,* which are ornaments like little silver buttons.

Ṣadrîyeh, a vest.

Ṭuḳṣîreh, a small blue jacket made of *jûkh,* a blue cloth. Sometimes a European jacket is worn or a sheepskin is used.

'Abâh (colloquial, *'abâyeh*), a homespun woolen overcoat, striped.

Ṣirmâyeh, a shoe, heavy or light according to the season.

Leffeh, a general name for the entire head-dress.

The leffeh consists of the following parts:

Ṭuḳîyeh, a cotton skull-cap.

Libbâd, a skull-cap of woolen felt put on over the cotton one.

Ṭarbûsh, a hat proper, usually a red fez-like head-covering, broad and flat, put on over the ṭuḳîyeh and libbâd.

Scarfs are wound around the rim of the ṭarbûsh so as to make a very heavy border (a thin scarf helping to pad out a heavier one).

Mendîl, a thin scarf used under a heavier one.

Maḥrameh, a white heavy scarf.

Kefîyeh, a yellow and fancy variety of scarf.

In the leffeh or head-dress are tucked, for convenience in carrying, the following articles:

Mirât, a mirror (a tiny glass).

Mishṭ, a comb for the beard.

Maṣṣâṣat, a cigarette holder.

Dukhân, tobacco.
Khalḳat (*aṣfat*), a ring (yellow) for the thumb (bahim).
Khâtim (*fuḍat*), a seal[1] ring (silver) for the little finger (*khanaṣet*).
Dubleh, a guard.

All these small articles following are in or about the girdle or belt:

Ghâb, a cartridge-belt.
Shibrîyeh, a dirk carried in the belt.
Ṣifn, tow.
Zinâreh, a steel for igniting the tow in striking a light.
Ṣuwâneh, a flint.
Mûs, a clasp knife.
Zaradeh, a chain to which the knife is attached.

The fellâḥah (peasant woman) wears the *Khurḳeh*, an embroidered dress of linen crash, with silk stitching. Over this dress she wears the *Khalaḳ*, or *Tôb*, a long veil of the same material as the Khurḳeh. But she is mostly distinguished by the

Uḳâ, a head-dress which is a snug little bonnet of cloth embroidered and heavily decorated with coins.
Ṣaffeh, a row of coins over the top of the head on the bonnet.
Shakeh, a row of coins or bangles across the forehead.
Iznâḳ, a coin of especial value which hangs by a chain from the head-dress, under the chin.

This head-dress is bound into the hair by strings and is worn night and day.

In the division of household labor the man goes to the market, field or on the road with the animals, leaving almost all the work about the house to be done by women and children. Indeed, these may often be called upon to assist in carrying to or from the market, in watching on the threshing-floor or in the vineyard and orchard, in helping harvest the crops or in gleaning, sifting and cleaning grain. Children sometimes carry food to the workers who are at a distance. The man may make repairs about his house, if skilful enough to do so. He drives the bargains and settles

[1] Gen. 38: 18.

business matters. Upon the woman falls most of the work of the household. It is often hard and long because of primitive methods and scanty means.[1] The older girls may help considerably, especially by taking much of the care of the children. The woman's day begins early with the grinding of flour for bread.[2] She probably cleaned the wheat on the previous afternoon while there was light. Grinding can be done in the early morning before daylight. The woman sweeps and cleans and cooks food for the family. She makes long trips into the uncultivated country about the village to bring home head-loads of brush, thorns or grass. She must make daily trips at least, and sometimes several a day, to the spring, or possibly to a cistern, for the water supply. She often keeps chickens. Gardening is the man's work, though the woman must often help in the little plot if there be one. Now and then a woman may find time to attend to her personal appearance. If her dress of linen crash be soiled she may take it with other washing to the spring or cistern. She first soaks her clothes and then laying them on a rock pounds out the dirt with a short club. If the silk embroidery on the dress makes it unadvisable to wet the cloth, she rubs off the dirt with bread-crumbs. She occasionally gets an opportunity to take off her head-dress of coins, clean the coins and comb out and wash her hair, or she may do the similar service of washing and head-cleaning for her children.

The peasant women are sometimes skilful in embroidering in silk, with a cross-stitch, on linen and on cotton. They make a good deal of basketwork from wheat straw, which they dye a brilliant blue, green, red, purple and brown. Cooking dishes, platters, bowls and jars are made of clay by the women. The women of any village keep to the making of such vessels and shapes as they have learned best. The Râm Allâh women make a reddish jar of huge size orna-

[1] *Cf.* Luke 10: 40. [2] Matt. 24: 41.

mented with a brown painted band of a basketwork pattern. This jar is known colloquially as *jarreh.* The smaller size goes by the same name or else by the term *hisheh.* *Hish* is a kind of red stone that is pulverized to make jar material. The long jar that is used for carrying water from the spring to the house is called *zarawîyeh.* The *zarawîyeh zerḳa* is a product of Gaza, and the *zarawîyeh bayḍeh* of Ramleh and Ludd. Another large variety of jar is called *zîr.* Any tiny jar used as a drinking vessel or for cooling drinking water may be called *sherbeh.* The little milk jars with a very wide mouth are called *kûz* or, by the fellaḥîn, *chûz.*

The peasant, when well fed, clothed and sheltered, is a fine specimen of physical humanity. When ill he is miserable indeed, and greatly to be pitied. Hospitals and other European helps are assisting of late where but a short time ago there was nothing but native ingenuity. Even now the very poor can hardly be said to be supplied with adequate assistance. In the more backward villages, farther from centers where physicians and dispensaries are available, the most curious shifts are made to drive off disease and win health. Among Moslems and Christians similar means are taken. Mothers pray at shrines and sacred trees, tying up bits of rag to keep the prayers in the minds of the saints who have been invoked. It takes kindliness and patience to win over the poorest and most suspicious of the sick peasantry. And it will take more than that to secure suitable nursing for invalids.

One child of Christian parents wore a bone from a wolf's snout about the neck as a charm. It was the gift of the paternal grandmother. A wolf's jaw-bone is a potent charm. A Moslem said that the wolf was a friend of his family and that if one killed a wolf with a knife and then wrapped the knife in a handkerchief or other cloth it would prove efficacious in time of sickness. For instance, if a child were ill with a cough it was only necessary to draw the back of the knife-blade across the throat in imitation of cutting and say, "Allâh and the wolf," "Allâh and the wolf," then make a noise like the growl of a wolf and the child would be well. The many superstitious remains of primitive religious notions are usually preserved among the women of the land.

Slips of paper, with verses from the Ḳurân written on them, are soaked in water and the drink administered to patients by the very ignorant. Burning and bleeding are frequently resorted to. More nauseating practises are the utilization for medicinal purposes of the froth that forms at the mouth of a maniac, or of a *derwîsh* (dervish) who, in the excitement of his exercises, has fallen down insensible. It is considered proper for the friends of the sick to call, and sometimes the room where the patient is lying is full of talking neighbors.[1] Fortunate is it if some of them be not smoking as well as making a noise. Figs are used as drawing plasters.[2] For soreness of the gums or teeth a dry fig is heated and laid on the spot. A relic of the days of quacks is found in the proverb, "Ask one who will try and not a doctor." Doubtless the next proverb in order would be the one running, " Patience is the key of relief." Of palsy the peasants say, " Palsy, then don't doctor it."

The following data, taken from accounts of medical assistance rendered to inhabitants of a score of villages in the country about Râm Allâh for a year are suggestive of the distribution of ailments. Leaving out of the account wounds, the chief ailments were classified under fevers,[3] malaria and typhus, with gastric troubles nearly akin. Then comes the second group of troubles, with influenza and pneumonia. Third in frequency was rheumatism. Enteric troubles were rarely mentioned. Eye troubles are common, but the physician is not resorted to as frequently as would be supposed. A few cases of abscess, dropsy and eczema were mentioned. May and June, October and November, brought

[1] Job 2: 11. [2] 2 Kings 20: 7. [3] Matt. 8: 14.

IN A DOORYARD. WOMEN CLEANING WHEAT

ON TOP OF AN OVEN. WOMEN SIFTING WHEAT

numerous cases of fevers. January and March exceeded in pulmonary affections, though they were pretty generally met with throughout the year. Autumn is a very unhealthy season. The dust blowing about the villages in the high winds is laden with abundant filth in pulverized form. Sunstroke is not unknown among the natives.[1] The reapers in the Ghôr are often stricken with deadly fever, probably because of the poor water supply, hot sun, cold nights and irregular meals. Contagious skin, scalp and eye diseases are to be dreaded. Because of the lack of facilities and knowledge in the care of children convalescing from measles, *ḥuṣbeh,* that disease is much feared, and the mortality among the young is great. The typhoid cases in the country are long and tedious, though not perhaps so violent as with us. Leben makes an ideal food for the patient.

Certain of the fountains of the country are provided with a more or less capacious catch-basin from which animals as well as people may drink. The fastidious are not to be blamed if they insist on seeing their own drinking water taken from the actual flow of the spring and under such conditions as shall not subject them to the washings of other people's mouths. Often at such places leeches thrive in the water, and where they are known to abound the natives seldom let their animals drink if other available water be near. People, too, are often bothered by the leeches lodging in the sides of the mouth or throat. Those that are swallowed cause no inconvenience, but when tiny leeches lodge in the side of the throat and grow to an uncomfortable size they have to be extracted. One day I was lunching with the local physician, Dr. Philip Ma'lûf, when a poor woman from el-Bîreh, not finding him at the dispensary, sought him at his home. She was troubled with a leech which had grown to uncomfortable size in her throat and was using up too much of the blood needed in her system. After the

[1] 2 Kings 4: 19.

parasite was removed she haggled about the price of the operation.

At another time I saw a little girl sitting on a chair in the sun in front of the doctor's dispensary. The doctor said that her leech was too difficult of observation and approach with his tweezers, but that in the warm sun it would be tempted within reach.

Medical assistance in the form of hospital or dispensary facilities is now offered at Hebron, Jaffa, Gaza, Jerusalem, Nâblus, Nazareth, Tiberias, Ṣafed, Haifa, es-Salṭ and Kerak. To these places the peasantry come from the country about, bringing their ills for treatment at the hands of foreign physicians. From the country around Nâblus, for instance, many patients come to receive the skilful attention of the surgeon at the Church Missionary Society Hospital in the city. Among these cases are many suffering with diseased bones.

The medical department of the American College at Beirut is an exponent of modern medical science for all Syria. There native physicians are trained in medicine and pharmacy and go to all parts of the Turkish empire, Egypt and the Sudan. The European hospitals in the country are in charge of expert physicians assisted by well-trained nurses.

Here and there one meets dumb people. In Râm Allâh is a dumb man, the well-to-do father of a considerable family. He is keen, alert and very skilful at making himself understood by motions.

The blind are receiving some attention. Schneller's school in Jerusalem makes provision for them. Miss Lovell, an English woman, has a small school for blind girls where she works assiduously for their welfare. The French Roman Catholic Sisters care for some.

The first hospital asylum in all Syria for the humane and scientific treatment of the insane was founded a few years ago and first opened to patients August 9, 1900. It is just a short drive out of Beirut, at a place called 'Aṣfûrîyeh, within the Lebanon government district. Its founders are Mr. and Mrs. Theophilus Waldemeier. Mr. Waldemeier was for over twenty years the superintendent of the English Friends' Mission at Brummana and other stations in Mount Lebanon. Advancing years seemed to make it wisest that he should relinquish the many-sided mission work. With his wife he planned a world tour in the interests of a work which he had thought over for many years. While friends were advising and expecting him to take a deserved rest he began to plan for this new enterprise, which he sweetly calls his " evening sacrifice "; a hospital for the right treatment of the insane, of which the country has many. The Waldemeiers visited successfully in Europe and America and returned with funds to build. They found a fine property of over thirty acres belonging to one of the *effendîyeh* class of natives, a Moslem who was in need of funds and good enough not to make too hard terms with these philanthropists. In the first two years the institution treated two hundred twenty-seven patients and sent away thirty-six patients recovered.

Mr. Waldemeier and his gifted wife treated us with the greatest cordiality, when we called on them, and showed us detail after detail of the work, the new building and so on, just as if they were enthusiastic devotees of an interesting new game; and so they are devotees of the old, the ever new game, of doing good. A large, well-equipped administration building, another for women patients and still another one for men were already up and fully used, forty patients at a time being the capacity. A new building was being erected to be used for the most violent cases. The story of some cases is a sad one. A surgeon of the Egyptian army was with us as we inspected the wards where the women patients are kept, filled mostly with young girls. He said, " I never saw anything so sad. The wounded and the dying on the battle-field do not make me feel like this." The causes of the troubles of these sufferers are various. Ten distinct kinds of mania are recorded on the books, among them cases resulting from alcoholic excess, from typhoid fever and those that are hereditary. No patients are received unless there is reasonable expectation of their recovery under treatment.

The nurses and attendants in the women's ward seemed to be much interested in their charges and to develop a real affection for them. There are no bonds in the whole institution. The severe cases are put to bed. As soon as their condition will warrant it they are set to work at something that will keep them busy, laundering or helping in various ways about the institution, always with ample supervision. One bright-faced patient possessed with the notion that the devil was in her nose made that member the object of her constant thought, keeping it always covered.

We saw a large, powerfully-made man standing behind the iron grating of one of the men's windows. He was an alcoholic case who was sent away from the hospital at one time apparently cured, but fell into the old ways again and now is hopeless, incurable.

Some of the patients come to the hospital in a most wretched state of filth. Some come loaded with the chains that the ignorant country people have put on them. Some have been isolated in caves and scantily fed, some have been beaten. Some have been made to drink water in which written texts of the Ḳurân have been soaked. Many are the ways with which the superstitious natives would treat these unfortunates. Sometimes the insane are looked upon with superstitious awe as of an order other than ordinary human beings and to be invoked. At other times the people are said to beat them in order to drive out the demon, but more often, according to their own saying, they let them pretty much alone. "For," say they, "God has touched him; that is enough; leave him alone."[1] All through the country this unconscious fraternity lives its life apart from men. Only their bodies are in contact with the world of reality. They are fed or beaten, caged or prayed to, in turn. We saw one of these unfortunates who had been groveling in a fit on the street in Jerusalem near the Jaffa Gate. He had a small cord drawn through a fleshy place in his abdomen, by working which back and forth well-meaning spectators had caused considerable blood to flow, thinking to relieve him. We have seen them wandering in the streets of Damascus with the freedom of the city, all making way for them; and well they might; we did, too, for I've never seen human beings more unutterably filthy. In the village of 'Ayn 'Arîk there was a dumb maniac who went about naked.[2] He was credited with being a wily, or holy man. Families having a sick person among them would sometimes send him presents of roast stuffed fowls and secure from the wily some of his hairs, which they would burn near the patient, hoping thereby to effect a cure.

The leprous generally congregate outside the cities and follow the trade of begging. Hospitals and asylums are provided for them, but many of them prefer the freedom which puts them obnoxiously in the way of those who can be teased for alms.

Death among the peasantry is an occasion for long mourning. The body is wrapped, and placed in the ground and protected from the falling earth as well as may be by the use of stones. On the top of the grave the heaviest stones obtainable are packed to make it difficult for the hyenas to secure the body. It is customary to watch the grave many

[1] *Cf.* 1 Sam. 21: 12–15; Matt. 8: 28. There is now a Hebrew asylum for the treatment of the insane patients of that race in Jerusalem called *'Ezrath Nashim.* It is supported by the Woman's Aid Society. See description of it by the American consul at Jerusalem, Dr. Selah Merrill, in *The Christian Herald,* New York, January 10, 1906. [2] 1 Sam. 19: 24.

nights to keep these creatures away.[1] The more advanced peasantry try to secure a wooden coffin for the body about to be buried. The natives are capable of much tenderness and consideration at these sad times. The many bearers take turns assisting in the carrying of the body on the way to the grave. Visitors from other villages come to assist in the mourning for the deceased. They are provided with food and shelter while they remain. The public mourning lasts as long as visitors continue coming to offer condolences, which may be for many days. At weddings the singers are men, but at funerals the women perform the part. The same native melody is used on both occasions. The death of a young man is an occasion for especial grief, since so many family hopes and prospects are thereby disappointed. A prop and stay in the tribe is withdrawn and the calamity is very severe. The women are sometimes seen on the threshing-floor marching slowly round and round, wailing out the dirge. One of the saddest cases that came under my observation was that of a young man who, leaving his family, emigrated to America in search of fortune. While in Monterey, Mexico, he heard of the death of an uncle in the home village and grieved over it. He was taken ill, probably with yellow fever, went to the hospital and died there in a short time. When the news reached Râm Allâh the grief was keen. It is customary at such a time for the women to go either to the threshing-floor or the cemetery to mourn.[2] But in this case, as the man was buried far away, the women assembled on a small piece of ground that was owned by some of the tribe where there was a fig-tree. They sat under this talking until the company increased to over forty women. They had all left their head-dresses, ornamented with coins, at home, and their hair fell in disheveled condition over their necks and shoulders. Some of them had daubed their

[1] Job 21: 32. [2] *Cf.* Time: Gen. 50: 3; Num. 20: 29. Manner: Deut. 14: 1; 2 Sam. 3: 31; 12: 16; 18: 33; Eccles. 12: 5; Jer. 6: 26; 9: 17; 22: 18.

faces with soot. Some were dressed in their oldest and poorest clothing; one had on a fancy Bethlehem costume, but her disordered hair was bound with crêpe. A circle was formed and the women marched to the accompaniment of the mourning song. Now and then a few would break from the circle into the middle and, tossing their arms above their heads, perform a funeral dance. The name of the deceased was Butrus (Peter) and the widow's name was Na'meh (Naomi). The following is a translation of the words which the women sang at the time:

O door of the house, fall down
For one who went and did not return;

For one who left his wife,
A trust remaining with me.

Butrus in the distant country calls,
" O, Ḥanna, take me back to my country."

The gun appears, but the lion appears not;
Lo, the strap of the gun is damp with mist.

The gun appears, but the lion comes not;
Lo, the strap of the gun is dripping with mist.

(At the time of the burial)

O my sorrow, there are his people;
Early were they at the burial place.

Early rose the sexton for the burial,
And the ḥarîm is soiled with dust.

The women of his kindred rend their finery
For Butrus who sank into the grave.

The women of his kindred tear their coverings.
Because Butrus is left in America.

(Impersonating Butrus)

Don't take me down into the ships,
My sister on the seashore is grieving.

Don't take me down to the foreign ships,
My sister on the seashore is calling.

(The mourners)
O my sorrow, they went on the seas and remained:
Oh, I wonder how they are, have they changed?

O my sorrow, they went on the seas and stayed the night:
Oh, I wonder how they are, or are they dead?

Bring me knowledge, O great bird, O little one;
America, is it far away and without a wall?

Bring me knowledge, O bird, O birds;
America, is it far away and without measure?

Greet them, O bird, O pigeon,
In their far country setting up the tents.

(Impersonating Butrus)
On the shore of the sea the gazels are browsing;
Oh, the descent to the ship, it is bad.

On the shore of the sea the gazels are airing;
Oh, the descent to the ship, it is bitter.

On the seashore, wondering whither to turn,
Appear, O Na'meh! the ship goes.

At the hospital I am thirsty, I want to drink;
Bid me good-by, my brother, the ship goes.

(The mourners)
Write on the flat slate,
"Thy time came; what could we do, my spirit?"

Write on the flat marble,
"Thy time came; what could we do, my precious one?"

O scribe, writing with a costly pencil,
Greet the absent one and clasp hands.

(Impersonating Butrus)
Thy robe is long, Na'meh, cut from it;
Have slight regard for fine appearance when we are gone.

Thy robe has a long trail;
Have little care for fine style when we are gone.

(*The mourners*)
The tassel on his head-gear dangles;
Tell his mother to continue mourning.

The tassel on his head-dress droops;
Tell Na'meh to quit fine dressing.

(*Introducing the refrain at the mill*)
Say to us, O Na'meh, in the night,
"How often have I worn the best of silk!"

Say to us, O Na'meh, in the afternoon,
"How often have I worn Egyptian silk!"

(*Closing*)
O ye strangers bearing the coffin,
Wait until his family arrive.

O ye strangers bearing the coffin,
Wait until his kinsfolk come.

The grave of Butrus by the road is in neglect;
He wants a guide to lead him home.

This beginning of public mourning was on November 23. On December 14 the funeral services were held in the village church, just as if the deceased were there. But the public mourning did not cease as long as visiting mourners from other villages came to condole with the family. It is customary for women in mourning to forbear changing or washing their dresses for months.

Graves are usually bordered with heavy broken stone partly sunken into the earth. For shaykhs and notables an oblong, box-like structure of stone and mortar is built over the grave, and perhaps a headstone erected, with an inscription in Arabic. The variety in the ornamentation of graves is very considerable, especially in different districts of the country.

Egypt was suffering from an epidemic of cholera in the summer of 1902. The news of cholera in Egypt makes one apprehensive lest through carelessness the disease should be brought into Palestine, although the quarantines are supposed to be enforced strictly on all lines of communication by sea or land. Toward the last of September the rumor got about that cholera was in the country and that cases had appeared as near as Hebron, twenty miles south of Jerusalem. By the middle of October rumor was persistent that Ludd and Jimzû were affected by the fell disease. English physicians in Jaffa published and circulated a poster instructing the people as to means of prevention. The Jerusalem government issued orders to the villages to clean the village streets and burn up the refuse. This would be a boon under any circumstances. The city streets were put into an excellent condition of cleanliness. Whitewash was freely used on the walls of the buildings, especially in the Jewish quarter. In a day or two Jaffa was reported to be infected by the cholera and, as the days went by, rumors came from one after another village that it was attacked by the scourge, which the natives call *the yellow air*. They give it this name because of their belief that it is a pestilential breath traveling in the air. One day, when the refreshing west wind was blowing up from the sea, a peasant in our village expressed the hope that the wind would change soon, as he feared that it might bring up *the yellow air* from the infected villages down in the Mediterranean plain. This ignorance of the real nature of the disease accounts, together with a fatalistic carelessness about observing the right precautions, for the awful hold that it gets on an Eastern country. It thrives best in the lowland country and least in the highlands, not being supposed to ascend over two thousand feet with any likelihood of persistence. But it was often carried to greater heights, causing much anxiety. Hebron, for instance, is over three thousand feet above sea-level. The bacillus has its greatest opportunity in running water, as at springs. In order to attack the human being it must enter the alimentary canal, usually, of course, by the mouth. A weakened constitution, excessive fear, nervousness and chills from great or sudden changes of temperature, make favorable conditions for its seizure of the individual. It usually begins with a diarrhea, which, if unchecked, is rapidly succeeded by the peculiar cholera discharges and a physical collapse that is as complete as the weakness induced by days and weeks of other severe diseases. Relief has to be prompt, the temperature restored and the discharges checked very soon in order to afford any reasonable hope of recovery. Most foreigners escape attack by attending very strictly and conscientiously to the proper precautions and heeding early indications, without allowing themselves to be disturbed by unnecessary fears. But they should be personally sure that only cooked food is eaten, no raw fruit or vegetables; that all water, for whatever purpose destined, be boiled, whether it is to be drunk or used to wash the person, hands, face, teeth or body, or used to wash clothing or dishes. When cholera is in the vicinity unboiled water should not be used for any purpose.

The people in our own village prohibited the approach of any persons from the village of Ludd. These local prohibitions through the country multiplied, making a set of quarantines that prevented travel and trade in many of the country districts. Our native village physician was taken by the government and placed in charge of the quarantine station at Bâb el-Wâd, which is on the Jerusalem-Jaffa carriage road. The railroad trains between Jaffa and Jerusalem were forbidden to stop anywhere between Bittîr and Jaffa. Some friends in Jerusalem feared to come out to visit us, only ten miles away, for fear that quarantine might be imposed at any moment, thus preventing their return to the city. However, that necessity did not arise during the whole time the disease was in the country. But to the north of us we were cut off from Nâblus, to the east from the

Jordan country, to the west from the villages and cities in the plain. Jerusalem was cut off from Hebron on the south. To have cut us off from Jerusalem would have made a very tiny island of our neighborhood. So long as we were part of the large island of which Jerusalem was the center, and our district remained free of the scourge, we were in a very happy case compared with what might happen any day. The peasantry in the villages west of Jerusalem depend a good deal on the sale of vegetables, fruit, bread and milk in the city, but soldiers prevented them from coming in to pursue their usual business.

October closed with very conflicting reports as to the nature of the sickness that was taking the people off, some declaring that it was not cholera, but only similar; that it was this and that other thing. The governor called together the merchants of Jerusalem and urged them to maintain regular prices, but they replied that this was their opportunity. He forbade any rise in wheat. However, prices on most foodstuffs and imported supplies began to rise. The train service on the Jaffa-Jerusalem line was discontinued. People rushed to the shops in the city and bought up canned goods and groceries. Camphor rose in price also, as the natives bought it to make little camphor-bags, which they would smell frequently. Men were stationed out on the paths leading to our village to prevent the entrance of people from suspected districts. In Jaffa some deaths were reported in the dirty section about the boat landings. Gaza reported the highest mortality, forty a day. Some of the inhabitants of Gaza moved out on the seashore and lived in tents. No deaths occurred among them. Ramleh set about providing its own cordon, and although it was very near some of the worst of the afflicted places, it kept itself free from the epidemic. Some Gaza men who essayed to reach Jerusalem were put under arrest.

By November 5 the general impression was that the

cholera was lessening its violence. The people of Ludd were getting straitened for food. The hospital and medical service of Miss Newton of Jaffa were a great blessing. She sent medical assistance to the people in Ludd also and was very prompt in getting in food supplies to the quarantined villagers. The dearth of food in Hebron threatened to cause a rise of prices beyond the reach of the poor. But some of the officials wishing to come to Jerusalem, the quarantine was lifted for a day to accommodate them, when some wheat slipped into Hebron from Jerusalem. In Jaffa the English church was open twice a day for special prayers for the cessation of the cholera.

We were greatly saddened toward the middle of November by the news that Mrs. Torrance, wife of the physician in the Scotch Mission at Tiberias, had fallen a victim to the cholera.

Some travelers who were having hard work getting through the country on account of the crisscrossing of the quarantines, were in a hotel in Nazareth when, during the night, a man came up to that hotel from Tiberias and developed a case of cholera. The hotel guests found in the morning that they were quarantined in the house. By the earnest use of talk and money they got the privilege of passing the time of their quarantine in some tents. They feared that, if they remained in the hotel and more cases developed, their detention might be lengthened indefinitely.

Some Jifnâ men who had been in Jaffa for weeks evaded the quarantine regulations and returned to their village, which was one hour north of us. Their own relatives were the first to drive them back with stones. The neighbors reported the facts to the police in Jerusalem and soldiers came out and shut up the quarantine jumpers in caves until they could be returned to the quarantine station at Bâb el-Wâd to pass the legal number of days.

On November 18 we heard of a man who had come from es-Salṭ to Jerusalem and died, of cholera apparently, in

Khan es-Sulṭân. This was the cause of some worry, but no cases resulted. On the 19th, as we were thinking that the colder weather would check the disease, we heard that it had increased considerably in Jaffa. On November 20 our village physician returned for a short visit to disprove to his family the report that he had succumbed to the cholera. He had about a dozen or fourteen people in quarantine at Bâb el-Wâd, who were taking that tedious way of journeying. The government provided tents at two and a half or three francs per day. Each person secured his own food by post carrier from Jerusalem or elsewhere. The claim is now made that the cholera got into the country through the faithlessness of the quarantine official south of Gaza. He is accused of having let through seven thousand persons at a bishlik (eleven cents) apiece. The story of how the cholera entered Ḳubâb is illustrative. That village and the village of Barrîyeh use the same fountain for water, the 'Ayn Yerdeh. Cholera was in Barrîyeh, and one mother who had lost a little child wished to keep its garments. She took them to the 'Ayn Yerdeh to wash them. Very soon a score of Ḳubâb people were victims of cholera, and three hundred in all died in that village. The doctor reported the people in the villages as very eager for instructions and obedient in observing them when the disease was at its height. He says that there were no tears, only great desire to escape the dreadful enemy. He went to the different villages near his station and, standing outside, summoned the shaykhs and chief villagers within hearing distance, where he exhorted them to use the necessary precautions. The Moslems have the custom of washing the corpses of their dead. This contributed much to the spread of the disease, as the flushings of water, vile from the body of the cholera victim, carried the germs all about the house floor and infected a considerable space. The physician's orders were to bury the deceased, clothing and all, and cover with six baskets of dry lime. Then all articles used or defiled by the sufferer were to be burned.

Friday evening, November 21, some Jaffa Christians sought to flee from their city and come to Râm Allâh, but the Râm Allâh people drove them back with threats and stones. Some of the Râm Allâh people recommended a cordon for all roads about the village, but the poorer inhabitants declared that they could not stand the increased price of living that would ensue. December 3 we heard that some Constantinople physicians had visited Jaffa and declared the disease not cholera but malignant typhoid fever. It made little difference to the generality what they chose to call it. By December 6 cholera was reported at Jericho. It was reported at an end in Ḳubâb but continuing in Jaffa with a very variable death-rate. By the middle of December six thousand deaths had been reported in Gaza. The reports from Jaffa always minified the number of victims. One physician stated that, when the reports said fifteen a day, he knew there were from fifty to seventy a day. It was said that Moslems were evading the government's orders regarding instant disposal of the corpses and secreting their dead, in order that they might carry out the custom of washing and otherwise preparing the body for burial. Hunger probably played an important part in the death-rate. The outside world never knew the facts. By the middle of January the cholera was announced at Turmus 'Âyâ, a little south of ancient Shiloh. But the disease had done its worst for the country for that season.

The work of Miss Newton in Jaffa and vicinity was very effective and impressed the Moslems greatly. One leading Moslem in Jaffa tried to collect money for the suffering, but met with no very generous response. He exclaimed of this English woman, "Do you mean to tell me that the Moslems, all of them, will go to heaven and this noble young woman will go to hell? Her shoe is purer than their souls."

CHAPTER V

RELIGIOUS LIFE IN THE VILLAGE

THE chief business of Palestine is religion. There is a religious instinct which must be reckoned with all the time. Its importance in Eastern life can scarcely be over-estimated. In Syria, there is, first of all, a Semitic core enshrouded by the specific religious faith and ritual of the time. In the peasantry, of whatever faith, this racial element is strikingly constant. Eastern life simply cannot be understood apart from religion. And yet the natives of the country are not, strictly speaking, theological in their way of thinking. They have little conscience as to doctrine. Church-membership is to them what citizenship is to us. Their great desire at present is, not to seek true doctrine, but to escape the persecutions of government and as many as possible of the uncertainties of life, by getting into official relation with a convent or other ecclesiastical establishment, a foreign consulate or a business under the protection of foreigners. Connection with such institutions affords a measure of immunity not enjoyed by the unattached native. Just so any member of a Christian church has the patronage of those at the head of his church, who are jealously alert to withstand state encroachment. In the treacherous waters of Eastern life ecclesiastical trappings are as life-belts, not to be discarded. There is little opportunity for the higher ethical considerations and religious growth so long as the solid footing of fair conditions of life and industrial freedom is denied. So long as the most lucrative and the securest positions are those of clients of some ecclesiastical establishment, so long will a religion of loaves and fishes, whatever the sect, prevail. When entering on a study of religious conditions in Palestine or in any other Asiatic country the Westerner should seek the equipment of a sensibly poised sympathy and unfailing courtesy.

Just as in the cities the mosks and minarets (properly called *mâdhaneh*) are the most notable religious objects presented to view, so in the country the eye is first caught by the white domes[1] and clustered trees of the shrines called *maḳâms* and generally designated by the peasantry as *wilys* or *shaykhs*. The holy place of the wily or shaykh of Ḳaṭrawâny will illustrate the significance of these places, which are usually situated on hills.[2] The shrine of Ḳaṭrawâny is a two-domed building, surrounded with trees, north of the village of Bîr-Zayt. A shaykh from the village of 'Atâra, north of Jifnâ, went down toward Gaza. He lived, died and was buried in a place called Ḳaṭrawâny (or Ḳaṭrah). But the belief came about that his spirit came back to this place near 'Aṭâra. So a sepulcher was built for him there on the hill where his spirit was supposed to be, and the place is now a shrine. On a ride to the north of this spot we passed two Moslem pilgrims who were, apparently, from middle Asia. They seemed to be making a tour of the shrines.

Other holy places are the reputed tombs of ancient worthies, as en-Neby Samwîl, the prophet Samuel, a mosk on the top of the hill of that name, which is about two easy hours from Jerusalem to the northwest. The tomb of Samuel is shown within, and the country of his activity is in view from the lofty tower above the mosk. Abandoned churches and mosks are resorted to as shrines.

Little oil lamps are often seen about specially revered places. These are made of clay in the shapes sometimes designated as virgins' lamps, though it is the general style of thousands of years back. It was originally a little saucer to hold oil, in which a wick was laid with one end on the edge. In making the saucer the sides were first pinched up a little;

[1] Matt. 23: 27. [2] Deut. 12: 2.

then more and more, until they covered the top, leaving two openings, one in a sort of spout for the wick, and one behind, through which the oil could be fed. A handle at the other end was sometimes added. Taste and ingenuity then varied the details of shape and decoration through the historical periods. These little lamps may be used as night-lamps in the houses, but are sure to be the kind employed at country shrines. Some of the poorest people make very crude little clay lamps somewhat after the ancient pattern. Sometimes they take the cover from a little tin box and pinch it into the customary shape.

In the walls of the vestibules of some of the larger and more famous ancient tombs are niches cut for the placing of lamps by devotees. At Tibneh the reputed tomb of Joshua has a vestibule which is twenty-nine and a half feet wide and over ten feet high. Its roof was supported originally, on the front, by four squared columns twenty-five inches through, cut from the rock of the place. Two of the columns, the one at either end, are engaged, and two are free. The three walls of the vestibule resemble those of a columbarium, having two hundred seventy lamp-niches, all fairly uniform, in even rows and with sloping tops. A little entrance two feet high and nineteen inches wide leads into the tomb chamber, which is thirteen feet eight inches by thirteen feet two inches in dimensions and has fifteen kokim.

At the tomb of Joseph, shown near Nâblus, there is a well-kept modern room enclosing the tomb. A dumb man was in charge when we visited the place. On receiving a bishlik, as we were leaving, he emitted the most weird sounds of anger and flung the coin on the pavement in pretended disgust.

Places once consecrated to holy purposes are apt to retain their sanctity. This is seen in the regard that the peasants have for the shrines and places of religious significance to any former people. The old church at Sebasṭîyeh (Samaria) is now a mosk. The ruin of the Crusaders' Church at el-Bîreh is venerated by Moslem and Christian. A man essayed, the story goes, to build a house out of blocks taken from this ruin, but his house fell, not once, but twice, a sign according to the native interpretation of the impiety of the man's act in taking those stones. In one of the apses of the church at eṭ-Ṭayyibeh there was a chromo picture on a board before which some Christians of that village burned oil in the little lamps. In the old Greek church at Râm Allâh, no longer in ecclesiastical use, are seen the lamps used by worshipers who reverence the old site superstitiously. In another part of the village there is a room, evidently once a mosk, which is now a shrine known as el-Khalîl. It is at the left of the west end of the long market street. It is fronted by a little courtyard in which are a mulberry-tree and the capitals of a couple of columns. The door of the room is at the northwest corner; at the northeast corner is an outside stairway by which one may go up to the roof. Over the door, serving as a lintel, is a piece of worked stone, evidently a small column. It is ten inches wide and forty-three inches long, including a round stone ball cut on the right-hand end, which measures six and a half inches. A raised panel design, twenty-nine inches long and three inches wide, is carved on the side. Into the right side of the doorway is built a voussoir of an arch. There are two pieces of fluted stone built into the wall of the building. In the northeast corner of the wall the corner-stones are of good size, the largest being twenty-seven by fourteen by eleven inches. The next stone under this largest is bossed. The upper part of the door works in a stone socket. Inside, the room is well plastered, the ceiling rather low, perhaps fifteen feet from the floor. A column is built into the east wall near the southeast corner. It is nine feet and four inches tall. There is a *ḳibleh* or prayer-niche in the south wall of the room. It is about thirty-nine inches deep and fifty-eight and a half inches wide. The outer facing of the ḳibleh is two feet wide on each side. In the west wall is a squarish recess like a closet. In the east wall are three little boards thrust in endwise and projecting to hold lamps. A large jar with a broken top contained some water. There were eighty-nine lamps in the room, of the little virgin-lamp style, for holding oil. The women of Râm Allâh are responsible for these, as it is their custom to go to this room and light lamps and offer a prayer to Ibrahîm Khalîl Allâh (*i. e.*, Abraham, the friend of God[1]) for the recovery of a sick child. Some say that Thursday, late in the afternoon, is the favorite time for women to go there and pray to el-Khalîl (*i. e.*, the friend or confidant, abbreviated from the above title). The building and yard are supposed to belong to Abraham. If a child too young or too ill-bred to observe the proprieties should molest the mulberries on the tree in the yard any passer-by would be apt to cry out to it to desist lest el-Khalîl should destroy it. Anything placed within the mosk or yard is considered as under the protection of el-Khalîl and perfectly safe from theft. Sometimes a quantity of lime is left in temporary store in this safe place. Perhaps the large jar that we saw with water in it had been left there by some one who had been working in lime.

All Râm Allâh pertains ecclesiastically to Hebron, which goes by the name el-Khalîl in Arabic geography, and to the famous mosk of that ancient city. In keeping with this the inhabitants of Râm Allâh, all Christians, look upon el-Khalîl (Abraham) as their patron saint.[2] Invocations are frequently directed to him in fear or distress. When it thunders the old-fashioned peasantry say that Abraham and St. George are racing their horses over the heavens and that the thunder is the noise of the hoofs. The peasants' invocation muttered on such occasions is, "Yâ Khalîl Allâh Salâm Allâh," which some interpret as a prayer that Abraham's horse may not slip. The other saint mentioned is Mâr Jurjus

[1] 2 Chr. 20: 7; Isa. 41: 8; Jas. 2: 23. [2] *Cf.* Matt. 3: 9; John 8: 39.

POTTERY

1. Jar for storing oil, olives, molasses or vinegar. 2. Style of water jar made in Sinjil. 3. Style of jar made in Râm Allâh for holding water or other liquids. 4 and 5. Smaller varieties of No. 3. 6 and 7. Jars for carrying water on the head. The next jar to the right of No. 7 is the kind commonly used for leben. 8, 9 and 10, and the three jars suspended by cords in the middle of the picture are all drinking jars; the two having neither spouts nor handles are for cooling water. 11, 12 and 15. Clay dishes for butter, jelly or milk. 13. Cooking vessel. 14. Charcoal braziers. 17. Salad dishes. (From Hartford Theological Seminary Collection.)

el-Khuḍr (St. George the Ever-living), to whom many Palestine peasants look for protection, and to whom considerable ecclesiastical property is dedicated. Mâr Elyâs and many other saints are spoken of, but perhaps the two above mentioned are as popular as any. Comparatively few Greek Christian foundations bear the name of the Virgin Mary (es-Ṣitti Maryam el-'Adhrâ). But to return to our little mosk, el-Khalîl. Report has it that the people of the village are much afraid that Moslems will lay claim to it sometime, and they are debating whether it would not be well to destroy the ḳibleh and with it all evidence of its once having been a mosk. The Râm Allâh people are much averse to possible encouragement of the introduction of Moslems or their customs into the village. The curious question remains, How can this mosk in a Christian village be accounted for? We might as well add that the Jews also, at Abraham's mosk in Hebron, pray to Abraham.

At the right of the entrance to the yard of el-Khalîl in Râm Allâh is a living-house that runs along the west side of the court and joins the mosk at the corner. This used to be the common *muḍafya* or guest-house for the entire village. The poor and strangers were entertained here. Families took turns supplying the food requisite for its maintenance. It was given up some years ago and there is no common guest-house now. Each of the different tribes has its own guest-room.

The reverence for sacred trees is another of the indigenous superstitions not essentially connected with any of the more modern faiths. Three hours out from Tiberias, toward Mount Tabor, a tree was observed with rags tied on its branches at the trunk. Large chunks of wood lay about under the tree. Some graves of Moslems were near at hand. A fine large sacred tree stands near Ṣurdah, the little village (ancient Zereda) between Râm Allâh and Jifnâ. Between Jifnâ and 'Ayn Yebrûd, shortly after passing Dûrah, the path goes by two fine oaks. The spot is known by the name Umm Barakât, the mother of blessings. Rags were tied to the branches of the older of the two trees. This tree was decaying, while the other was young and flourishing.

Some curious pulpit-shaped rocks near the trees doubtless helped to give the place its sacred character. We saw remains of fires near by. In a crevice of a rock there was a broken black jar with fragments of charcoal in it.

The locality of a murder has a sort of fascination for the peasantry. Less than an hour out from Bayt 'Ur eṭ-Ṭaḥta (the lower Beth Horon), on the road to Ramleh, there is shown a fig-tree near which, fifty years ago, a Râm Allâh man was killed by a Moslem. A pile of stones covers the actual spot.[1] Near the path from 'Ayn Yebrûd to eṭ-Ṭayyibeh, east of the Nâblus road, is a stony, barren tract called the Wastîyeh. Into one of the cisterns found here the body of a murdered man was once thrown; consequently those who have to pass the place do so with trepidation.

There is a notion current that the sins of a slain man come upon the slayer. Sometimes, therefore, they say of one who persists in wrong-doing that at last he will get some one to kill him and so escape the consequences of his own sins.

Superstitions by the score, common to those of different faiths, might be discovered among the people, such as the cutting of the hair and the hanging of an egg and garlic, and perhaps also blue glass bracelets, over the doorway of a new house. Some peasants will not eat food which another man has desired lest harm might come of it. "For," they say, "the soul of the man who wished the food has entered into it." If a man takes food in his hands to eat, and the food falls, he will say that it was not meant that he should eat it. Fear of evil spirits or, more specifically, of the evil eye, is an ever-present dread. It seems to arise from the notion that too much prosperity, health, pleasure or any good thing, or

[1] 2 Sam. 18: 17.

the signs of such, may arouse malignant activity on the part of some jealous spirit. An appearance of poverty, of forlorn misery, even of uncleanness, especially in a child, is thought to lessen the likelihood of unwelcome attention from the evilly-disposed spirit. Blue beads and blue tattoo marks on the face are utilized to avert the evil eye. The evil eye may be in the steady gaze or stare of a stranger, or in his photographic camera, which the more ignorant dodge fearsomely.

It is common for women to pray for offspring, and there is great faith in visits to certain shrines and localities for this object.[1] The warm springs at Tiberias on Lake Galilee are looked upon as peculiarly efficacious bathing places for barren women.

It may be said of every site of Old Testament times, that is known or supposed to be known, and of many later sites, including crusading remains, that the superstitious reverence of the peasantry clings to them. Add to these the shrines of modern origin, departed Moslem shaykhs and holy men, dervishes and the insane, which are often revered as devoutly by Christians as by Moslems, and one begins to recognize the existence of powerful religious influences quite independent of the teachings of Christianity or Islâm.

Even that temper of mind known as fatalism, and ascribed particularly to the Moslems, is a common characteristic of all the peasantry. The belief in a set and immutable time to die, for example, is as firmly held by many Christian peasants as by Moslems. One also meets the conviction that early death is the special mark of heaven's disfavor, and that the pious need not expect it. After the death of a young man who had emigrated to America, and while gloom hung over the village because of it, I was talking with an old man, a Greek Christian, whose sons contemplated going to America. He said that as he, with all his family, was devout, he had no fear that his sons would die in America. He believed that

[1] 1 Sam. 1: 10, 11.

no harm could befall those who did right and observed prayers.[1]

Among the Moslems of a country population in villages where no pretentious buildings can be erected, and on the desert where no such building would be of any avail, the one thing that holds the daily attention of the faithful is the institution of prayer. Five times in the twenty-four hours this ought to be performed, with preliminary bathing, the formulated utterances and the prescribed prostrations. This is the tie that binds. At the appointed time the horseman dismounts, spreads his cloak for a rug and upon it performs his devotions.[2] Soldiers go a little way from the barracks and in some open space offer their prayers. Dignified effendis proceed to pray, whoever may be about.[3] At large springs, as at el-Bîreh and Lubban, small stone platforms are provided for those who are near at hand when the hour of prayer comes upon them. The apparent oblivion which overtakes a devotee at any of his exercises seems impenetrable. Riding out northward from Jerusalem in a carriage with Moslem passengers, I had an opportunity to note the sort of spell that came over one of them, a dervish, during his devotions. He wore a pointed cap of quilted felt and a green *keffîyeh.* He interrupted his conversation at sunset to begin a singsong of certain offices, his memory being assisted by a note-book. He half closed his eyes and, turning his head now this way and now that, in utter unconcern about his appearance or surroundings, he wailed out his cry as the carriage rolled along. Afterward he resumed the conversation. Once on the same road a dervish, apparently a simple fellow, ran a considerable distance behind our carriage. He was armed with a sort of javelin. The peasants chaffed him as they would a child. The stated hours of prayer for Moslems are just a little after the sun has set, two

[1] Eccles. 7: 17; Job 4: 7; *cf.* Psalm 55: 23; Psalm 91. [2] *Cf.* Psalm 55: 17. [3] *Cf.* Matt. 6: 5.

hours after sunset, a little before dawn, just at the turn of noon and in the afternoon about midway between noon and dark. These five regular times for prayer are denominated respectively, *maghrib*, *'asheyeh*, *ṣubḥ*, *ḍuhr* and *'aṣr*. There may be extra or supererogatory prayer seasons, but these are the stated ones. Wherever there are *mûadhdhins* (muezzins), as in all the larger places, they ascend their towers and call out the hour of prayer. At Jenîn our room was near the mosk and mâdhaneh (minaret). The call of the mûadhdhin there between three and four o'clock in the morning was the most varied and melodious intonation that I heard in the land. It was peculiarly rich and sweet, and I felt instinctively that the man's soul was in an ecstasy of religious fervor.

The complicated prayer of the Moslems, in a characteristic form, has received classic description in the superb work of the great Orientalist, Lane, in his " Manners and Customs of the Modern Egyptians." People interested in Arabic civilization do themselves an injustice if they omit the careful reading of that book.

An occasion of keen interest to all the villages where Moslems dwell is the annual Neby Mûsâ (prophet Moses) pilgrimage in April to the hill reputed among Moslems to be the place of the burial of Moses.[1] It lies due east from Jerusalem and southwest from Jericho. From Jebel Nâblus and Jebel el-Khalîl (Hebron and environs) and all the country about contingents arrive in Jerusalem. Banners are carried to denote the delegations. Dervishes are in attendance to excite the religious emotions by dancing,[2] howling and self-mutilation. Soldiers are there to represent the authority of the government. All assembled at Jerusalem, the procession starts from the Ḥarâm esh-Sherîf on Friday and, proceeding out through the St. Stephen's Gate (Bâb Sitti Maryam), goes down into the Kidron Valley and off by the

[1] *Cf.* Deut. 34: 6. [2] 2 Sam. 6: 14.

Bethany road. Spectators throng the hillside east of the gate. Groups of women, huddled in out-of-door ḥarîms, sit on the edge of the high embankments by the roadside. Venders of toys and delicacies ply their trade. Some of the dervishes have spikes, with filigree iron heads, thrust through their cheeks.[1] Drummers and singers and the marching pilgrims pass on, accompanied a part of the way by dignitaries in carriages. As the banners pass between the high embankments on the sides of the road the spectators sitting there are apt to take hold of the floating folds and kiss them, or rub their faces with them, afterward passing them on to friends.[2] The pilgrims spend a week at Neby Mûsâ, where they have a sort of camp-meeting and religious revival. It is an opportunity for the venders of supplies. On the following Friday the procession returns to the city with drumming, shouting and shooting of firearms.

During the month of Ramaḍân a strict fast is observed by Moslems in the daytime. They are allowed to fortify themselves for it by indulging during the nights. As the Moslem calendar, made on the basis of lunar months, shifts about the seasons, Ramaḍân comes, through a course of years, in all seasons, wet, dry and intermediate. It can readily be understood that such hardships as there are in the observance of the day-fast through Ramaḍân will fall to the lot of the poor, the largest percentage of whom would be peasantry. In the cities a signal is provided to warn the people of the approach of daylight and of the close of the day. This allows them time to provide for suitable observance of the day-fast and the night-time indulgence. In Jerusalem, for instance, a cannon is discharged for the signals. In Hebron both a gun and a drum are used, but at different times. The gun is fired at sunset. In the morning about two o'clock a man goes about with a drum and sings out his warning to the people to arise and prepare their meal before the coming of

[1] *Cf.* 1 Kings 18:28. [2] *Cf.* Mark 5:27; Acts 5:15; 19:12.

the light shall make eating unlawful. The devotees are not supposed to eat or drink anything after the time when the coming light allows them to distinguish between a white thread and a black one. This time is usually a little later than 4 A.M. Many of the peasants hear the signals from afar, but to those unable to do so their best judgment must be the warning.

One evening as we journeyed homeward from the city we saw a group of Moslems squatting around in a circle on the ground eating their first meal for that day. They had been overtaken by the proper time while on a journey. We made a visit to Teḳû'a and Herodium on the last day of Ramaḍân. We were gone from 7 A.M. until late evening. Our Moslem guide fasted all day. On the way back, after dark, as we passed through Bethlehem, he took a small quantity of food. Later, as we were going up the road from Bethlehem to Jerusalem, the guide broke out joyfully, " Ramaḍân finished; not a day left," and soon after we heard the Jerusalem guns ushering in the feast of Bairam.

Doubtless the strongest visible cord of union among the native Christians is the priesthood. Most priests feel themselves to be soldiers of the faith as well as expounders of its doctrines. They are exceedingly jealous of prerogatives. The hand-to-hand fights between Greek and Latin priests at the Church of the Holy Sepulcher, the feuds and wars between Maronites and Druzes in the Lebanon, the tireless rivalry all through the country of those who represent the native churches, witness to a sense of rights and also of a commission in a militant order. Any newly discovered ancient site of especially religious significance, such as the ruins of a church or a monastery, is seized, if possible, with avidity. The Orthodox Greek Church is easily the master of the situation in Christian Palestine. The wealth and influence of this church are great and its presumptive rights are unquestionable, since it is the church that was in possession of the land before the Moslem conquest and the church with which the conquerors have dealt. On the other hand, the Roman Catholic Church represents the faith of the Crusaders, who held power for over a century in the country, and to-day the interests of this church are upheld by French, Italian and Austrian influence. Wealth has poured in and a secure place has been won for this Western church in the cities. In the village progress for it is difficult. The Roman Catholic organization is closer than the Greek, and their representatives in Palestine are well educated, as a rule.

For the Orthodox Greek Church the patriarchate at Jerusalem is the ecclesiastical center in Palestine. The chief ecclesiastical positions are filled by foreigners speaking Greek. In any village the church, if large, is under the care of a foreign head priest, called *raîs*, assisted by native priests called *khûrys*. These khûrys must know a little, presumably, about reading and writing, in order to read the services in Arabic; but, as a matter of fact, some of them would be put to it if handed a bit of sight reading in their own tongue. In Râm Allâh, when a vacancy occurs in the number of these native assistants, each tribe nominates one candidate and the village elders choose one from the number. The chosen one goes to the patriarch in Jerusalem for his authority, regalia and induction into office. Each khûry assists in the prayers for a week in turn. They receive a monthly stipend from the patriarchate paid through the raîs. This may amount to between six and ten dollars. The Râm Allâh people pay into the church a fee of one and a half or two dôllars for a marriage, forty cents for a funeral and about twenty-two cents for a baptism. A khûry may have been a tradesman before being chosen to office and have no special preparation for his work. He may be a married man when chosen and in such a case would retain his wife. The patriarchate in Jerusalem is possessed of great revenues from rentals and business interests and is disposed to be generous to its members and to make sure of their loyal adherence. Free quarters, provisions and other assistance are granted when such concessions will do good in cementing the allegiance of the communicants.

The native Greek Christian has no zeal for the conversion of a Moslem to Christianity. Some abhor the thought of giving the Christian gospel to the unbeliever, and some believe that the nature of the Moslem is irredeemable. Most of the natives, however, believe in a division or allotment [1] of religions to the peoples, that the gospel is for Christians and the Ḳurân for Moslems and that this is a very proper arrangement. The lack of interest on this subject is probably the result of centuries of habit and sentiment. Certain it is that few, if any, Moslem renegades would be allowed to live in Palestine. Two converted Moslems have been baptized in recent years and shipped to Egypt for safety. Moslems now and then convert Christians. In the mixed village of 'Âbûd some Christians have turned Moslem.

The Christian year in Palestine, among the Greek Church peasantry, is according to the Julian style. Whenever a fast is the order of the Greek Church calendar those who heed it refuse resolutely any animal food, or food that is cooked in fat or that contains any amount whatever of butter, milk or other animal substance. Once while out traveling, during Greek Lent, we wished to share our lunch with a Christian native who attended to the riding animals. Among other supplies were some cookies. These were, of course, a new style of food, but sufficiently near to what the natives call *"ka'k,"* cake. Being a little uncertain as to how such a thing might be made, the conscientious man had to inquire, and on our confessing that there was some animal substance in the article, he felt it necessary to decline it.

Easter goes by the name of the " Great Feast " among Oriental Christians, and its approach and occurrence arouse

[1] *Cf.* Deut. 4: 19.

the keenest ecclesiastical activity during the year. Weddings, not being allowed during the Lenten fast, come in rapid succession after Easter Day. On a Palm Sunday we saw girls dancing on the threshing-floor of the village.[1] In the week preceding Easter come the ceremonial of feet-washing[2] before the Church of the Holy Sepulcher in Jerusalem, and the descent of the Greek fire at the Sepulcher, inside the same church. Good Friday evening is such a time of general attendance at church for prayer that it offers opportunities to those not of the faith to break into the village houses and steal.

The feasts constitute a convenient calendar, marking the seasons for the peasantry. For instance, in the autumn three of the feasts are connected in the minds of the peasantry with the coming of the rain. At the Feast of the Cross, towards the end of September, the peasants say there is rain on one hand and summer weather on the other. At the later Feast of St. George (el-Khuḍr), observed especially at Ludd, it is expected that the rain will come in an amount sufficient to enable the farmer to sow and plow. At the Feast of Burbâra (Barbara), in December, they say the rain will come in through every mouse-hole in the house, that is, in an exceptionally heavy downpour. On the first and last of these feasts, The Cross and St. Barbara, parents like to make for their children dishes of boiled wheat with little candies stuck around the top.

The Roman Catholic priests are zealously cultivating the native Christian population, and trying to increase in influence, though the feeling against them on the part of the Greeks is one of bitter hostility. They are forced to adopt a missionary policy and their growth in the country villages is very slow. They have established excellent monastery accommodations for the shelter of such of their pilgrims as pass through the country.

[1] *Cf.* John 12: 13. [2] John 13: 5.

The United Greek Church, which is so important in the north, is making a small beginning in Palestine. It uses the Arabic language in the service. It is that section of the old Greek Orthodox Church which was won over to papal allegiance, and is being used as a sort of bridge between the Greek Church and the Roman. Protestants find the Greek Orthodox Christians much less hostile than the Roman Catholics. However, a priest of the United Greeks (Roman Catholic) has been known to bring boys to one of the Protestant boarding-schools for entrance for the sake of the training there afforded.

The Greek monasteries in the lonely country districts are often penal establishments, such as those in the Wâdy Ḳelt, on Mt. Quarantana (the traditional site of the temptation of Jesus), and at Mâr Sâbâ.

Though they are so small a sect as scarcely to be counted in the enumeration of present-day religious bodies in Palestine, yet the Samaritans, because of their historical connection with the country and its religious genius, have a significance for us and a description of their great feast may be interesting.[1]

About 5.30 o'clock in the afternoon of May 1, 1901, a small party of us who had been riding all day through the hill-country of Ephraim, came in sight of Jacob's Well,[2] or rather in sight of the walled enclosure about the premises, which the Greek Church has secured. For the first time in some weeks we saw also a line of telegraph poles and wires, that from Nâblus to the east of Jordan. We rounded the lower slopes of Mount Gerizim and in a short time were going down the valley, having Gerizim on our left and Ebal on our right. This valley, in which modern Nâblus, ancient Shechem, lies, runs east and west. The city of over twenty thousand inhabitants is about eighteen hundred feet above the sea-level, picturesquely lodged between the two moun-

[1] 2 Kings 17: 24–41; John 4: 9, 12, 20. [2] John 4: 6.

tains. The valley is narrow, so that a few minutes' ride from the center of the city would lead one to the slopes of either mountain, and an hour's climb to the top of either. The ascent of Gerizim is a simple matter; that of Ebal would be less pleasant on account of the prickly-pear (cactus) which grows very thickly on its sides. Approaching the city as we did from the east end of the valley, one sees an attractive group of cheerfully tinted buildings, some quite high for a Palestinian city, built rather towards the Gerizim side of the valley. Several tall palm-trees stand among the buildings. A little to the right, and quite prominent, is a Moslem cemetery, its graves covered with stones set up to look like small sarcophagi. The first building reached contains the barracks of the soldiers who do the police duty of the country round. Presently we join the road from Jacob's Well, which forms a V with our own. Rooms were secured at the Latin monastery. We had timed our visit so as to be present at the Passover celebrations of the Samaritans. The once powerful sect, constantly diminishing, is now confined to this one city. Friends living in Nâblus report it as numbering but one hundred and twenty souls. The next day, as we rode up the mountain to the Passover, we passed the little graveyard that receives the different members as they fail from the congregation. It looks like a bit of plowed ground, with its simple broken surface. The Samaritans we found near the top of the mountain. There they were at their great camp-meeting of the year, living in tents near the place of sacrifice, which is just below and a little west of the very summit of Gerizim. Moslem and Christian spectators woro sitting or walking about the encampment, and here and there among these were Moslem soldiers, the inevitable accompaniments of Eastern religious celebrations.

As there was time before sunset, we went to the summit, a few minutes' walk above the camp. It is a good situation for a citadel and fortification, and we found the ruins of one

ON THE WAY TO JERUSALEM FOR THE NEBY MUSA PROCESSION

A NEBY MUSA CONTINGENT ARRIVING WITHIN THE JAFFA GATE, JERUSALEM

strewn all over the cap of the mountain. As one stands at the northeast end of the very summit, near a Moslem wily (small memorial building to some saint), the view is superb; mountains on every hand, among them Hermon, farthest yet grandest of them all. Just below us, like a velvet carpet of regular pattern, is the fertile plain of Makhna, running north and south. True to Syrian religious custom, according to which every sect or religion makes a convenient grouping of all its holy places, we have only to look around to see the celebrated places of sacred writ. Here, the Samaritans claim, is the true Shiloh, the true Bethel, and also Mount Moriah. Over there to the southeast, across the Makhna, is the little village of Rûjib, which they say is Ai, while the village of 'Awarta is the burial-place of the sons of Aaron. Not accuracy, but convenience and monopoly, seem to guide Eastern religionists in identifying holy places. Near this the northeast end of the mountain is a portion of the foundation of the ancient Samaritan temple. A little to the south, on the east side, is a large expanse of rock, sloping westward. Here, they claim, was the true site of the tabernacle, the altar being the rock, the slope of which allowed the blood of victims to flow into the pit at the lower end. At the west end of the ruined castle are shown twelve huge stones which, they say, are the ones that Joshua took from the bed of the Jordan.[1] At the northwest side is an old pool.

Returning now to the encampment, which was in excitement over the coming ceremony, we found a sunken space about three feet deep and about twenty by forty feet in area. It ran north and south and was enclosed by a wall. A tent had been standing in the southerly end as we went by on the way up the hill. This was now taken down and allowed to lie flat on the ground, affording a good-sized space for the priests, who came into the enclosure with some twenty other men with their prayer-rugs. These Samari-

[1] Josh. 4: 3–5, 20.

tans were fine-looking people. I think that they had the finest faces I ever saw in such numbers in the East. They had well-formed heads, and there was quite a variety of facial types, some round and chubby, others long, some dark and others light. They all, old men as well as little boys, had clear, delicate skins. The high priest was tall and slight. His beard was gray and his countenance very pleasing. The second priest was a larger man, heavy and well proportioned, with a brown beard. In the middle of the enclosure was a little pit with fire over which were three large kettles of boiling water. Near it were seven lambs ready for the sacrifice, nosing around and chewing contentedly. The enclosure soon filled up with the Samaritans. The high priest and the men with him took their places on the canvas facing the east, towards the rock of sacrifice just mentioned and began the ritual of the Passover. The high priest wore a long green robe. The others were dressed in white. The rest of the men and children stood about, inside the enclosure, taking part in the service. When about half through with the service the high priest turned and faced the two irregular rows of worshipers behind him and began the prayers, among them one for the Sultan. We noticed on the breast of the high priest a badge said to be the gift of the Sultan. After the prayers all except the high priest went to the other end of the enclosure while he began reading the twelfth chapter of Exodus. The sun was about to set. The Passover moon, like a silver globe, came over the top of Gerizim in front of us. Just as the priest came to the word *kill*, at a certain place in the chapter, the eager look on the faces of the Samaritans gathered about the animals became very intense, and as the fatal word was pronounced with unusual emphasis the knives of those in readiness were set to the throats of the sacrificial victims and the high priest turned his face again towards the east in supplicatory prayer. The blood was caught and a little of it was daubed on the faces of some of the children. Then hot water was used to help pull off the wool from the sheep, as they were to be roasted in their skins over the large fiery pit, which all this time had been in preparation just outside the enclosure to the southeast corner. Men had been continually replenishing it with fuel until the rocks were very hot. A rustic frame of crossed sticks was provided to cover it when all was ready. Long wooden spits were brought and the lambs, with heads on but the right fore limbs removed, were fixed for roasting. The refuse parts were destroyed by fire. Unleavened bread, a sort of thin, rolled pastry, was passed about in little bits with bitter herb rolled inside. As it was late and the ritual over, the actual consumption of the lambs, which comes along towards midnight, being said to be a very ordinary affair, we started down the mountain for Nâblus. The moon, now golden, flooded the beautiful valley with its light. Such a night! We soon reached our rooms in the town and said " good night " all around.

READING LIST

Curtiss, Samuel Ives: "Primitive Semitic Religion Today."
Jessup, H. H.: "Women of the Arabs." N. Y., 1874.
Masterman, E. W. G.: "Studies in Galilee.
Mitchell and Hanauer: "Tales Told in Palestine."
Finn, James: "Stirring Times." (C. Kegan Paul & Co., 1878.)
Hogarth, D. G.: "The Penetration of Arabia."
Muir, Sir William: "The Caliphate, Its Rise, Decline and Fall."
Smith, W. Robertson: "Kinship and Marriage in Early Arabia."
Gibbons, Herbert Adams: "The Ottoman Turks."

CHAPTER VI

THE BUSINESS LIFE OF THE VILLAGE

THE Palestine peasant can do hard work. When half starved, anemic, hounded and terror-stricken he naturally enough fails to be as brisk and as inventive as he might otherwise be, but with half a chance he is industrious and thrifty. There are the lazy and the active as in other countries. As a general rule it might be said that the Palestinian is accustomed to work hard, but not steadily; liking to rest occasionally, not understanding, nor benefiting by, a system of sharp espionage or, more properly, " nagging." This latter frets him and destroys his efficiency, and ought not to be practised on him. A good-natured firmness that holds him to the letter of agreements in simple, plainly understood terms is much better.

The country life of Western Palestine to-day is organized on the basis of farming. The original estate of the Arab is to own flocks and tents, with the auxiliary pastimes of raiding and hunting. This life is represented to-day by the nomad tribes of the Syrian desert and of Arabia. They still roam over Eastern Palestine and penetrate into Western Palestine, but their range is being narrowed in these regions by the pressure of the Turkish government, which is organizing the country more closely in favor of its own authority. The transition stage between herding and agriculture may be seen in the Jordan Valley and eastward, where the nomads and the village peasants go into partnership together to raise grain. Ordinarily a desert nomad scorns the farmer and villager, but there are Bedawîn farmers who are a sort of industrial bridge between the civilization of the villagers and the primitive freedom of the dwellers in tents farther

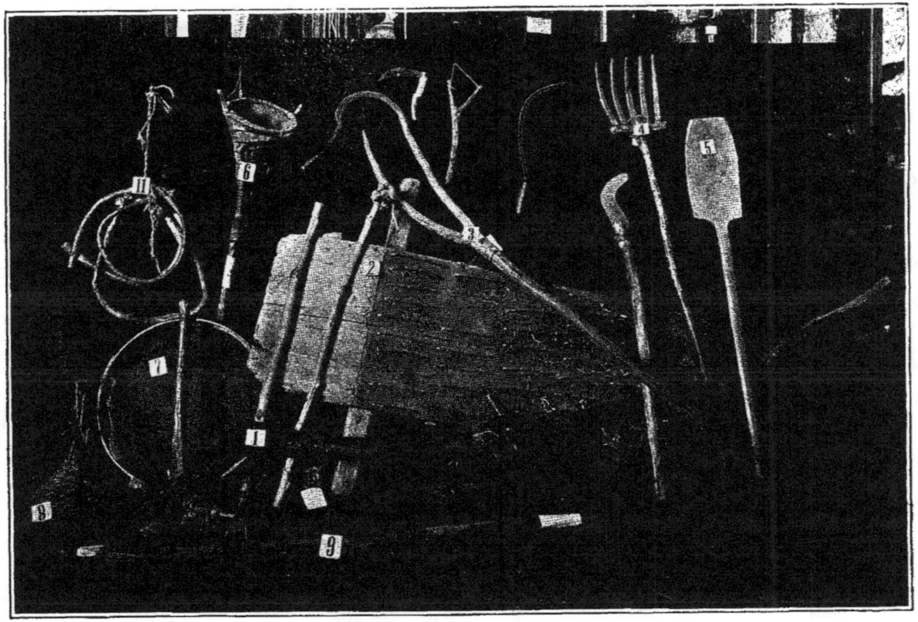

FARMING IMPLEMENTS

1. Plow. 2. Threshing sledge, showing the under side. 3 and 4. Grain forks. 5. Wooden shovel or fan. 6. Seed-tube. 7. Sieve. 8. Dung basket. 9. Goad and share cleaner, the iron-shod end being used as the latter. 11. Yokes. Pruning knives and sickles are also seen in the picture. (From the Hartford Theological Seminary Collection.)

east and south.[1] The breeding of horses and camels falls to the nomad, while the rearing of sheep, goats and cattle is the vocation of the villager. It is hardly necessary to say that a scattered farm life, with dwellings far apart, as in Europe and America, is not known in Palestine, since the country is not yet secure enough to encourage it.

The farmers (*fellaḥîn*) are the foundation of the village population. Their lands lie out around the village and may extend a considerable distance from it.[2] It will be well to understand the system of landholdings in Palestine. There are three kinds of landholdings to be distinguished, *wakf*, *mulk* and *mîreh*. *Wakf* land is land that is held in perpetual and inalienable right by some ecclesiastical establishment, as, for instance, the properties of the Jerusalem Mosk, "The Dome of the Rock," or the landed properties of the Hebron Mosk, which is a very wealthy foundation. Or *wakf* land may belong to a school or other institution, or to a family. *Wakf* land is supposed never to change its character. If it belongs to a family there is an elder of the family or some representative who is the wakf administrator.

Mulk land is absolutely free and transferable land. It is usually in a city or a village, or it may be in a certain border around such a place of, say, forty yards in width. This is house and garden property for the actual needs of city or village life. It can be sold or otherwise transferred at the pleasure of its owners. Such a piece of property pays an extra tax where a house is built on it, as the occupancy of the land by a building prevents that land from yielding taxable produce.

Mîreh land is domanial or state land. The ultimate title is with the state, to whom it reverts in the event of the failure of proper heirs. There are nine degrees of heirs eligible as owners of such land, children, grandchildren, brothers' children and grandchildren and so on; lastly the wife of the

[1] *Cf.* Job 1: 1–3, etc. [2] Josh. 21: 12.

owner, if all the other degrees fail. If the land is sold, then the degrees count from the new owner and go right through the nine degrees from him. So it is very possible that mîreh land may be in continuous ownership other than the state's.

Village cultivable lands are mîreh lands. In cases where they are village lands they are held as communal lands. In villages like Râm Allâh and el-Bîreh the land that is held thus in common as cultivable land is divided into three grades according to quality. Then each grade is divided into *feddâns*. A *feddân* is, in the first instance, a team or yoke; in Râm Allâh, four yoked cattle. Feddân then comes to mean the amount of land apportioned to the owner of such an equipment, which amount is presumably as much as the feddân of cattle could plow in a day. Finally the term feddân is used by the peasants to indicate the acknowledged right of a village farmer to own and work his plow and team and participate in the annual divisions of the arable land of the farming community. The feddân is the unit, but one feddân may be shared by several owners, each partner contributing his share to the outfit and being recorded as entitled to privileges in the feddân. These legal fellaḥîn, then, receive by lot as their assignment for the year some of each quality of land. Hence the man, or family, or company interested in one *feddân* may have land here, there and in a third place. A deep furrow, the width of a plow, marks the boundary between the different strips. Or a succession of small heaps of stones may mark the line.[1] The workers on such a strip or strips pay the government taxes or tithes on the produce of their land.

To obtain a place in the list of such fellaḥîn and share in the use of the communal lands is a matter of some complexity and difficulty and, perhaps, of serious discussion amounting to a quarrel. A stranger coming to the village to live cannot

[1] Deut. 27: 17.

A SOWER

CHILDREN GLEANING

ordinarily enter into the land privileges. A newcomer may occasionally be worked into a privileged family by marriage. The old families of the villages, having had these land rights for years, hold them tenaciously. Newcomers are ordinarily compelled to turn to some other business, to open a shop or go into some kind of manufacture. By a difficult procedure, eased with money, communal land may become the private property of one person and be made into a vineyard or an orchard.

It is customary, under intelligent management, to let the village grain lands rest every other year.[1] Dressing the land is not resorted to. The limestone in the soil supplies to some extent this lack. Distinctively farm-buildings, such as barns, etc., are scarcely to be seen unless it be at some farm-school or foreign colony.

Wheat and barley are the common grains. The peasant knows nothing of oats. Of hay, as the Western farmer raises it, he is likewise ignorant. Large quantities of *dhurah* are raised. This is a kind of millet. The early part of the winter is the time for sowing wheat, or, as the natives say, "When the thirst of the land is quenched."[2] Barley, which matures quicker, is sown a little later than wheat. In broadcast sowing of grain the farmer sows first and plows afterward.[3] He starts early with his companions for the field, a little donkey carrying the plow and the seed-bags. The plow animals are usually unencumbered while going to and from the fields. Arrived at the field the donkey is turned loose to browse,[4] the men throw aside their upper garments and tuck the corners of their skirts into their belts. The sower[5] goes ahead, tossing the grain as evenly as possible over the ground, while the plowman follows and turns it under. There is generally a good deal of shouting on the part of the plowman in directing or stimulating his animals.

[1] *Cf.* Jer. 4: 3; Hosea 10: 12. [2] *Cf.* Psalm 63: 1. [3] *Cf.* Isa. 28: 24, 25. [4] Job 1: 14. [5] Matt. 13: 3.

This talk to the domestic creatures is interesting. Here are some samples: To start a mule the expression used is *dîh*; to stop it, *hûs*. To start a donkey, *ḥe*, and to stop, *hîsh*. An ox is encouraged to go by *imshi* or *iṭla*, and commanded to stand by *huwwa*. So there are appropriate words or sounds for the different creatures. To make a camel kneel the driver says *ikh;* to make him rise, *ḥawwil*, and to walk, *ḥay*. A horse is stopped by *hûs* and started with a sucking sound of the tip of the tongue back of the front upper teeth. Dogs are called with *kity* and sent away with *wisht*. Cats are called by *bis, bis*, as one rubs thumb and finger, and scared away with a rough *biss*. Hens are gathered with *tî'ah*, chickens with *sîs*; both are driven off with *kish*.

If the rains be fairly good the wheat springs up soon, varying as to luxuriance with the richness and depth of the soil. Sometimes one will see a donkey nibbling at the tender tops of new grain or animals walking through it without rebuke from the owners. They seem to think that such things will not materially hurt the crop if done during the early weeks of newly springing growth, but that more rain and the later growth will make up for the slight setback. But when the grain is fairly up more care is exercised. The peasants are fairly respectful of the rights of the owners of the grain that grows near the paths and roads.[1] One seldom sees a passing native allowing animals to disturb the green grain, though sometimes an insolent soldier will ride his horse right into an unreaped field. For wheat, especially, the peasant has great regard, considering it a sin to damage the growing wheat or to waste the kernels and flour. His respect for this breadstuff is almost awe. A donkey-boy in attendance on a party of tourists who were going to the Valley at Mukhmâs (Michmash) was greatly perturbed because one of the forward animals in the cavalcade began to nibble some green wheat by the wayside. The boy

[1] Deut. 23: 25; *cf.* Matt. 12: 1.

shouted out *Ḥarâm Allâh, Ḥarâm Allâh* (forbidden of God) and stopped the creature as quickly as possible. Many peasants are so poor that they have to substitute barley bread for wheat, but ordinarily wheat is the food of the properly fed peasant and barley the choicest food for horses, donkeys and mules. Chopped straw is also fed to these animals.[1] For other animals, *kursenneh,* a grain resembling lentils in appearance, is a common food. Tares[2] (*zawân*) often make their appearance in the grain, especially if the seed is not carefully separated before sowing. If the tare seeds are not taken out of the wheat before it is ground, any considerable proportion of it in the flour is apt to cause dizziness and nausea. The tares are of some use, being sought as food for young chickens.

It is especially favorable for the farmers if mists prevail at night during the time just preceding the harvest. The moisture keeps the heads of the grain from becoming brittle and so allowing the kernels to rattle out too easily. Then, too, the work of reaping, hard at best, is much pleasanter if the cooler weather is on for a few days. It is commonly ordered that the farmers shall proceed to reap simultaneously, and it is often forbidden to go out to the fields to reap until all are ready. By this arrangement the assessment of the tax on the crop may be made with more uniformity and thieving is rendered difficult. In all these matters, requiring the regulating authority of recognized overseers, it is the so-called *ukhtiyarîyeh,* or as we should say, selectmen, the chiefs of the tribes, who decide questions from the day that the land was parcelled out to the feddâns until the crop is gathered. The beginning of the harvest is a time of merry singing and industrious work.[3] Women as well as men go to the fields[4] and often the babies are taken along in cradles. Some of the reapers sleep in the field. The

[1] Gen. 24: 25. [2] Matt. 13: 25–30. [3] Psalm 126: 5, 6; Isa. 9: 3. [4] Ruth 2: 8, 9.

barley harvest always precedes the wheat harvest by a few weeks.[1] In reaping, the stalks are grasped and cut low down with a sickle.[2] A bunch is tied with a straw and thrown into a heap to make a shock. The grain is carried to the threshing-floor by donkeys, mules or camels.[3] The animals have much hard work during this season. The threshing-floor is usually a smooth plot of ground near the edge of the village, beaten hard. Very often a natural rock floor may be utilized. At Baytîn (Bethel) the immense ancient pool, now dry, at the southwest of the village, makes an excellent threshing-floor. On the floor the grain is piled up in what look like huge walls, each family's crop by itself.[4] Watchers sleep on the floor at night to prevent theft[5] and fire. When all is ready the families owning grain on the threshing-floor throw down circular beds of the shocks and drive the animals around upon it. In the middle highland country the hoofs of the animals are depended on alone as threshing instruments.[6] But in the north, and in some other sections, a sledge is drawn about by the animals. In the bottom of the sledge teeth of iron or stone are inserted, which tear the straw.[7] At Samaria we saw threshing being done with the sledge and animals on the third of May. In Râm Allâh, where they use animals only, and where the season is later, it may be observed in June and possibly in July. Even down on the plain between the Shephelah and Jaffa we saw the peasants at work on the thirtieth of June, sometimes with a camel and a donkey hitched together. The animals generally used are the plow cattle, but all animals available are liable to be drafted into the service. Horses, donkeys, cattle and mules are to be seen hitched together promiscuously.[8] The mouths of the animals are often muzzled with sacking.[9] Their drivers follow them

[1] Ruth 1:22; 2:23; 2 Sam. 21:9. [2] Mark 4:29. [3] *Cf.* Micah 4:12. [4] Joel 2:24. [5] 1 Sam. 23:1. [6] *Cf.* Hosea 10:11; *cf.* Micah 4:13. [7] *Cf.* Isa. 41:15. [8] Deut. 22:10. [9] Deut. 25:4.

up with a kind of basket on the end of a pole to catch the manure and prevent its falling into the grain. When threshing begins the heap of stalks and heads may be four feet high and fifteen or more feet across. Midday is the best time for threshing, as the stalks are then brittle. When thoroughly ground and beaten by the hoofs of the threshing animals the heap may be but a foot deep. When the process of threshing is completed the resulting mixture of chaff and grain is tossed into the air so that the wind may carry off the chaff,[1] while the heavy grain falls directly under the fan or wooden fork which the laborer is using. The women then sift and clean the grain with different grades of sieves [2] and the men put it into sacks. Another more thorough sifting and cleaning is necessary before it is ground. The chopped straw, called *tibn*, is used as a fodder for animals. Some of the worst of the refuse is burned in the ovens. The fine dust-like chaff, called *mûṣ*, is also swept up and used in a mixture with clay with which the roofs are covered. A camel-load of wheat-tibn, two huge sacks, may cost from fifteen piasters to twenty-three according to cleanness and the size of the sacks. The lowest price that we ever paid was thirteen and one-half piasters. This is the Jerusalem market piaster, which equals about three and four-sevenths cents. The great wheat-field of the country continues to be the Haurân, east of the Sea of Galilee. From that region caravans of camels bring the sacked wheat into Western Palestine as far south as Jerusalem. The local wheat supply is entirely inadequate for the needs of the large villages, to say nothing of the cities, and must be supplemented from the fields of Esdraelon, the Maritime Plain, the Ghôr and the Haurân. When quarantine cuts off district from district, as in cholera times, the suffering is considerable. The ordinary country store-place for grain is a cemented cistern underground. Lentils, kursenneh and chick-peas, *ḥummuṣ*, are subjected

[1] Psalm 1: 4. [2] Amos 9: 9.

to threshing in a way similar to that in which wheat and barley are treated.

The grape season is the happiest of the year. It begins late in July and reaches well on towards the rainy season, the first of November, or possibly even to the first of December. It includes the time for ripe figs, pomegranates, quinces and almonds. Comparatively few of the grapes are turned into wine except on foreign initiative. The Jewish colonies that have come into the country make considerable wine. A native spirit called *'araḳ* is made from refuse grapes. A grape molasses, *dibs*, is made. The fresh fruit is consumed in large quantities. Donkeys loaded with box panniers of grapes go as far as Jaffa, thirty-five miles from the grape regions. Hebron and Râm Allâh are famous for their grapes. Râm Allâh is ten miles north of Jerusalem, and Hebron (el-Khalîl) nearly twice as far south of the city. The Jerusalem market is kept abundantly supplied with fresh grapes from these two places. Whole families go to live in the vineyards during the season of ripening grapes.

A very important manufacture from grapes is the raisin. The business is growing and the raisins are exported from the country through Jaffa. The grapes, when picked from the vines, are washed, given a bath in a mixture of lye-water and olive-oil, and then spread out on a cleanly swept space of ground. The lye makes the skins tender and the oil tends to keep off insects. The siroccos of September are of great assistance in raisin making, though not at all good for the unpicked grapes, as they are apt to turn them into raisins on the vines. The favorite raisin of the country is that made from the little seedless variety of grapes from es-Salṭ, east of the Jordan. These grapes go by the name *banât esh-shams*, that is, daughters of the sun. The next in favor are those of Hebron, where the larger varieties of grapes, reddish and white, are raised, and where the raisin making has been carried on for some time. Third in quality, perhaps, come the raisins of the Râm Allâh district, including Jifnâ, Bîr ez-Zayt, Silwâd, etc., where the industry has but made a beginning. In this district the grapes are usually greenish white or white, that is, somewhat similar to the Malaga variety. Native business men of Râm Allâh go about the district paying from two cents to three cents a pound for the raisins, subject to a discount of ten per cent for waste. The German contractors provide wooden boxes for packing the raisins. Women and girls are engaged to sort them, as they are brought into Râm Allâh from the country around, at a daily wage of from seven to twelve cents. Something less than a third of a cent a pound is paid for camel transport to Jaffa, to which must be added the charges at that port. On board ship the German contractors pay for the completed consignment about three cents a pound, possibly a little more. The native vine owners think that they are discovering that the early picking of the grapes for raisin making prevents waste and saves the strength of the vines.

After the season the vines should be pruned and the vineyards plowed and dug over, once in early and once in late winter.[1]

In vineyards and fig-orchards one will notice the stone huts called *ḳaṣr*,[2] plural *ḳuṣûr*. Between seasons, when they are not in use, they swarm with hungry fleas. Near each of them is a tiny sunken pit, walled on three sides, which makes a little fireplace. A similar pocket makes a hiding-place for dry figs which are left here under slight pressure beneath a flat stone. The latter place is made to look like the ground about by covering with small stones so as to mislead thieves. Such a hiding-place is called a *mikhba*. Most of the fig crop is dried for later use. The smaller varieties are most suitable for this purpose. The fruit is picked into small baskets and spread out on

[1] *Cf.* Isa. 5: 6. [2] Isa. 5: 2; Matt. 21: 33.

the ground. Sometimes the fruit is crushed by the hand to hasten the drying.

The olive crop is ready late in the autumn. The trees are beaten [1] with long poles by the men, while women and children gather up the berries from the ground. Seldom is care exercised to select and sort the best of the berries. They are piled in heaps inside the house, where they often become heated through, thus producing an inferior quality of oil. The berries are first put into a circular stone bed, where they are crushed, seed and all, by a sort of millstone set on edge and run like a wheel around a central pivot by a shaft. The crushed mass is then put into gunny sacking or coarse baskets and carried to the press. The oil-presses have always been very primitive, bungling affairs, but of late iron screws are being introduced.

When the grapes have all been picked from a vineyard the sheep and goats [2] are turned in to eat the leaves from the vines. The flocks are allowed to feed in the wheat and barley-fields, also, after the harvest. Goats and sheep are very often seen together in flocks.[3] Their keepers, who are their inseparable companions through the day, take care to secure safe folds for them at night. A party of us were at Teḳûa on the 30th of December, 1902. After examining the ruins we turned our attention to the modern aspect of the place. The caves and recesses about the ruins were used by shepherds, who were living there and caring for large flocks. As the sheep and goats came home late in the afternoon, the little lambs and kids, whose tender days forbade their accompanying their mothers to pasture, were hungrily awaiting them. There were about sixty of these young ones skipping about. When the plaintive cries of the little ones were answered by the motherly calls of the returning elders there was considerable excitement and motion on both sides, until by some mysteriously hidden sense families were

[1] Deut. 24: 20. [2] *Cf.* Isa. 5: 5. [3] Matt. 25: 32.

THRESHING

A THRESHING SCENE IN THE OLD POOL AT BETHEL

united and all was quiet again as supper progressed. A few days later, on our way in from Mâr Sâbâ, we saw the new-born of the flocks in the desert places where animals were browsing. The shepherd usually carries the newly-born in from the fields.[1] Very rarely is one missed. Once, in the valley called Wâdy el-'Ayn, between eṭ-Ṭayyibeh and Dayr Dîwân, I traced a little kid by its bleat, and seeing no flock about carried it home in my saddle-bags, hoping to rear it; but, missing the peculiar quality of the new milk of its mother, it did not survive many hours. Sometimes, in order to curb the inordinate appetite of a young kid for the milk, the shepherd puts a little bit in its mouth, made by two pencil-like sticks and secures the ends by cords crisscrossed over the sprouting horns.

The sheep of Palestine have immense tails, which often weigh fifteen pounds and more. In the Lebanon this weight is doubled on the sheep that are specially fattened for the winter supply of meat. These sheep, called *ma'lûf*, are fed on the remains of the mulberry leaves not devoured by the silkworms. As the worms eat only the tender parts of the leaves, the sheep are given what is left. When the animal is so surfeited as to refuse more food, an attendant makes it her business to roll it up in leaves and force it into the unwilling creature's mouth. The sheep attains an almost incredible size under this treatment.

The goats have very long flapping ears, which often get torn in the briers as they hold their heads down to feed. On some breeds the ears nearly, if not quite, touch the ground as the goats walk along. Goats and sheep are allowed to overrun all the wild places for pasture, so that any shoots of trees or shrubs that start are nibbled off. They browse upon some of the driest and least promising ground. They flourish best in the time of the rains. As the country's surface is burned over with the hot summer and autumn, the

[1] Isa. 40: 11.

flocks are driven to the few moist valleys.[1] Most frequently a boy is in charge of a smaller flock.[2] He whiles away some of his time on a reed flute.[3] If his animals get too far from him, or go in the wrong direction, he heads them off with a call and by dropping a stone from his sling,[4] or hand, just beyond them in the forbidden direction. The shepherd's usual weapon is a heavy oaken club, called locally *dibbûsy* from its resemblance in shape to a pin, the long handle being ended in a round, heavy knob. This club is under three feet in length and weighs from one to two pounds. It is a powerful weapon. Often, too, a shepherd will carry one of those long, rickety, brassbound muskets that look very dangerous, — for the manipulator. A leathern pouch, flint and steel, a knife and a sling of woolen yarn complete the outfit, except the actual clothing. The main garment is a long cotton shirt that comes to the knees, belted with a leathern belt. For sleeping and for rainy weather the homespun woolen overcoat, called an *'âbâyeh,* is worn. Shoes and head-dress finish off the man, who is the loneliest of Syrians, though he sings and plays and talks to his animals. Sometimes, as you see him in silhouette against the sky-line, he seems to be transfixed on the club or musket on which he leans, so long does he stand unchanged. When he moves it is with singularly slow movements.

Besides meat and milk, which both goats and sheep provide, the sheep produce wool. Considerable raw wool is bought by the weavers of the village. A man in Râm Allâh, whose house abuts unpleasantly on more valuable property, refuses to sell it to a well-to-do neighbor[5] because it is on the outskirts where he is in a position to get first chance at those who come into the village from that direction to sell fleeces. The wool is washed, combed, dyed and spun into thread by the villagers. We had occasion to purchase

[1] Psalm 23: 2. [2] *Cf.* 1 Sam. 17: 28. [3] Judges 5: 16. [4] 1 Sam. 17: 40. [5] *Cf.* 1 Kings 21: 3.

1.—HAND SPINNING 2.—REELING
3.—STRAIGHTENING THREADS FOR THE LOOM

a lot of wool in fleeces for mattresses. We bought five hundred and ten pounds at eleven cents per pound, but after a thorough cleansing we found that the lot weighed four hundred and twenty-six. Having purchased ticking for mattresses, quilts and pillows, and cotton for filling the quilts, our next step was to engage the services of the mattress-maker from Jerusalem. His name was Baruch, a Spanish or Sephardim Jew, tall, wiry and dark, with stooping shoulders and remarkably successful in getting hold of one's hand and planting on it a reverential kiss before his object was discovered. The kiss felt and sounded like the bursting of a smoke-ball. He came for a few days' stay, bringing his tools and a boy helper with him. The most novel of the implements was one shaped like a huge bow which is used in fluffing up cotton or wool. It might be compared to an attenuated single-stringed harp. It is held in the hand by the wooden part, the string resting in the cotton. By striking the cord with a wooden mallet, a vibration is set going that twangs musically and throws the cotton into a light, billowy mass. He is very skilful with his needles. He would sew and quilt nearly twenty hours out of the twenty-four in his haste to complete the task and get back to Jerusalem. We were put to it to feed him properly, as certain things were unlawful for him to receive and eat from our hands. But eggs, olives, bread and tomatoes were acceptable. In case of a doubt concerning an article of food we simply asked him whether it was lawful or not. He was very gentle and pleasing. We had to be careful to see that he did not go to sleep among his inflammable materials and leave the lamps burning according to Oriental practise.

When otherwise unemployed a villager will spin off a ball of yarn by hand. Two sticks, like thick pencils, are laid one across the other at right angles. This makes the bobbin. The upright one is notched at the top to catch the thread when needful. A hank of clean wool is disposed over the left forearm. A little of this is started through the fingers of the two hands. It is then caught on the notched end of the bobbin, which is given a whirl and allowed to hang down, while the hands play out the twisting yarn to govern the thickness. When the bobbin carrying the spinning yarn has reached the ground, the amount of yarn already made is wound up on it and caught at the notch. The whirling, feeding out and spinning go on until a ball of yarn is produced.

The looms are primitive and heavy. They are constructed in the dark room which serves as the weaver's house. A pit is made for him to sit in, and only the light from the door falls on his work. Cotton and wool fabrics of heavy texture are produced. The heavy woolen 'abâyeh is the chief garment made by the peasant weavers. The light-weight cloth for the other garments is purchased from the city shops. Coarse rugs are made on a still more primitive loom, which is often seen out-of-doors, especially among the Bedawîn.

The land of Palestine bears abundant evidence of a higher state of cultivation once upon a time than that of the present day. Remains of villas, terrace walls and numerous cemented cisterns to catch rain-water are observable. The soil lacks only water to produce abundantly. For the most part the list of things grown has narrowed to those requiring the least care and capital. Where springs are plentiful, and where the people have a little ambition, a variety of vegetables and fruits are cultivated. But because of the uncertainty of the amount and incidence of the tax there is little incentive. In the neighborhood of Jaffa some of the finest oranges in the world are raised. The Sidon oranges come next in desirability. The Jordan Valley is one of the richest garden spots imaginable. The vine is perfectly at home in the lime country of the highlands, as are the fig and the olive.[1] This same region is excellently well adapted to silk

[1] Deut. 8: 8.

culture, and might exceed the Lebanon in this respect, though scarcely a dream of such a possibility is indulged in Palestine. The gardens of Urṭâs, near Solomon's Pool, of 'Ayn Kârim, of Silwân (Siloam) and of Jenîn might with encouragement be matched hundreds of times. Around Haifa, and on the way to 'Athlît, the Germans have shown what improvements are possible. There is also the fine agricultural farm at Jaffa, called Mikweh Israel, or Natur's, under French management. By pools and cisterns, conduits and irrigation, the peasant farmers could make garden spots where now to the eye of the stranger all looks hopeless. The peculiar powdery effect of lime rock, and the countless tons of small stones constantly breaking up and showing on the surface of the ground, look, but are not necessarily, forbidding.

The market of a village is usually its chief street, in which the buyers and sellers meet each other, where the laden animals from the country about come with goods, and where people bent on business are most apt to meet those who can serve them. Shops and storerooms line the market street. The Arab name for this interesting locality is *sûḳ*. Thither the gardener takes such of his produce as he cannot himself use, and if he be not a merchant himself, puts it into the care of one who is, on commission. Venders of fabrics, pottery, breadstuffs and meats assemble here and display their goods. The shopkeepers naturally seek localities in the market street and, when space fails there, in the adjacent streets. If there are a number of tribes in the village, each tribe, in its own section, may have stores for the supply of the simple stock of foodstuffs required. A shop or store is a little room from six to a dozen feet square, with a door, seldom a window, a counter and the necessary bins and shelves. What we should call a grocery store will keep in stock sugar, flour, oil, matches and possibly grain. Some simple candies, some spice, starch, dried fruit, coffee and rice may complete the list. The scales will be on the counter. No wrapping-paper need be used, as the purchaser brings his own dish if he be purchasing a liquid, and if not, carries his purchases in the skirt of his dress or in a handkerchief. The sugar comes in a huge loaf covered with blue paper. Salt is heavily taxed by the government. Tobacco is a government monopoly and to be sold only by a specially authorized merchant, who wears a brown coat as a sort of uniform designating him and his rights. Such a shop as has been described may add cotton cloth and thread to its stock. Shoe shops confine themselves to the making and displaying of peasant shoes. The weaver of cloth and ʿabâyehs ordinarily has no separate place of sale, but sells from the loom-room or else makes a journey to the villages about and displays the goods in their market streets. The shops have their regular customers, to whom they sell on credit, with some favor and less haggling than is customary with other purchasers. The butcher hangs his freshly-slaughtered sheep on hooks in the side wall of the market street and sells at a uniform price per ruṭl or *oḳḳîyeh* any part of the creature. Perhaps he has not killed until there is a likelihood of demands enough for meat to warrant the venture. If local restrictions do not hinder, the butcher may kill and dress his animals right in the market street.

The traders are keen and allow no points of advantage to escape their notice. In fact, the conversation of the common people of the country is in terms of the currency and concerns the ins and outs of bargaining, loss and gain. Sometimes, in the heat of trading, the parties appear to rise into a frenzy of altercation. But nothing is ever settled at this high tension. After a few seconds of comparative calm the haggling and controversy begin again and an attempt is made to find a common basis of argument in which neither party may yield too much. The difference between wholesale and retail business is not very clearly recognized in the villages. Few peasant producers know what their own expense has been in the production of their commodities. Striking a bargain is a tedious process to the stranger, but an exercise of great interest to the native and full of possibilities. He declares that the business arrangement shall be as you like, utterly. He is a servant of God, he seeks not money but your happiness, your good-will. Is not that the sweetest possession, the love and favor of brothers? If it is a house that you are trying to rent at a decent price, he says, "What is such a thing as that between us? Take it for nothing."[1] An utter stranger once came to my door with a young gazel which he had found in the wilderness. He declared that it was a present to me. I offered him forty cents for it and he demanded sixty. I gave him the forty, however, promising the other twenty if the little creature lived.

Measures and weights vary as between villages. In the cities the French system prevails, but in the country the peasantry persist in the use of the variable weights and measures. Many things are weighed which with us are measured, as, for example, olive-oil and vegetables. The *oḳḳîyeh* approximates a half pound. Six of these oḳḳîyehs equal an *oḳḳa*, and two oḳḳas equal a *ruṭl*. One hundred ruṭls equal a *ḳonṭâr*. The linear measure of one *dhrâʻ* or *drâʻ* equals about twenty-seven inches. The grain measure, called *ṣâʻ*, is the least regular of all. The Râm Allâh ṣâʻ, for example, is a little larger than the Jerusalem ṣâʻ and more than double that of Ṭayyibeh.

In theory the coinage of the country consists of the Turkish gold pound of one hundred piasters, the silver *mejîdeh* of twenty piasters, the half and quarter silver mejîdeh, the silver double piaster, piaster and half piaster. There are also coins of nickel and copper alloy, one called *bishlik*, which equals two and a half piasters, a double bishlik, called *wazary* in Jerusalem and *zahrâweh* at Haifa, a half bishlik, a half

[1] Gen. 23: 11, 15.

piaster and a quarter piaster. There are some copper coins of small value. This list and these values are according to the government standard, which is called *ṣâgh,* and they hold for all payments of taxes, for the post and telegraph and for legal business. For ordinary trade in the country, though these same coins are used, different values are assigned to them. Thus Hebron, Jerusalem and other places have their own systems of reckoning. In Jerusalem the tariff *sherk,* or market, as it is called, makes the mejîdeh twenty-three piasters instead of twenty as in government reckoning. The result is a diminution of the piaster and an increase in the number of them in each of the coins mentioned above. The Turkish gold pound is not seen in the country, but the gold twenty-franc pieces of the Latin Monetary Union are frequently seen and go by the name *lîreh fransaweh* or *nubalyôn* (Napoleon). This coin equals one hundred and nine piasters according to the Jerusalem market rate.

Change is seldom made for the large coins except in the better city shops, but must be purchased of the money-changers who sit behind their little tables at different points on the main streets. A very common rate for change is the charge of a piaster and a half for changing the Napoleon into small money. In the villages the storekeepers sell change.

The peasants refuse to accept damaged coin or any coins that arouse their suspicions as to genuineness or weight. A few coins are less acceptable in some sections than in others. The big copper coin called the *ḳobbuḳ,* worth five *paras* in Jerusalem, is not used in Beirut, and conversely the *neḥâsy* of Beirut and vicinity is not used at Jerusalem. When the new style *metlik* had been issued by the government and had been in use in Constantinople for some time, it was slowly gaining favor in Beirut and was being refused in Palestine except in a few places, where it was taken at a discount of one-fifth from its legal value.

A primitive method of keeping a record was seen at the village of eṭ-Ṭayyibeh. A small bow was made from a twig and on the cord was strung a lot of paper slips. Every slip contained the names of five Ṭayyibeh men. The whole village was thus divided up into groups of five. Whenever soldiers coming from Jerusalem were quartered on the villagers one of these groups was responsible for feeding the soldiers. Each group took its turn. Another bow, string and bunch of written slips represented the order of turns of the citizens for feeding the soldiers' horses.

Money lending is common among the country people and often the rates are very high. Seldom is the rate less than ten per cent, and more often it is twenty. A clever man possessed of a small capital multiplies it rapidly by judicious loans, though it must be confessed that the gambling element enters pretty largely into the business. Some possessors of ready money invest it in the form of advances to owners of future crops, taking their pay in the crop when harvested. This is often done when soldiers, representing the government, descend on a village and demand the taxes. The peasants in seeking the ready money with which to pay are compelled to dispose of barley and other produce cheap.

Often of an evening one will hear the crier publishing something of general concern to the villagers. In Râm Allâh this officer, called *nâṭûr*, and chosen by the shaykhs, receives a yearly allowance of seventy mejîdehs. The tribal elders decide upon some matter for general observance and the crier makes it known. For instance, when an especially dry season was on, the village crier was heard proclaiming that no woman should draw more than one jar of water from the springs at a time. If any woman were caught offending the extra jar would be broken and a fine of a bishlik (eleven cents) imposed. At another time it was forbidden the people to harvest the olives until a certain date. Lost articles are advertised by the criers, and those lounging about in the evening are kept in touch with business news, as the voice penetrates all quarters of the village.

The go-between, or *wasîṭ*, is a familiar figure in Syrian business matters. A merchant from Nazareth explained to me the popularity of this intermediary thus: " If there are two men, each wanting something of the other and neither wishing to express his whole mind before the other has done so, they can avoid the difficulty by employing a third person to whom each unbosoms freely, and this third person, possessing the secrets of both, knows how to approach either one with the business of the other."[1]

The village shaykhs are agents in many business matters. The shaykh is chief of his family or tribe in all matters needing a representative. The position often goes from father to son, if the ability which secured the position for the father be a characteristic of the son. Or it may go to some other near of kin to the former shaykh. The shaykhs are sometimes chosen by acclamation or by general consent and are recorded by the general government. The shaykh is in charge of the guest-room of his tribe. Here it is that out-of-town business men are taken, especially if they have come to buy commodities of the village. When the soldiers are sent by the government to a village with a levy they are entertained at the guest-house. The shaykhs of the different tribes in the village deal with the soldiers. The amount of money asked of the village is apportioned between the shaykhs representing the tribes. Each shaykh distributes his apportionment to the members of his own tribe. If any man prove obstinate in meeting his obligations he is turned over by the shaykh to the soldiers, who may beat him or carry him off to prison. If the government seeks an offender in the village it does so through the shaykh of the offender's tribe.

Where there are a number of shaykhs, in dealings with the

[1] *Cf.* Job 9: 33; also Gal. 3: 19; 1 Tim. 2: 5; Heb. 8: 6; 9: 15; 12: 24.

VARIOUS ARTICLES MADE OF SKIN: BOTTLES, BAGS, POUCHES AND BUCKETS
The background is formed by a large straw floor mat, such as used in the guest rooms.
(From the Hartford Theological Seminary Collection.)

government, the village is represented by one or more of the number who go by the name *mukhtâr*. So in Râm Allâh there are three of these mukhtârs, one for the Greeks, one for the Roman Catholics and one for the Protestants of the village. The last two are a concession to the interests of those who might not be fairly represented by the first mukhtâr.

The stone and building trades are highly respected industries among the peasants. In a typical peasant house there is scarcely any woodwork to be done except to set up a heavy door. The windows, if there are any, are small light-holes merely. Quarrying, stone-dressing and construction are carried on in every large village. The highlands have yielded inexhaustible supplies of building material from time immemorial. Limestone may be found and burned anywhere.[1] The kilns are usually built in valleys or on their sides, where it is possible to dig a good-sized pit before building up the circular stone walls, and where the draft will be good.

A *ḳonṭâr* of lime is one hundred twenty ruṭls (seven hundred fifty pounds) instead of the usual one hundred ruṭls, and costs about a dollar delivered. The master workers in lime and stone and cement receive from seventy-five cents to a dollar and ten cents per day in the villages. Their helpers receive from twenty-five cents upwards, according to the grade of work.

As the common name for stone is *ḥajar*, the place where stone is found, the quarry, is called *maḥjar*, the prefix *m* conveying the sense of locality. Rough, undressed stone blocks are called *debsh*. Those roughly squared, but undressed, are called *khâmy*. Dressed building-stones are called *ḥajar*. Flat flagstones are called *balâṭ*. Stone cut for arches goes by the name *maḳâdam* (singular, *maḳdum*).

The limestone of the country is found in several grades of

[1] Isa. 33: 12.

hardness and desirability for different kinds of building. The very best stone for house building is a hard white limestone which holds well with lime cement and is known as *mizzy ḥulu*. *Mizzy aḥmar* is very similar, but of a brownish-red color. The softer limestone is called *kûkûly*. The stronger kind is yellowish, *kûkûly aṣfar;* the other kind, a white stone, *kûkûly abyaḍ*. *Malakeh* is a pretty, brilliant, white stone used decoratively in finishing over doors and windows. The very hard flint *ṣuwwân* would ordinarily be unmanageable for building purposes. *Nâry* is a soft, easily crumbled stone that cements together in a compact mass with lime and is used in filling in the core of house walls and in arches supporting the house floors (*muṣṭaby*) above the cellars. *Hethyân* is similar to *nâry*, but even softer and reddish. *Huwârah* is really decomposed stone, very soft, used as a top dressing in building roads, where it settles into a natural cement, mingling with broken rock and soil. Soil is called *trâb* and a derivative from it, *trâby*, is used colloquially to designate clay and wet earth as materials in building. Lime is known as *shîd* and mortar as *ṭîn*. Cement goes by an imported name *shementu*, or *ḥomrah*, literally the *red* dust of pounded pottery. The hard cement, called *kaḥly*, used in pointing the house walls, is made of lime, *ḥamrah*, that is, pounded pottery, and *nehâteh*, the dust that falls from the work of the stone-dressers' tools. Plaster is called *ḳaṣâreh* or *iḳṣâreh*, and whitewash, *trâsheh*. Tile and brick go by the name *ḳermîd*. The heavy iron hammer with which rough stone is squared into workable shape is called the *shaḳûf*. The *râs* is a heavy sort of iron hammer with pointed ends of steel used as a pick. The hammer used to drive the chisels and occasionally to do slight dressing by pounding the edges of a stone is called *muṭraḳeh* and is quite unique in shape. Its two faces are set obliquely on the central part of the head and a short handle supplied. By this adjustment of the faces a downward stroke is more easily effected.

It is of steel and about three pounds in weight. The *shâḥûṭeh* is a heavy double steel hammer toothed at both ends. One edge may have more, and the other edge less, than twenty teeth. Two grades of face dressing may be given to a block of stone with this one tool. The *maṭabbeh* is a very heavy hammer made of a rectangular bar of steel with ends about two inches or less square. These ends or faces are supplied with numerous points, making anywhere from eighty-one to one hundred and forty needlelike teeth, according to the grade of work required. The *shôkeh* is a pointed round steel chisel and comes in various sizes. The *izmîl* is a flat, bladelike steel chisel of differing sizes used in dressing the sides of stone where, in building, a close joint is desired. Stone is gotten out of the quarries with wedges, heavy hammers and the râs. The shâkûf is then brought into play. Mizzy stone may be dressed with the shôkeh (chisel), then with the shâḥûṭeh and lastly with the maṭabbeh. Kûkûly may be pounded with the râs and then dressed with the shôkeh and shâḥûṭeh, or, when quite soft, the shôkeh's work may be done by the preliminary dressing with the râs. The trade of stone dressing is known as *daḳâḳeh* and the workmen as *daḳḳîḳ*, both terms being connected with the verbal root *daḳḳ*. The builder or mason is known as the *bannâ*. The more pretentious title *muhandis* or *muhandis bannâ* is given to those competent to undertake and judge of immense works. Such are often foreigners, resident in cities, who are called out on jobs demanding expert opinion and advice. The muhandis is highly respected as a master of the whole art of construction.

Foot travel is the rule among the peasants. Those whose business takes them away from the home village walk the entire day with about the same endurance that they work in the fields at home.[1] The few who own donkeys or mules walk behind their loaded animals, carrying produce between

[1] *Cf.* 2 Sam. 2: 29.

the villages. Hence it comes about that donkey paths make up by far the great majority of the paths and that the transport of bulky and heavy articles is difficult in the interior. The government roads increase slowly, but are very great conveniences when constructed. The road at present under construction from Jerusalem to Nâblus (Shechem) is being made in sections by contract. The contractor hires the natives to bring the materials, broken rock, lime dust and pulverized stone, and an excellent carriage road results. The natives along the way then begin an irregular carriage service which creates a business. Seats for citizens range about twenty cents apiece for a ten-mile journey, though the price depends somewhat on the number of passengers clamoring for, or indifferent to, accommodations, and the apparent ability of the applicant. As in many other kinds of bargaining, the engaging of a carriage seat is made more sure by receiving a pledge from the owner that he will keep his word with you. This *'arrabôn* is frequently demanded by the party to a business arrangement who has the greater interest in its fulfilment and would suffer the greater inconvenience in the event of default. In the case in question perhaps half a fare will be demanded from the carriage driver as a pledge that he will perform the required service, and if he wants business badly enough he will entrust the sum to the keeping of his prospective passenger. Now and then, when a family is carrying a quantity of bedding and other household goods, copper vessels, baskets, boxes, their chickens and children, the carriage may seem a little crowded, but usually for men travelers the accommodations are fairly comfortable. Frequently some of the peasant passengers will become nauseated by the motion of the carriage and hang their white faces out the carriage door. The carriage will continue to be a luxury for some time in the country districts. Sick people and children are greatly convenienced by a carriage service, since in rainy weather it saves unnecessary

A MARKET SCENE: PEASANTRY NEAR DAVID'S TOWER, JERUSALEM

exposure. Now and then a lone pedestrian will succumb to the raw chill of the rainy days and die on the road. During heavy rains the Russian pilgrims, if caught out in the dismal weather, suffer and lose some of their number by death.

Camel trains are used in transporting grain. Camels can be used only in dry weather, as their large, spongy feet slip on the muddy ways and they are apt to fall spread-eagle fashion and be hurt fatally.

In the village of Râm Allâh the customary width of a road is but three meters.

A case has been known where a man, who owned land on both sides of the road, desired to consolidate his properties, and accomplished it by building in the road and deflecting traffic to such an extent that it left him on one side of its course.

The trades that need a large patronage for support are usually carried on in the cities, though the craftsmen go on tours through the villages, doing such work in their line as has accumulated since their last visit. So carpenters, glaziers, tinsmiths, cleaners and whiteners of the copper cooking vessels (*tungerer*), sellers of ready-made garments, etc., itinerate among the villages. The gipsies are the country blacksmiths. In the cities native blacksmiths are found. In shoeing a horse the custom is to place the foot to be shod on a small block and have an attendant hold up the other foot of the same side to prevent kicking.

Ready money is scarce enough to be a very strong influence in favor of any occupation that can offer it. Many men and women from the villages about Jerusalem go into the city to sell their produce or their labor. Sitting about the streets near David's Tower may be seen the Silwân women with vegetables, milk and eggs. Some men who own donkeys or mules act as messengers between their villages and the city, carrying produce into the markets and returning with purchases for the village. Some Râm Allâh men go into the city as mechanics, but more go for domestic service in the houses and convents. When women servants are needed they are usually secured from Bethlehem, which is only five miles from the city.

The peasants use the word *antîky* (plural, *antîkât*) for any antique object, such as a bit of carving, an inscription, an old coin or a piece of glass or pottery. Indeed, some friends of ours met an extension of the use of the term in Egypt. A girl, very eager to sell them some oranges, after following the carriage a long way and being continually refused, hit on what she thought would be a successful method. Thrusting the fresh fruit close to the Americans she cried, "Antîky, antîky." Seldom can the peasants really comprehend the strange delight that foreigners take in ancient objects, unless perchance the material be precious metal or stone, but they have learned that antiquities command a price. So with a money stimulus the mischief is augmented. Certain of the country people go hunting for old objects, rifling ancient tombs and scattering the contents far and wide in order to gratify the hideous taste of curio purchasers. Fearing lest they may be traced in their philistinism the peasants give wrong information as to the places from which the articles came so that their "finds" lose much of their value as historic data. Could the place and conditions of their age-long burial be known they might give archeological information more precious than the intrinsic value of the objects themselves. Sometimes a "find" is more or less injured because it is supposed to be valueless.

The provisions of the Turkish law regarding antiquities are very strict and operate to make scientific research difficult when not impossible. But the administration of these laws is not skilful enough to prevent an immense amount of sly pilfering from old tombs and suspected localities. Ancient tombs are completely covered from observation by soil.

After heavy rains these sealed tombs are often betrayed by a slight sinking of the earth about them, and thus possibly a whole series of tombs will be discovered and their contents disposed of in the distant city.[1] These opened tombs may be seen all through the country, staring from the hillsides and among the terraces like ghastly eye-sockets. In the house which we hired for a boys' school the builders had placed in one room as a floor stone an *antîky* of which they were proud. It was an ornamented and inscribed slab which they claimed to have found at Dayr Dîwân.[2] The inscription in Greek read

✠ *ΥΠΕΡ ΑΝΑΠΑΥCΕΩC CΗΛΑΜΩΝΟC ΠΡΕCΒS* ✠

For the repose of Sêlamôn (Solomon) Presbyter.

[1] *Cf.* Matt. 13 : 44.
[2] Described in P. E. F. Quarterly, October, 1904, page 382.

CHAPTER VII

THE SOCIAL LIFE OF THE VILLAGE

KINSHIP, religious association, party traditions and proximity, these four influences are important in the order named in helping to form society. Among the people whom we are considering the fact of kinship is the first determining cause of social relations. In fact it is so important that the farther we get away from a city the more does it tend to become the sole basis of friendly association. In the villages kinship overshadows all other considerations. In the desert there is practically no other bond in which is the possibility of society. The law of hospitality is really an invention of necessity, the guest becoming by a fiction a temporary kinsman.[1]

As men come to live more closely together they are compelled to heed other considerations than blood relationship, and so in the village, while kinship dominates everything, yet there must be some regard to other claims. One might live in a village a long time without realizing the fact, but a little inquiry would elicit it, that any happy social group of people is almost certain to be a group of kindred. The village will have as many distinct sections, or, as we should say, wards, as there are tribes. One does not discover much that is comparable to society existing between members of different divisions of the village.

Religious association counts for something, however, in making society for the villager, though this is less the case than in the cities. The celebration of feasts, pilgrimages and ecstasies gives the Moslem not only society but a deal of entertainment. The Christian population finds an important

[1] *Cf.* 1 Kings 20: 32, etc.

social center in the church, and in the festivals and celebrations of the church much of its pleasantest entertainment.

Party traditions, such as those which have divided the villages of Palestine into Yemen and Ḳays, have besides their divisive effect a social significance in an interest which is engendered between the villagers the country over belonging to the same party. As the old enmities die out this broader social spirit may persist and even offer a basis for wider interests.

Proximity might seem at first thought to offer only added occasion for hostility between those whose family or religious differences keep them apart, and so, no doubt, it often does have this effect. But it was noticeable that, when a squabble arose between Christians living in el-Bîreh and others in Râm Allâh, the Bîreh Moslems threw themselves into the question in favor of the Bîreh Christians, and the united Bîreh populace came over in a rage to take vengeance on the Râm Allâh people. It was not that Bîreh Moslems welcomed an opportunity to fight Christians even to the extent of assisting other Christians, but it was a pure case of neighborliness with the nearer neighbor. Ordinarily Râm Allâh and el-Bîreh are neighborly enough, both being of the Ḳays faction.

The diversions of the Syrian peasant are extremely simple. Doubtless conversation is the chief social delight. Pictures, books and formal entertainment are out of the question. It takes most of the time to earn the sustenance of the family. The idea of spending money for pure amusement is scarcely to be dreamed of by a sane person. Young men often take pleasure in the possession of a silk head scarf or a black, thin overgarment, articles of dress which are not strictly necessary, and yet sufficiently useful luxuries. The children play merrily if they are healthy. The old men sit about and talk in the shops and market. Visiting in each other's houses is almost unknown unless the persons be near of kin. The men see each other in the market. The women see each other at the springs and at the ovens. News goes about with extraordinary rapidity from lip to lip. The entertainment of visitors and guests is a matter of honor. Conversation is lively and the little points of etiquette much regarded. Among the well-to-do the visitor is served with preserves, fruit, lemonade and, lastly, coffee. Before the serving of the coffee the visitors are hardly at liberty to withdraw. If an early departure be imperative the coffee will be hurried and served early. It is said that among the Bedawîn a full cup of coffee is a sign of enmity. So the cups are not quite filled to the brim. The coffee-cup (finjân) is a tiny affair, usually without handle or saucer. Sugar is not commonly added, milk never. When sugar is used it is ordinarily cooked with the coffee.

It is customary to make calls of courtesy upon the occasion of any gala day or feast day of special significance. For instance, the leading men in a village may call on the government representative, say the *mudîr*, on the occasion of the Sultan's birthday. Or Moslems may call upon the church officials in honor of the great church days. The natives honor foreigners by calls if they learn that some day of great significance to the foreigner's home country is at hand. It is customary to call upon a neighbor who has returned from a journey immediately and felicitate him and hear of his experiences. Upon entering a house for a call, if it be among their own neighbors, little formality is indulged. The burden of that is on the host, who should greet the comers with "*Fût*" (enter), or "*Foḍḍel*" (welcome). Among the more pretentious visitors the preliminaries of calls are smoothed through the medium of servants. The passing over the threshold may be made the occasion of the expression of much hospitality and courtesy. The seat of honor is the one farthest from the door, but modesty dictates that one should sit down in the humblest place, that nearest the door, until expostulation and entreaty prevail on one to take the place of honor. The first questions are concerning the health of the host and his family. In a Moslem's house it is not customary to ask concerning the man's wife. The conversation may be made sprightly by the keenness of the interest shown in these objects of inquiry, or it may be disagreeably dull on account of the perfunctory manner in which they are mentioned. A matter of business, if there be such, is kept back until other subjects of conversation fail. The introduction and carrying on of a conversation may be a very graceful and interesting thing, but if either party be boorish,[1] and the purpose be to demand some advantage, as when official business brings together those of different religious beliefs, the meeting can be a very strained and uncomfortable affair. Such an occasion would be the meeting of a proud city Moslem with a Christian peasant, or even with a Moslem peasant. But between village peasants themselves, though of different faiths, there is more real courtesy than elsewhere. Not many of the people like trouble and hard feeling. Most of them like the atmosphere of good-will and at least the externals of good fellowship and generous treatment.

Invitations to a hospitable meal or feast are often sent out shortly before the actual hour, if not just at the very time.[2] It is commonly the case that a courteous host seeks to dissuade the guest from bringing the call or visit to a close.[3] The departing guest usually says something like "*A khâṭrak,*" "By your leave," to which the host answers, "*Ma' Salâmeh,*" "[Go] with peace."[4] The first speaker responds to this with "*'Ala selmâk,*" or "*Selimt.*"

[5] Greetings in the market-place and on the road are formal but graceful. The common greeting of "*Salâm 'alaykum,*"[6] "Peace be on you," is replied to by "'Alaykum es-salâm,"

[1] Prov. 18:23. [2] Matt. 22:3, 4. [3] Judges 19:5–8. [4] *Cf.* 1 Sam. 25:35. [5] Matt. 23:7. [6] Gen. 43:23; Luke 24:36.

" May the peace be on you." In strictness this is the salutation of Moslems, though it is commonly used indiscriminately. Now and then one may hear of a bigoted Moslem who would not return this salutation to a Christian, but would mumble out " Peace be on the faithful ones," in which class he would include, of course, none but his coreligionists.[1] More characteristic are the rustic salutations, " Marḥabâ," " Welcome "; " Mîyet marḥabâ," "A hundred welcomes "; " Kayf ḥâlak," " How are you? "; " Ḥumdillâh," " Praise God "; "Allâh yofathak," " May God preserve you "; " Ḥumdillâh salâmeh," " Praise God, you are well," or, " I see you well "; " Salâmtak," " Your peace." The peasant's early good morning salutation is " Ṣubâḥkum b'l-khayr," to which the response is, " Yâ ṣubâḥ el-khayr." When the day is well on the pleasant greeting is, " Nahârak sa'îd," " May your day be happy," to which the gracious reply is, " Nahârak umbârak," " May your day be blessed." The evening salutation is, " Mesâîkum b'l-khayr," answered by, " Yâ mesâ el-khayr." At night it is, " Layltak sa'îdeh."

An evasive answer to one asking a question as to another's destination in traveling is to reply, "A(la) bâb Allâh," "To the gate of God."

In addressing foreigners the peasants use the term *khawâjah* for a man and *sitt* for a woman. In speaking to a superior of their own race they employ the term *sayyid*, *lord*, or *sir*, or *effendy*. Among themselves they use the word *shaykh* for an elderly, a learned or a holy man. To their equals in age and station the peasant's titles of address are numerous. " Yâ shaykh " to such is used in expostulation or derision. "'Ammy," " My uncle"; " Ḥabîby," " My dear "; " Mu'allim," " Master " or " Teacher," or the first name of the one addressed are used in conversation. If the talkers are uncertain of each other's name they may say, " Hayû, shu ismak? " " Eh, there, what's your name? "

[1] Matt. 5:47.

though this is rather contemptuous. In rough conversation the speakers may grace each other with such address as " Yâ bârid," literally, " Thou cold one," meaning foolish one; " Shu ente," " Who are you anyway? "; " Majnûn, ente? ", "Are you mad? "; "Ana ḥamâr? ", "Am I a donkey? " *i. e.*, " Do you take me for a donkey? " or, sarcastically, " Shâṭrak," " You are clever." To boys, " Yâ ṣuby," or " Yâ weled," and to girls or any unmarried woman, " Yâ bint," are the simple forms of address. " 'Amty," " My aunt," is often used to middle-aged or elderly matrons. A father will often call his child by the relation which he himself sustains to the child, " Yâ aba," literally, " O father! " A maternal aunt has been heard to call her niece or her nephew by the relationship which she holds to either, viz., " Yâ khâlty," meaning literally, " My maternal aunt."

A very graceful salute is executed with the right hand touching lightly first one's breast, then the lips and then the forehead. The one saluted answers by the same set of gestures. In Damascus I once saw a group of citizens who had gathered in a tiny room for conversation executing simultaneously a similar salute, except that they first swept the right hand downward towards the ground in lieu of the touch on the breast. This variation is more elegant or more humble than the former way, according to circumstances.[1] I once saw a villager presenting a paper to be read to one of the official class. The peasant made a sweeping motion toward the ground with the hand holding the document.

In meeting, the native seizes the hand of his superior and endeavors to bring the back of the hand to his lips and forehead. The other, however, generally succeeds in withdrawing his hand before more than a touch of hands has been accomplished. On meeting, especially after a separation, the custom has obtained among women friends

[1] *Cf.* Ruth 2: 10.

of kissing each other first on the right cheek and then on the left. Men salute each other in the same way in some localities. Strangers enter into amiable conversation with each other without the necessity of introductions.

The guest-house of the tribe makes a place of rendezvous for men, where congenial companions may be met in a social way. Song and story are much enjoyed by the men. Those who have a knack for story-telling, or who can sing to their own accompaniment on the *rabâb*, a kind of fiddle, or on the *'ûd*, a kind of lute, are assured an appreciative audience. The social and kindly amenities may be seen here at the guest-house after a funeral. The nearest of kin to the deceased among the men is constrained by his men friends to accompany them to the guest-house where, by preparing food and supplying a stream of conversation, they try to divert his mind from his grief. They may seek to entertain him thus for several days. I accompanied one such group of mourners and sympathizers to the guest-house where we sat cross-legged upon the floor. A man and his wife who lived in the same house and kept the guest-room in order prepared coffee. Green coffee berries were roasted in a long-handled iron ladle over the coals in a clay brazier. The roasted berries were put into a wooden mortar and pounded with a long wooden pestle. When they were quite fine the odor was very pleasant. The coffee was then put into a tin pot having a long handle and allowed to cook over the brazier until it swelled up in the pot several times, when it was served in handleless cups, of which there were but two in the company. They handed me the first cup, but I passed it on, refusing to drink before the old men had partaken. The cup that I used was washed after my predecessor had drunk from it, but I noticed that for the others the cups were refilled without washing. It was most delicious coffee. Some of the men had previously refreshed themselves with cigarettes. The talk had been general and

WOMEN AT THE SPRING

FOUNTAIN AT NAZARETH

lively and an air of comfort and good-will had filled the place. I admired those good-hearted men and their simple and sensible way, as with the fumes of coffee and the interest of their talk they beguiled their friend and themselves for several hours. The female friends of a woman in grief assemble at the house where she lives with the object of comforting her. So with all the great events of life, birth, marriage, death, a feast, a return from a journey, the friends, who are usually related, distantly at any rate, gather together for the pleasure of conversation and discussion, to drink coffee and, as they say in the native idiom, to "drink tobacco," for they always describe smoking as drinking.

Often in a conversation where there seems to be a likelihood of ill feeling, as, for instance, in business matters, the one who is leading the conversation will pronounce the opening salutations and addresses all over again. So in the middle of a conversation that does not appear to be "getting anywhere," he may break in suddenly with "Good morning, sir; how are you?" This repeated several times during a long talk has the effect of a fresh start with the erasure of what has passed. Sometimes a man who is being pressed, as he thinks, unduly, will break out into vituperation, pass his hand over his brow in sign of weariness and the unreason of his opponents, even weep a little with vexation. Meanwhile all the other talkers about him observe him soberly and silence may rest on them for some minutes before the subject is resumed. All these things make little difference with the results of the business in hand, however. He who has the advantage holds it unmoved, though he may be as diplomatic as possible in forcing the conclusion. Any exhibition of passion or impatience usually betrays the weaker side in the discussion. Such conversations may be continued at odd times through days.

When there are visitors at the guest-house who are to be fed, the people take one of the huge dishes known as the *minsaf*, fill it with food, generally rice and mutton, and several help to carry it to the guest-chamber, supporting it in a large piece of sacking, which they hold by the four corners.

One of the gala times to which the neighbors look forward is what might be called a roofing-bee. When a house which is in the course of building has been finished except the roof, the master mason in charge becomes practically the head of an open-air festival, for besides his usual helpers the whole neighborhood turns out to assist. The women bring stone and mortar, the men stand in line to pass it, and amid shouting, singing and the firing of guns the work goes on merrily to completion, when the mason is supposed to receive as a present a new robe and the merrymakers are feasted on rice.

Among the rich, women as well as men smoke the *nârjîleh*, which is supplied with *tumbâk*, a Persian variety of tobacco.

A great deal of entertainment must be afforded the natives who come in contact with foreigners, as these latter attempt, and mangle, the language. But with imperturbable and polite deference the native listeners betray no sense of our blunders, even declaring our gift in acquiring the tongue remarkable. The eager learner is fortunate indeed if the natives do not answer back in the same broken Arabic which he is perpetrating. Such an excess of accommodation hinders advance in the difficult idiom. A missionary friend told me of the amusing experiences of herself and another worker in their early attempts to force their ability at talking in Arabic. They were almost totally ignorant of the language, but they went to a garden where there was a group of women and boldly essayed to tell the story of the rich man and Lazarus. One of them knowing a word for *man*, *zelameh*, said it, and was followed by the other, who said the word for *poor*, *fakîr*, and pointed upwards. The first then said *zelameh* again, when the second, who also knew the word for *rich, ghany,* said that and pointed downwards. That was the extent of their exposition. Some one, hearing of it, asked our friend if she thought any impression was made upon her hearers. She laughingly replied that she didn't know, but that some one had stolen her pocket-handkerchief during the performance.

There is play for all ages. The feasts, the weddings and even the funerals are practically occasions of play for the adults. The young men often play a game similar to our *duck-on-the-rock.* The old men sitting in the streets about the doorways are often seen playing a game called *sîjeh* or *lîwan.* In the dust or on the flat surface of a stone slab forty-nine or twenty-five squares are marked off, as on a checker-board. The markers or men are, perhaps, small stones. The one suggesting the game says, "I'll take the lîwan" (hall), which is the central square of all, and places one of the markers in a space next to the lîwan. Then each player in turn places a marker in a vacant square anywhere on the diagram, the central lîwan excepted, until all but that one are filled. The first player then, he who claimed the lîwan, moves his nearest marker into it. The player next in turn jumps the marker which the first player moved. The third player moves into the lîwan and is jumped by the following player. Jumping must always be towards the lîwan and is allowable whenever there is a marker in the lîwan, one or more empty spaces between the jumper and the lîwan and an empty space beyond the lîwan into which to jump. The game continues until there is but one marker left on the board, and that in the lîwan.

The more vigorous game called *dôsh* is played with pitching stones. The two players try for the first turn by seeing which one can come nearest, with a throw of his stone, to some mark. Keeping the positions in which they land in this trial-toss, the first player (the one nearest the mark) throws his stone at the stone of the other, trying to drive it as many feet as possible. He continues until he fails to drive his opponent's stone, measuring with his feet the ground over which he has driven it and adding up the score. The other then tries to drive his opponent's stone in the same fashion. The one first driving his opponent's stone a total distance of forty feet is the winner and is entitled to be given a ride on the back of the defeated player.

The village men greatly enjoy motion songs, with dancing, swaying, clapping of hands, etc. Many of these exercises are combined in the *mil'ab*[1] at wedding celebrations. When clapping of hands is the prominent motion, the song may go by the designation *ṣaḥjeh.*[2] When a sort of dance, which consists chiefly in stamping the foot forward, characterizes the motion, the accompanying song is designated as *dabkeh.*[3] In this latter the dancer or dancers, for there may be one or several in line, hold handkerchiefs fluttering in the hands and stamp forward first with one foot and then with the other in groups of three stamps or steps with each foot, changing gracefully from one foot to the other.

There are strolling gipsies who go about entertaining by dancing and thrumming on instruments. Sometimes a man with a baboon or a bear comes to a village.

The native enjoys hunting. Gazels, partridges and wild pigeons are the chief game, but he does not despise smaller birds.[4] He seldom has anything like modern arms, and therefore unless hunting is his business often misses the object of his aim. Still he enjoys the noise of his gun.

Quarrels are of too painful frequency among villagers. They are always costly affairs, for the officials mulct both sides, unless the trouble has been hushed up before soldiers are sent to investigate. There has been considerable improvement lately in the general order and security of the country. Even within ten or fifteen years, it is said,

[1] See page 56. [2] See page 184. [3] See page 186. [4] Gen. 27: 5; 1 Sam. 26 :20; Prov. 12 :27.

the roads have become more safe, outrages much less common and villagers more peaceable. Formerly the peasants went heavily armed and altercations were likely to lead to bloodshed. As I am rewriting these notes there come letters from friends in Palestine bringing news of a quarrel of serious proportions in one of the large villages. A score or more of the men have been put into the nearest city prison and great expense and continued ill-will are inevitable. A marriage had been arranged to unite young people of two different tribes. This unusual event was not allowed to proceed without very great jealousies and some disagreement as to minor terms among the relatives. The trouble culminated on the day of the wedding; and for some hours a battle raged. From housetops, windows, doors and in the alleys of the quarter of the village where the tribes lived stones were hurled and wounds inflicted.

To take revenge is known as *akhadh ith-thâr*, or *astad ith-thâr*. The blood-revenge is called *ith-thâr id-dam*. A family or tribe feels that it has been humiliated when any of its members have been assailed by outsiders. If blood has been drawn or a fatality has ensued the disgrace must be wiped out. The accomplishment of this is expressed as *nafy il-'âr*.[1]

[1] Gen. 9: 6; Num. 35: 21; Deut. 19: 21; 2 Sam. 3: 27; *cf.* Matt. 5: 38, 39; 27: 25.

CHAPTER VIII

THE MIND OF THE VILLAGE

The state of learning in Syria and the Levant seems to have been steadily on the decline for some centuries. At the beginning of the nineteenth century it must have been at a very low ebb. Once flourishing literary centers were dead to scholarly impulses. Famous institutions and foundations for learning had vanished. The French campaign in the Levant, the assiduity of German and French scholars, but even more effectively of late the presence of the Western missionaries, have all been stimulative to a renewed literary activity in the Arabic language. One of the most noteworthy names in this nineteenth century revival is that of the poet Yâzijy (Shaykh Nâṣîf ibn ʻAbdallâh al-Yâzijy) of the Lebanon, who is much esteemed as a sort of modern Hariri. His " Majmaʻ al Baḥrain " (" Where the Two Seas Meet ") is a great favorite. He wrote on literature, logic and grammar. His works are used as text-books in the Syrian schools and his poems are available to readers. The presses of Beirut and Cairo have put forth a large number of works within the last century by both old and new authors. The services of the American Press in Beirut have been of very great value and influence in the near East. Excellent work is done also by the Jesuit and other presses in the same city. The press is not so restricted in Egypt as in Syria; hence the activity in journalism in the former country as compared with the latter. The periodical press of Egypt is quite varied. Though some of the journals there published are under the ban of the censor in the Turkish domains, yet subscribers in Palestine receive them by the French post. Beirut is the intellectual hub of Asiatic Turkey as it is also a chief center of trade. American and English educational enterprises have done much for Turkish subjects. Among the Syrians their influence has been very conspicuous. In Palestine proper the educational missionary work is largely in the hands of the English people and their church societies. Wherever missionary effort has been put forth it has stimulated local effort and lifted the educational standard. The old system of village boys' schools under the care of the *khaṭîb* is about as weak as it can be and not actually vanish. The Greek Church schools in the Christian villages are in about the same condition. In such places only a few leading men will ordinarily be found able to read and write. But where missionary schools have entered the native schools have multiplied and improved. Robinson mentions a straggling school for boys in Râm Allâh, in 1838, where five or six boys were considered educated when they could read the Arabic Psalter. To-day things are considerably different, for some hundreds of the Râm Allâh children are in school, being educated in all branches of elementary education and some of the studies of secondary grade. The most notable difference, however, between then and now is that there are almost as many girls as boys in the schools of the village mentioned. Stimulated by the provision of the American Friends for the education of girls, the native Greek Church also has opened a school for the village girls.

We are reminded here of a story of the American scholar and missionary, Dr. Van Dyck, who, while on his way to a village in the Lebanon, was accosted by a Moslem, who asked after his errand. Dr. Van Dyck replied, "I am going to the village of A—— to introduce three schools." "Three schools," said the surprised questioner; "why, that is a good many for so small a village." "Well," said Dr. Van Dyck, "I am to open a school, but if I do that the Greeks will open one and the Roman Catholics another, so that I consider that

I shall really be responsible for three schools." At Schneller's school for orphan children in Jerusalem are some hundreds of boys. They are divided into *families* of from twenty to thirty, with a monitor or group-father over each. The forenoons are taken up with schoolroom exercises and most of the afternoons are devoted to learning trades. Shoemaking, carpentry, pottery, printing, wood-carving and dairying are taught. Blind boys are taught to seat chairs and weave straw mats. The chief hindrances in the promotion of school enterprises in Palestine are all reducible to legal disabilities, which are the occasion and encouragement for many other petty annoyances. It is at times very difficult to secure valid titles to purchased property and more difficult to accomplish safely the erection of suitable buildings.

Of foreign tongues there are many to be heard in the country. Some friends in Jerusalem were one day discussing the numerous tongues and dialects used in a conversational way in and about the city. They began to count them up and reached something over fifty. Not all of these are heard by the country people, but many of them are heard occasionally as pilgrims and other travelers pass. Until comparatively recently the leading foreign tongue was French, but lately its influence has been lessened in favor of English and German.

The language of the people is Arabic. It is a virile tongue and destined to increase in use rather than diminish, though it may never again have the ascendency enjoyed in the days of the caliphates. One is tempted to say that the Syrian finds his nationality in his faith and his politics in his church only. But it would also be true to say that, to many, their clearest bond of national feeling is in their boasted language and in the masters of their old literature. The Arabic classics hold an equal sway over Christian and Moslem natives. If there is any possible place or condition in which

A HOUSE-ROOFING BEE (ET TAYYIBEH)

the bitterness of the rival faiths can be assuaged it is in the discussion of Arabic lore. The language and its masterpieces are the source of much intellectual and esthetic delight to the people. In these they must find all the gratification that in Western societies is realized in the pursuit of the liberal sciences and arts.

The country and desert folk of Palestine and Arabia are justifiable in much of their pride in their really beautiful language. Some of the gutturals may seem unduly harsh, and when fully pronounced the word endings may at times seem monotonous; but rightly rolled and molded there is nothing more beautiful and clear than a well-spoken chain of Arabic sentences. One must prefer the country to the city speech. There are twenty-eight distinct letters in the Arabic alphabet. The first two letters *alif* and *bay* correspond to the *aleph* and *beth* of the Hebrew, also to the *alpha* and *beta* of the Greek, from which comes our word "alphabet." The two letters *lam* and *aleph* written together are sometimes reckoned an extra letter. Many of the other letters are variants of each other phonetically, such as different kinds of t's, h's, d's, s's and k's. Dialectical variations account in part for these numerous sounds and for others which were not given a distinguishing sign after the alphabet stiffened into its classical form. For instance, there is a character pronounced to-day by some *ḍha*, by others *za*. Another is pronounced *koff*, but by others *aff*, and by the Bedawîn, *goff*. In Egypt the sound for the fifth letter of the alphabet is hard *g*, while in Syria it is *j*. The fourth letter *th* tends to become a plain *t*, as in *katîr* for *kathîr*, or in *talât* for *thalâth*.

There is a historical instance of such dialectical variance among Palestine country people (Judges 12: 6) where *s* and *sh* in sibboleth and shibboleth are the sounds in question. Both of these are represented in Arabic, the language of modern Palestine, in the letters *sîn* and *shîn*. This instance helps to suggest how close are the tongues of ancient and modern Palestine, Hebrew and Arabic. Aramaic was the historical bridge between the two.[1]

Many of the place names to-day in use are probably not Arabic at all, though sounding very much like it, but old Aramaic or Hebrew names adapted to Arabic-speaking mouths. One of the adaptations thus made to render the ancient tongue palatable to the modern pronunciation is the change of final *l* to *n*. So Israel becomes Israin. Similarly, Gabriel is frequently heard in Arabic as Jibran. Instead of Bethel the modern Palestinian says Baytîn, there being in Arabic no softening of the letters b, g, d, etc., after a vowel as in Hebrew. The Arabic language early lent itself to the grammarians who, with great skill, wrought out its inherent symmetry and logical possibilities. To look at the language as they have developed it and systematized it is quite a novel experience for one who has known only the European family of tongues. Stress is laid upon the substantial quality of almost every word except the mere particles, exclamations, etc. But the tendency is grammatically to refer the words to triliteral verbs. In the arrangement of verbs in paradigms the third person singular of the past or, rather, completed action or state of the verb, is made prominent. Inflection is managed by preformatives and afformatives denoting the person, number or gender; also by infixes and significant vowels to assist in determining voices and modes of action. The noun is similarly modified to denote gender and number. Verbs and nouns both take pronominal suffixes. There is a tendency to pleonasm in the use of pronouns and prepositions in connection with such suffixes. The dual is in constant daily use in the language.

What to us would seem like very picturesquely figurative tendencies in common speech are the relationships introduced by the use of such words as *ab*, father; *umm*,

[1] 2 Kings 18: 26.

mother; *dhû*, master or possessor; *ibn*, son;[1] and *bint*, daughter. This is carried to such an extent as really to include nicknaming.

Arabic has a large vocabulary and permits considerable further expansion. In remoter regions the borrowed words are few, but among those who hear other tongues they are numerous. In this respect the tongue has had an experience not different from others. Still it retains considerable independence, as languages go, and covers a wide empire. Even where Arabic is not actually spoken, its influence has been considerable. It has loaned large numbers of words and its script has covered many other languages, as, for example, Turkish, Persian, Hindustani, Malay, the African dialects, etc. The influence of the Ḳurân and Islâm has been the real force in this expansion of idiom and script. Prominence in the written language is given to the consonants. Owing to its easily cursive form and the customary omission of vowels it can be written with great rapidity. For these very reasons it easily degenerates into a scrawl scarcely legible, but perhaps no worse than English or any language carelessly written. A piece of writing is called *basîṭ* when the vowels are left out, and *mûshakil* when they are written.

The vowel signs are three, *a*, *i*, *u*, but according as these are preceded by a heavy or light consonant, or followed by such or by one of the semivowels, they admit of considerable modification. The vowel sounds in Arabic, therefore, are numerous. As the consonants are prominent in writing, so are the vowels very significant in speaking. Especially in speaking long distances in the wild country, across ravines from hillsides, etc., a peculiar and effective stress is placed on the vowels.

There are dialectical variations between the common spoken language of the peasantry and that of the city; also

[1] *Cf.* John 12: 36; 1 Sam. 2: 12, A. V.

between both of these and what is termed church or high language, which is really a near approach to the classical Arabic; finally between the language of women and children on the one hand and men on the other.

One very peculiar custom is that in the use of the personal pronouns the order is always first, second and third. Not as with us, *you and I*, but *I and you*, or *I and he*, would be Arabic usage.

More closely significant in a study of the Palestinian peasant are those local turns of the language which we find in his colloquialisms, exclamations, etc. There is also a very fruitful field in the proverbs, songs and stories of the peasantry. A choice collection of stories as gathered by a life-long resident of the country, Rev. J. E. Hanauer, has been edited by Dr. H. G. Mitchell.[1]

The word *hôl* is used in Râm Allâh and its environs to mean very or very much, that is, as a colloquialism for *kathîr*. *Hôl* means, literally, *frightful*, so its use is equivalent to the analogous use of *awful* as a superlative in English. The Râm Allâh peasants would say *Shughal hôl*, "An awful lot of work"; *tîn hôl*, "very many figs."

The Bîreh people use *fôḳ el-fôḳ*, which means, literally, *the up of the up*, to express *first-rate* or *excellent*, instead of the customary *'âl*.

In Palestine the word *shellaby* is very commonly used to mean *excellent;* also to signify assent, like *all right*, instead of the still more common *ṭayyib*, literally, *good*. Syrians in America, when conversing in Arabic, sometimes use instead of either of the above words the English *all right*, which they clip into *orrite*.

Shu b'amal fîh? equals "What shall I do about it?" or, literally, "What shall I do *in* it?"

Yâ abayyeh, literally an intensification of "O my father!"

[1] "Tales told in Palestine," Hanauer and Mitchell, Cincinnati, 1904, Jennings & Graham.

is used in the face of difficulty as a sort of expression of dismay. *Yâ ibn Âdam*, is used in expostulation, *son of Adam*, equalling *man*.

Of an exclamatory nature are the following as samples of peasant usage: *Hayû*, "There you are," as we might say in answer to a question as to the whereabouts of a tool or other article. *'Un* is a sort of grunt to express proof of one's own efficiency or honesty. If you infer that a workman is not doing his work well or skilfully, he will put in stroke after stroke under your eye, each stroke accompanied by a self-approving *'Un, 'un*, as if to say, "See that and that. Don't I know how?" Or if one complain to the man who is bringing a load of fire-wood that it is filled with dirt and is not well dried (it is sold by weight), he will throw out piece after piece of choicer wood with a grunt at each one, as much as to say, "Look at that, and that and that!" If you wish to convince him, you pick out piece after piece of the inferior wood and hold it up before his very eyes with a *'Un, 'un* in each case. *Eḥ* is a sort of aspirated *e* which means, "Yes, that's the way," or better, "That's it, so." For instance, if a boy or any one else is told to do a thing and he seems to be interpreting his instructions well, the one who is directing him will say encouragingly, *Eḥ, eḥ*, the equivalent of the colloquial Arabic *Ay na'am* (or *aywa*) *hayk*, "That's it," or "That's right," or "Now you've got it." A long-drawn *'Um* is used to mean "I comprehend," or "Is that the way of it? Yes, I see now," after an explanation has been given. *Uff* is sometimes expressive of astonishment, but often of contempt in the sense of "What a fibber you are!" or "I can't express my opinion of you." *Uḥ* is used in some such case as this. I ask a native, "Are the apples of Zebedâny (near Damascus) good?" He, knowing that they are famous for quality, will preface his affirmative with a breathy *Uḥ*, as if to say "Nice? Well, I should say!" "Of course they are," or, "Better than they do not exist." Then, perhaps, he will show their size by the circumference of a circle which he makes with all the fingers of one hand held up. *Shi* or *Hiḥ* is expressive of a little surprise or weak objection; or it may be merely a gratuitous exclamation thrown in where we should expect no expression, or might even think it saucy. It is used much like our " Humph." If a child is set a task or a lesson and wishes to say, " It is very hard," he is very apt to slat the fingers of the hand together and exclaim, *E-e-ee* with much the same force as *Yâ abbayeh* above. *Thk,* a sort of suck with the tongue and teeth means, " No." Sometimes it is joined with *Mâ fîsh,* " There is not," or " I have nothing," and the speaker may snap his thumb under the edge of his upper teeth in emphasis. *Thk* is very often given with an upward toss of the chin to mean, " No." *Hiss* is used by a mother or older person to hush a child. It equals " Keep still " or " Enough of foolishness."

In beckoning children the hand is held about as high as and near the shoulder, the palm downwards and the fingers shutting back and forth to the palm while " Come, come " is said. To hold all the fingers together and the hand, palm upward, about the height of the hip, means a threat like " You'll see."

Of curses [1] there is a very great variety, expressive of animosity,[2] disgust [3] and impatience.[4] Many of the formulæ are shortened until only the direction and object of the curse are left in the expression. So, should you hear some one say impetuously to another, " Your father," " Your eyes," " Your breast," or " Your faith," you might know that a curse was intended with these as the objects. The verb *la'ana, yal'anu,* which signifies cursing, is generally understood. The curses are sometimes very indirectly aimed at the victim, as, for instance, when a donkey driver cursed a stumbling donkey with *Abu jiddak,* literally, " Cursed be the father of your grandfather." The curser may in this circular

[1] Prov. 26: 2. [2] Num. 22: 6. [3] 1 Sam. 17: 43. [4] Job 3: 1.

way of attack reach even himself without apparently minding the implication, as when a man driving donkeys along the road became angry at one of them and shouted, "May your owner go into the grave."

Colloquialisms and stories tend to pass into proverbs. The East is very rich in proverbial expressions, and the Arabic language has been used for the utterance of many thousands of them. The apt introduction and quotation of proverbs is considered an elegant accomplishment by conversationalists. Some of the proverbs are accompanied by explanatory stories telling how the proverb in each instance arose. Then there are expressions that are tending to the proverbial form. Some of these latter will be mentioned first.

Moslems are accredited with the saying that the bobbing *ḥirdhôn* (lizard) is praying.

When three or more persons in one place are found to have the same name the people say, "There must be a treasure about."

Of the kind of young man slangily known among us as a *masher* the Palestinian says, "He has a heavy shadow."

Of a miscellaneous pocketful of things, such as a boy might carry, they say, *Mithl jerab il-ḳurdy,* "Like the Kurd's pocket." This is from the story told of a Kurd who had lost his wallet-pocket by theft. When the thief was found the Kurd was asked in court to describe the pocket and its contents. He described the pocket accurately enough, but in telling the contents he named over thing after thing until he had mentioned a catalogue of much that the world contains.

With reference to the infection of yawning the story is told of a man who was riding a camel in the desert. The camel yawned and then the rider yawned. The rider said to the camel, "I took my yawn from you; from whom did you take yours?"

In a class of native youth learning the English language one of the boys lost his bearings and was unable to follow what the rest of the class was saying, so he mumbled *Mithl akhras fy zeffeh.* He meant, " I am like a dumb man at a wedding procession." On such occasions a ready tongue is quite necessary.

When one does a foolish or witless thing, another is apt to say impatiently to him, *Kathîr minnâk thîrân*, that is, freely, " There are many oxen of your kind."

When one shows lack of grace, they quote, " The bear stood up to dance and killed seven or eight persons."

An ignorant or dull person is accused of not knowing his elbow from his wrist.

A rather cynical and unsentimental way of describing the effect on a man of the loss of his wife is that, " It is like knocking his funny-bone."

Of course rain would never be expected in July. Such a thing would be called *zelket fyt tammûz*, " a slip in July," and this expression is used proverbially to describe any prodigy or any very surprising occurrence.

That good actions may be spoiled is expressed by the statement, " If a cow yields a large quantity and then kicks over the milk-pan she is not praised."

An obstinate person is described by *râs-hu yâbis* or *râs-hu ḳawy*, " His head is dry or hard."

Gift-taking, that is, bribery,[1] is described as a sickness to which all officials are proverbially subject. Such a man is described by *Butnhu wâsi'a, byokul kathîr*,[2] " He has an expansive stomach, he eats a great deal."[3] Of an official whose power is limited they say, " His arm is short."[4] Orders from headquarters in Constantinople not carried out by an under-official are said to have been " put under the carpet."

[1] Prov. 15: 27; Isa. 5: 23; Amos. 5: 12. [2] Neh. 5: 15. [3] *Cf.* Hab. 1: 13; Mark 12: 40. [4] Isa. 50: 2; 59: 1.

" When the salt blossoms " denotes improbabilities, for which the following is also heard, though I should not want to vouch for its absolute impossibility, " When the goat climbs to the top of the minaret." I have seen goats in very unlikely places.

The following list of proverbs gives a sample of expressions in common use among the peasantry of central Palestine.

Abu Ḥashîsh fy ḥâlat ghalbân: "Abu Ḥashîsh is overcome of his own matters." This is used when a man already crowded with duties is asked to do something more.

Ḥabîby bḥibhu walau kân 'abd âswad: " I would love my love even though he were a black slave," illustrating constancy.

Lâ taḳul lil mughanny ghanny walâ lil raḳâṣ yarḳuṣ: " Never tell a singer to sing nor a dancer to dance," signifying natural obstinacy.

Tub il-jarreh 'ala fimhâ, taṭla' il-bint mithl imhâ: " Turn the jar on its mouth, the daughter comes up like her mother." The first part of the saying is put in for rhythm, and the whole is one way of expressing family resemblances.

Labis el-'ûd yajûd: " Clothe a stick of wood and it will do well (or look well)." The 'ûd is the wooden frame on which the bridal trousseau is rigged and carried in procession when the wedding garments are purchased for the bride. The proverb compares the clothing with the man who wears it and rather insinuates that clothing makes the man.

Idhkur idh-Dhîb wahayay lahu il-ḳadîb: " If you think of the wolf, get the stick ready for him."

Il-harîbeh thulthay il-marâjal: " Running away is two-thirds of strength." (Notice the dual, without ending *n*, in the colloquial.)

Yâmâ kassar hâ il-jamal baṭṭîkh: " Oh, how often the camel broke melons." It is said of one who, having done well, ends by spoiling all. It is also applied to one who, in making purchases, at last buys something quite beyond his means.

Or it is used to indicate that the man is well known as a blunderer and that no one ought to be surprised at a fresh sample of his failing.

Ḳallil il-ḥaky tirtâḥ wakuththirahu faḍḍâḥ: "Diminish the talk and you will have rest; increase it [and have] disgrace."[1]

Mâl ḳalil majmû'a khayr min mâl kathîr mubaddad: "A little wealth in hand (gathered) is better than much wealth scattered abroad [*i. e.*, on loan]."

Kul shay 'ind il-'aṭâr illâ min ḳûl ḥabbany: "Everything may be found at the spice-sellers' except the saying 'love me.'" This is to the effect that real love is the one thing that cannot be purchased.[2]

Ish-sharaf aḥsan min khazâyn mâl: "Nobility is better than treasure-chests of wealth."

Âb ikṭa' il-ḳuṭf walâ tahâb: "In August cut the bunch [grapes] and fear not [its being unripe]." Everything in its proper season.

Id-dâr ḳafrat wal-mazâr ba'îd: "The house is empty and the visiting place is far," meaning we are out of whatever it is that is needed and the place where more may be had is far off.

Iṭlab il-jâr ḳubl id-dâr war-rafîḳ ḳubl iṭ-ṭarîḳ: "Seek the neighbor before the house and the company before the route." Make sure of good neighbors and companions, as they are more necessary to your welfare than the mere house or road.[3]

Ta'allam il-bayṭarah fy ḥamîr il-âkrâd: "He learned to shoe horses among the donkeys of the Kurds." This is a contemptuous way of indicating that one's preparation for the trade or profession followed was inadequate.

'Ala ḳadar firâshak midd rijlayk: "According to the measure of your bed stretch your legs." This is quoted in favor of living within one's means.

[1] Prov. 13: 3; 21: 23. [2] *Cf.* Prov. 15: 17. [3] *Cf.* Prov. 21: 19.

Il-ghâib jihathu ma'hu: "The absent one has his excuse with him."

Fâlij la tu'âlij: "Palsy, don't doctor it." This one has a hopeless touch.

Ish-shay matta zâd nuḳṣ: "Anything carried to excess diminishes." This proverb advises against overdoing.

Mâ fy kabîr illâ il-jamal: "Nothing is large except the camel." Compare this with "Comparisons are odious."

Il-walad walad walau kân kâḍy balad: "The boy is a boy though he be judge of the country."

In kân râyḥ kaththir min il-ḳabâyḥ: "If one be going away, increase the mischief." This may refer to an official who becomes reckless on the eve of his discharge, or possibly to the people who, in view of the near departure of their superior, take advantage of the fact to perpetrate mischief. Compare, "When the cat's away the mice will play."

Mâl il-majânîn lil-'aḳâl: "The wealth of the crazy is for the wise."

Kalb hâmil khurj mâl: "A dog carrying a saddle-bag of wealth." This refers to an unworthy owner of wealth.[1]

In râḥat ghannat wan jât ghannat: "Whether it goes or comes I shall sing." The one so saying declares that he will be joyous despite circumstances.

Bayn hânâ wamânâ râḥat lihânâ: "Between this and that the beard went." In case a man is given conflicting orders he quotes the above to the effect that between coming and going one's beard is in danger of flying off. The syllable *na* on the end of the last word is added for euphony merely.

Hâfitha 'ala iṣ-ṣadîḳ walau fil-ḥarîḳ: "Succor your friend though he be in fire."

Khayr il-âmûr l-wasṭ: "The good of things is in moderation."[2]

Ziyâdeh il-khayr khayr: "Increase makes good better."

Iṣ-ṣubr miftâh il-faraj: "Patience is the key of relief."

[1] *Cf.* Prov. 11: 22. [2] *Cf.* Prov. 25: 16.

'Allamnâk ish-shiḥdeh sabaḳthanâ 'ala il-bâb: "I taught you begging and you got to the door before I did." This was a beggar's proverb originally and illustrates the fact that the pupil may outdo his teacher.

Mithl azîmeh il-ḥamar lil-'urs: "Like the invitation of a donkey to a wedding." This is applicable when one who is invited as a guest is asked to work. The donkey's function on festive occasions is to fetch and carry.

SONG OF THE SAḤJEH

Good evening, all ye who are present;
In the middle of the garden is a green bird chirping to you.

O mother of the only one, bless thee for what thou didst for him.
On his wedding day thou didst grind his flour at Zerḳâ.

Were it not for love we'd not come walking,
Nor would we tread on your ground.

Good evening, thou owner of a silver rosary!
After starting lovingly, why is there this hatred?

Good evening, O possessor of an amber rosary!
After starting lovingly, why dost thou fight?

The sand cannot be kneaded, nor thorns trodden,
Nor the secret displayed to all the people.

How many palms have we climbed without ladder,
And how many offenses of friends have we overlooked!

O sweet, O beautiful, thy letter came to us;
As we read it how our tears flowed.

O excellent, sweet, moving thy lips,
Thou hast wounded hearts; we beg thee let us come to thee.

For my friend, friendship should abide;
As for the disloyal the day of judgment shall find him.

For what reason dost thou close thine eyes without sleepiness?
Thou pleasest not me but other people.

I shall rush on you at noon, you who are in my mind;
With the sword shall I [over] throw you with high windows.

With the sword shall I charge you in the darkness of the night;
I'll take my sword and cause the blood to flow.

O beloved, O beloved, thou whom the heart desires,
Since the day of thy departure my heart counts the nights.

Thou oughtest to be sorry for leaving us,
Thou wilt weep tears of grief when thou seest us.

I passed by their house and said not a word;
The tears of my eyes dropped before me on the stone.

The tree of love is cast out by the gate of Damascus;
I was dying and my friend came not to me.

The tree of love at the gate of Damascus is swaying;
I was dying and my friend did not come to ask.

O tree of love, at the gate of Damascus, it is green;
I was near to dying and my friend came not once.

Do not think that good style consists in ample clothes;
Good style is providing dishes for the men.

Do not think that good style consists in elegant robes;
Good style consists in large trenchers, in kindness and generosity.

O Egypt, O how far off art thou, in whom is the beloved!
If I live another year I must surely live in thee.

O sweet one, bring thy bottle and we'll drink and fill it;
Thy people are far and thy country's water is scarce.

What brought thee forth, O gazel, to roam?
To look on thy country, O sweet, and return.

What brought thee from thy country, single, alone?
I want to look on thy country and I want a friend.

Our dear ones, because of their ambition, they left us;
Because of scarcity of money they traded among us.

O heart, leave them, count them as dead;
I put them in my eye and they did not fit.

O seller of coffee, I want a ruṭl of thy coffee;
Yesterday afternoon I saw the woman who bought of thee.

O daughter of the Arab shaykh, O wearer of the blue mantle,
Thy father is an Arab shaykh ruling o'er the Belḳâ.

O daughter of the Arab shaykh, O wearer of the black mantle,
Thy father is an Arab shaykh ruling o'er the 'Aujâ.

O daughter of the Arab amîr, O Turcomany,
Untie the fastenings of the shoes and walk.

O daughter of the Arab amîr, we can find no fault in thee;
Thy father is a pasha and thy uncle is an Arab shaykh.

The eyebrow of the eye deserves burning,
Of that one who winks at a low fellow.

SONG OF THE DABKEH

O man with the forelock tossing,
Thy speech is very choice.

The love of thee o'ercame me!
My strength cannot [resist].

The love of thee o'ercame me;
May the Lord of Heaven establish thee.

O graceful one, wear thy robe
With the knot turned behind.

O beautiful, O father of Shôrâ,
Thy cheeks are as crystal.

Thy love into my very heart
Dug [its way] and made a pit.

O beautiful, holder of a handkerchief,
Thy signs burned my very heart.

O beautiful, I am not thy equal;
Thy price is that of precious wood.

I've never seen so excellent among the Arabs,
O beautiful one of sweet manners.

Thy breast is as the tablet of the Khaṭîb;
O that fate would bestow thee on me!

Thy breast is as the tablet of the Khaṭîb;
Upon it are the letters unknown.

Thou causest me worriment and suffering,
Thou who art to me unlawful.

A RÂM ALLÂH MATRON AT HER OWN DOOR
(From the collection at the Semitic Museum, Cambridge, Mass.)

CHAPTER IX

THE LIFE TO-DAY AS ILLUSTRATED BY ACTUAL VILLAGES

Such tourists as have a student's interest in addition to a desire for mere sightseeing will find the value of their Palestine visit doubled if they will allow some days for visiting villages. If one will go in as quiet and unobtrusive a way as possible, and with the aid of an introduction to some householder of the village, one will be able to learn much. Certain of the missionaries in Jerusalem as elsewhere devote themselves to itinerating among the villages and are fully acquainted with conditions of which it would be well for a novice to be informed. The village of Râm Allâh is one of the most satisfactory places accessible from Jerusalem for the purpose of seeing well-developed Syrian village life. It is ten miles north of Jerusalem and is now reached by an excellent carriage road. It is one mile from the much smaller village of el-Bîreh, which lies on the main carriage road from Jerusalem, northwards toward Nâblus (Shechem). This slight remove from the main line of tourist travel, its considerable size and the superior intelligence of its inhabitants have joined to produce a good, wholesome sample of a native village, neither so metamorphosed as some of the larger places nor so squalid and degenerate as many of the smaller villages.

It was in May, 1901, that the road mentioned was opened up for use from Jerusalem to el-Bîreh, a distance of fifteen kilometers. From the Damascus Gate, where the Bîreh and Râm Allâh carriage owners stand, the route leads out past the Dominican Compound, within which is a church of St. Stephen and a theological school conducted by the eminent French scholars of the order. On the left, opposite, is the large milling property leased for many years by Mr. Bergheim. Next on the left is an olive grove, and a little way farther on the pleasant garden and large square building of the English Church Mission, where the society conducts a collegiate institute. Next on the right, beyond an olive grove, is the costly and well-built compound of the High Church Anglican bishop for Jerusalem and the Near East. On the left opposite are the new school buildings under his auspices. Just beyond the Anglican Compound, at the fountain known as Bîr el-Kelb, a street coming from Herod's Gate, Jerusalem, intersects the main road. Just up this street a few steps on the left is the entrance to the so-called Tombs of the Kings, one of the places well worth looking at. The next largest building on the right before coming to the minaret is occupied by the community of " The Overcomers." They control property on both sides of the highway. A little beyond this point the road makes a long loop to the right in order to save a steep climb by the old bridle-path which goes straight on past the houses of some Moslem officials of Jerusalem who prefer the more ample and comfortable liberty of suburban building sites. Here one has a pretty view of the upper part of the Kidron Valley. On up a slight hill and then down a long easy descent, and one is brought to the foot of another steep bridle-path, which the road avoids by another curve to the right toward the Mount of Olives and a loop to the left on to the top of Mount Scopus. From Scopus there is a charming view of Jerusalem. Beginning at the far right (north) of the suburbs, one sees the black, formerly blue, dome of the Abyssinian Church; then to the left the delicate, shapely, blue cupolas of the church in the Russian Compound; then just inside the northwest corner of the city wall, the sharp spire of the Roman Catholic Church, the low black dome of the Church of the Holy Sepulcher, the whitish tower of the German Church and the domes, red and blue, of the great synagogues. To the left and farther over is the large dome and symmetrical building of the Ḳubbet eṣ-Ṣakhra (sometimes called the Mosk of Omar) in the southeastern corner of the city. Turning now from the city one will see some six miles northwest of Jerusalem the lofty minaret of Neby Samwîl, on the hill thought to be the Mizpeh of Samuel. This place can be seen from many points of old Judea. The village in the foreground almost due north and by the side of the carriage road is Sha'fât. The name is thought to be the last two syllables of the name Jehoshaphat. Nearly opposite Sha'fât some find the site of Nob, the city of the priests of Saul's time. If one had time to go to the top of the hill between Scopus and the Mount of Olives, where the large buildings are placed, one could see the peculiar formation of the hill-country that leads down back of Jerusalem to Jericho and the Dead Sea. The Dead Sea and the table-land the other side of the Jordan would be visible. In fact, but a few minutes north of Scopus, on the carriage road, one may see the bluish Moab hills looming up in an even line beyond the Jordan River, whose bed is hidden because it lies over three-fifths of a mile lower than the level of this spot though less than twenty miles away. That is a very considerable drop in levels for so short a distance, as one realizes when one goes by carriage from Jerusalem down to Jericho and the Dead Sea. But to return to the village of Sha'fât already mentioned, one sees beyond it on the right a peculiarly shaped hill with an artificial look about its incised top which is regarded as the site of Gibeah of Saul. Off to the left is the village of Bayt Ḥanînâ. After a long curve or two one begins to descend more swiftly. From this point one can see far to the right on the northeast a prettily situated village on a sharp hilltop. It is eṭ-Ṭayyibeh, of which more later on. To the left as one proceeds appear remains of an old Roman road. It is noticeable all the way from Scopus and from here to el-Bîreh, though at times as now it takes a short cut where the present road makes a curve. The old road intersects the new where the latter crosses the bridge at the bottom of the valley. This bridge is called the half-way bridge between Jerusalem and el-Bîreh. There is a good stream under the bridge in rainy weather. The small village that rises on a hill just beyond the half-way bridge to the north is er-Râm, possibly the Ramah of Samuel, though Râm and Ramah mean simply an elevated site. Just by the left (west) side of the road as one comes opposite the village is an arched ruin. About it are other evidences of decay. After the ruin comes a long level stretch and another little bridge. Along here of an evening one sometimes sees a fox. The village to the left (west) is Ḳulundyeh. To the right (east) runs a path that will take one past er-Râm to Jeba', and so to Wâdy Mukhmâs (Michmash) or to 'Ayn Fâra and the Jordan. At the place where the road bends to the right around the truncated hill of 'Aṭâra there is a dismantled lime-kiln and a rough donkey path leading off to the left (north). This rude path is the old road to the village of Râm Allâh. It goes to the west of the hill of 'Aṭâra, while the carriage road goes to the east of it. The carriage road allows one to reach el-Bîreh easily in twenty minutes. It passes between 'Aṭâra and another hill on the right (east) of it along a pretty stretch of valley. At least it is pretty toward evening, when perhaps one will see a little owl among the rocks. The stream of 'Ayn Nuṣbeh is trickling or splashing, according to the season, down the side of 'Aṭâra near a little bridge. One evening I rode out towards this place from Râm Allâh on our saddle animal "Daisy" to meet the carriage. Daisy was very loth to travel away from home, but very glad whenever I turned her head about. The evening was lovely. As the light went out over the hills toward the western sea the changing color on the horizon on the near hills, on the rocks all about, and the quietness cast a spell of peace unique to these surroundings. After the reds had faded out of the soil and rocks, a somber ink color, dark purple, black, came on. A clump of dry brush topping a little watch-tower on a near hill seemed to belong to a farther hill behind it and, as I rode along, to be a human figure moving on that far hill. I met the carriage after dark near 'Aṭâra and came back in front of it.

At the top of the next long slope one has the vineyards of Râm Allâh on the left and el-Bîreh on the right. The little village of el-Bîreh, rich in shrubbery and the choicest spring for many miles around, lies on a gentle slope facing the south. First among its trees are some figs, then come gardens, walls and the spring with the little domed building. Beyond on the right are the ruins of its ancient khân and then the straggling village houses of stone. Pomegranates, figs, etc., are scattered through the place. The new khân is on the carriage road at the top of the village. The little shanty on the left of the road across from the spring is a sort of coffee khân merely and a lounging place for passers-by. Half-way up the road before it swings to the right towards the new khân with stables, the Râm Allâh road goes off to the left (west) over the rising ground that hides the village from view. It is less than a mile to Râm Allâh, and the path to it traverses a different part of the country from that which is seen on the carriage road. All along the highway one feels that but a few paces anywhere would take one to views of the deep cut of the Jordan Valley and the Dead Sea region, with the ever-enticing blue and hazy line of Moab's hills beyond. But here is another side of the country of Palestine. This rise in the ground between el-Bîreh and Râm Allâh is on the watershed of Western Palestine. On the outskirts of the village is the land for the Boys' School, the property of the (American) Friends (Quakers), who for many years have done most significant and practical work in the training of youth.

The inhabitants of Râm Allâh are industrious and thrifty,

and most of the village land is under excellent cultivation in choice grape vineyards and orchards of figs and olives. The needs of Râm Allâh are so much in excess of the lands which are legally recorded as belonging to it that its people have bought tracts here and there all about the country. The lands right around the village are so much more valuable as vineyards and orchards than for raising the grains that the farmers have pushed out and acquired these outside fields from the lands of a dozen or more villages as far as 'Ayn Ḳânyeh, Mukhmâs and Dayr Dîwân. For such outside lands the Râm Allâh people have no government deeds (*kushân*, plural *kuwashîn*), the title resting, so far as the government records are concerned, with the original village owners, and so the taxes are collected from them. But it is perfectly understood among the people in whom the ownership in fact rests, and these actual owners pay the yearly taxes for the land to the former owners. The government collects land taxes directly from Râm Allâh for those lands only which are within Râm Allâh's legal boundaries, which are much narrower than its acquired boundaries. A kind of private deed suffices as part of the evidence of transfer between the peasants.

On the east of Râm Allâh as one enters the village the legal or, better, original boundary corner is marked by an underground cistern known as Bîr esh-Sherḳeh (The East Cistern). It is on one's left in approaching the village, some rods before the property of 'Abdullâh Ṭoṭah, which is on the other or right-hand side. The next house and property are those of 'Isâ Shaṭâra. Then comes a small vineyard, opposite which is the Ḥarb house on the left. From the top of this building one has a view of the Mediterranean on one side and of the Moab hills on the other. Next on the right is the large monastery property of the Franciscans, on the left the house and chapel of the Church Missionary Society. Then (left) is passed the house of a dumb man, father of a considerable family and owner of a well-cultivated garden plot. He is quite ingenious at a pantomime method of talking and story-telling. His trade is that of roof-mender, which craft is in demand, as the cemented joints between the flat stones of the native roofs have to be kept in good repair against the soaking rains of winter. Next on the left is one of the entrances to the Friends' Girls' School property. The particular bit of their land that touches the road here goes in all the neighborhood by the name *el-Khums*, that is, *The Fifth*, because in some past division of the land it represented that fraction of a larger lot. Next by turning the bend to the left one comes into a street about three hundred twenty-five feet long and a trifle less than thirteen feet wide, in which are seven houses on the south (left) side and eight houses on the north (right) side. Among their tenants are four weavers and one dyer. The dyer is a tall, strapping fellow from the north, a Moslem who came to the village in 1901. At that time he was the only Moslem in the place. By a little jog to the left at the end of the street one avoids running into a building which for years has been used by the Friends' Mission as a primary schoolroom and a Sunday meeting place of the congregation that attends the Friends' meetings for worship and the Bible School. Nearly opposite this building is the dispensary of the native physician, Dr. Ma'lûf, a graduate of the College of Medicine in Beirut. Thence one may go southeast to the front entrance of the Girls' Training Home (Friends') or west along the main axis of the village, the market street, which is a continuation of the street by which we just entered the village, except for the slight jog to the left in coming down hill. These very jogs, of which many may be seen about the village, are illustrative of a principle, or the lack of one, in the community life. Streets and paths grow up by common consent of the householders, who feel the need of such conveniences for egress or ingress, but they are allowances from private property or, better, communal property. Sometimes a builder finds it convenient to set his house somewhat into the road, thus destroying the alignment of the street. Walls of stone and mortar are permanent structures, and the line cannot be corrected by any legal means.

The main part of the market street runs between the property of the village church on one side (south) and a row of shops and houses on the other (north). There are ten provision shops, five shoe shops and two weaving-rooms along this street. A great deal of local marketing is done in the open street. Here the wheat-laden animals from the country northeast of Râm Allâh bring their burdens. Huge camels, with a back load of clay jars held in a rope net, or carrying sacks of melons or grain, are made to saunter in and kneel. Women with head loads of vegetables, eggs, snails and other food products, and men from Nâblus with ready-made *kinabîz* and other articles of men's wear, stand ready for customers. Fruit venders, buyers and sellers from all the villages about are apt to be found here, for Râm Allâh is what might be called a county-seat. Some one from eṭ-Ṭayyibeh or from Kefr Mâlik will come to sell oil or other produce, and buy some necessities, perhaps a pair of shoes, to take home. This main market street of the village is about three hundred feet long (from Dr. Ma'lûf's curb to the entrance of the Greek Church yard) and for the most part about fifteen and a half feet wide. About two-thirds of the distance down there opens from it on the right (north) the entrance to the village khân.

Owners of camels, mules or donkeys buy up supplies of oil, dried figs and wheat from the villages and sell them in the village markets, or carry them to Jerusalem and Jaffa. From Jaffa they may bring up rice, sugar, kerosene, oranges and wood to supply the Râm Allâh merchants. Such articles in bulk are very apt to come from the seashore direct, but others are brought out from Jerusalem.

There are something over two scores of shops in Râm Allâh, counting eight shoemakers', a dozen weavers' and several butchers' stands. There are a good many quarriers, stone-masons and stone-dressers, plasterers and roof-menders. Most of the people have work of some kind on the small farming plots, vineyards and orchards. There are a few presses for making the oil and several cisterns for storing it. A few public carriages have been introduced since the opening of the way to Jerusalem for vehicles.

A butcher's fixtures consist of some iron hooks in the wall at the street side. Sheep have for years been killed right in the streets, the carcasses being hung up against abutting buildings, dressed quickly and divided to waiting customers. Perhaps a little girl is waiting to carry home some scraps in her sleeve. A member of a larger or richer household buys a larger piece, which is held in a scrap of brown paper or, more likely, a vessel brought from home. Sometimes, however, the purchase is carried off as it is. The matter of price is a simple one; it is the same for any part of the creature. Haggling may vary it a trifle, unless the demand for meat on a given day is unusual. Ordinarily the killing of a sheep is deferred until a market for the meat is fairly well assured. The price in Râm Allâh ranges from eight to twelve cents a pound, according to the season of the year and the scarcity of sheep. Goat meat is cheaper. Sometimes beef is offered, but one usually suspects the health of a cow that has been killed and prefers lamb. In Jerusalem fair beef can be obtained, but seldom can it be had in the country.

From a point a little beyond the end of the market proper a street turns to the left (south), passes the back entrance to the Greek Church property and goes off towards the largest village threshing-floor. On this road there are twenty-two houses, one store and one silversmith's shop. Seven hundred eighty feet along this way is the threshing-floor. Not quite half-way to the threshing-floor is an open space used as a sort of secondary market for such things as would take up too much room in the main street. From the beginning of the threshing-floor one hundred thirty feet onward brings one opposite an interesting place. It is a little sanctuary in a cave and is about a short stone's throw to the right (west), under a large tree which can be seen from the road.

After passing a few more houses one is well out of town on the road which leads between vineyards towards Baytûnyeh, 'Ayn 'Arîk and Ramleh. Most of the vineyards are to the southwest and south of the village. The Khulleh, or valley, at the southwest has the best stretch of vineyard land. Most of the fig-orchards are to the west of the village and most of the olives are on the northwest. Lately some fine vineyards have been made to the northwest near 'Ayn Miṣbâḥ, and there are some to the northeast around the 'Audy property and east of the Latin (Franciscan) monastery.

From the watershed Râm Allâh slopes away in a westerly direction, draining towards the Mediterranean. North of the village is a deep valley that heads on the east at the watershed and falls away on the west toward Kefrîyeh. The country falls gradually towards 'Ayn 'Arîk to the northwest and to the Balû'a or sunken meadow, where a winter pond stands near Baytûnyeh to the southwest. To the south, southeast and south-southwest the land rises into hills towards 'Aṭâra and Khurbet Suwaykeh.

Our first visual impressions of Râm Allâh were received on an afternoon early in April, 1901, before the completion of the carriage road, as we approached it by the old bridle-path already mentioned. By this path Râm Allâh is hidden from sight until one rises to the summit just to the south of the village, where many of the villagers have vineyards planted. Between this hill and the village lies a soft depression which, beginning at the watershed to the east of the village, dips away to the southwest towards the little village of Râfât and beyond, disclosing a beautiful view

LITTLE GIRLS OF THE VILLAGE

of ancient Gibeon (el-Jîb) and Mizpeh of Samuel (Neby Samwîl). There the village of Râm Allâh rested partly in the edge of the valley, but mostly spread along the opposite ridge. The gentler rays of the afternoon sun brought out the creamy tints of the stone houses standing in their cubical solidity. Here and there rose a taller building; at the left was the red-tiled roof of the Greek Orthodox Church. But by far the choicest bit of the panorama was the house and grounds of the Friends' Mission property. The house had one of the rare, tiled roofs evidencing Western influence among the flat and domed structures of the truly Oriental style. The well-constructed stone building was the home of the Girls' Training Home, a boarding-school for young Syrian women, supported by the New England Yearly Meeting of Friends, and named after two of their honored members, "The Eli and Sybil Jones Mission." I had seen pictures of the place and so knew it at once, though there was now added the charm of colors. The building sat in sweet Quakerly composure among numerous trees and vines. Tall, pointed cypresses, pines and various fruit trees abounded, which once so delighted the gaze of a little girl in the village that she boldly declared that she knew where heaven was. She thought she had seen it when she looked through the Mission Gate on the well-kept grounds filled with beautiful green. Such gardens could be duplicated all over the country at a small price beyond patience.

Just above the Friends' grounds is the house owned by the English Church Missionary Society, who make Râm Allâh headquarters for their work in different villages of this region. For more than a quarter of a century the agents of the society had been Mr. and Mrs. George Nyland, who, in their early years, went out from Holland to Egypt as missionaries, but after a few years entered the Church Missionary Society work in Palestine.

The nearest neighbor at the front was the so-called " Old Man at the Gate." He had earned this title, suggestive of unpleasant nearness, by a certain ability to introduce himself when no one else did so. It was a practise of his to come up through the grounds into the house once or twice each year to ask for an envelope and paper. The sensation was like the imposition of a tax. He assured us of his great friendliness and his usefulness to the Mission. He often spoke of the piece of land near the south gate where the small cistern was as an evidence of his goodness to us, in that he had sold it to us for a very small price, though the traditions of the mission were that he had received a very good price for it. I recollect the way in which one of his sons disappointed us. We had as guests over night some missionaries who depended for their start the next morning at five o'clock on our promise to secure the animals to take them on to Nâblus. We bargained with one of the old man's sons to provide us a saddled animal and considered our business done, but about nine o'clock that night he came around and calmly repudiated the bargain, demanding better terms. We ought to have been thankful that his impatience to get the better of us had prevented his saving this bit of annoyance until the last moment before starting. As it was, we still had some hours of night to provide ourselves.

Across the street from the schoolyard was a family which some of our people had dubbed " The Clean Family." Our butcher lived directly in front of us. He was an honest, burly fellow who usually wore a sheepskin coat, wool side in. He had been a friend of the mission inmates for many years and an attendant and helper in the mission congregation. To the north of us were some Protestant natives who were pleasant neighbors, and across the street from them dwelt some English women, mission workers, who gave their time to works of mercy among the women of near-by Moslem villages. We were to become much indebted to them for comfort and society.

Just south of the Friends' property is the little chapel of the Greek Catholic body which claims a few people of Râm Allâh, and just south of that runs a little path, through the vineyards, called the *Ṭarîḳ el-Majnûny, The Road of the Crazy One.* One of the old men told how in former years along that road the oak woods were so thick that a cat could not pass, and that if a piece of bread were dropped from above, the thickness of the foliage would prevent it from reaching the ground. This is interesting as pointing to traditions and to the kind of figures used by the natives in descriptions.

And so our neighborly resources continued. We gratefully acknowledge that the best lesson that we learned during our intimate acquaintance with the village community was that, joined with varying accidents of speech, dress and advantages, human beings are much alike everywhere and possess many admirable traits.

To the westward of Râm Allâh there begins with an abrupt head the Wâdy Ṭarafîdya, which runs nearly north and south and leads to Wâdy el-Kelb. One of the paths to 'Ayn 'Arîk bends around it. Just under this path to the eastward, between it and the wâdy, is a little spring, 'Ayn Ṭarafîdya. Most of the land hereabouts has been purchased by Râm Allâh people of Baytûnyeh, the latter reserving the spring and some olive land. The taxes are paid through Baytûnyeh. Forty-two feet down from 'Ayn Ṭarafîdya is a reservoir with thick, heavy stone walls, the corners being at the four main points of the compass. The northeast wall is ninety-seven inches thick and the northwest wall sixty-six inches thick. The reservoir is nearly forty feet square. The southeast wall inside is forty feet long and the northeast wall lacks three inches of the same measurement. There is a broken descent into the old dry pool at the west corner. I was here on a soft, gray December morning when the sky was hung with ready clouds. There was a sweet quiet under the olive-trees. The earth was red beneath. The black wet trunks and moss-covered branches showed through the gray-green mantle of the trees like a core through filigree. On one side of the valley the steep wet cliffs were decked with Christmas green. On the other side were terraces holding leafless fig-trees that stretched up their many fingers like candelabra to the mist. Down through the valley were seen round, stone watch-towers with brush tops. Pink daisies, narcissus, the little white and lavender crocuses and creepers were already showing. In the tiny scrub-oaks were twining green leaves.

Wâdy el-Kelb has two heads, the one to the north being called Shayb ed-Dars, the one to the east going by the name Baṭn el-Hawâ. Wâdy el-Kelb and Khullet el-'Adas are favorite grounds for anemones of various colors. Every little cut or crest of the surface hereabouts has its local name given or continued by the peasants, who spend many hours in these orchards, vineyards and pasture-grounds. The next depression beyond Baṭn el-Howâ is Wâd Karom Shutâ, which rises in Karom Shutâ and between the two wâdys thrusts out the little headland known as Ḳurnet Mûsâ. Above the Karom Shutâ are the Karûm Senâsil, named from the terraces that characterize the piece of vineyard there.

The burj, or tower, of Râm Allâh is in the southeast of the village near the very high house that is so prominent to one viewing Râm Allâh from the eastern hills. It is said that here was the former stronghold, and that under the place is a powerful spring called 'Ayn el-Burj. The property over it is owned by Ab ul-Bâbâ, of the tribe of Shaḳara, who, when he built there three or four years ago, found a good cemented canal coming from what was evidently a strong spring. Over the canal was a flat stone covering. The owner filled in the place at night, concealing it with masonry for fear that the government, if aware of such a spring, might open it to the public and he receive less than its value or nothing at all. Here, if the story be true, is the treasure that Râm Allâh lacks to make it a well-watered village. This 'Ayn el-Burj is said to be the source of the water that flows into the reservoirs near the property of the United Greeks' (Roman Catholic) Chapel.

The chief fountains about Râm Allâh are known as 'Ayn Miṣbâḥ (spring of the lamp), 'Ayn Minjid (spring of help), 'Ayn Mizrâb (spring of the conduit or channel) and 'Ayn Umm el-Kerzam. The spring at el-Bîreh, though a mile away, is in frequent use by Râm Allâh people. 'Ayn el-Ḳaṣr, towards Kefrîyeh and three miles away, is almost too far to be reckoned with the Râm Allâh water supply.

One October afternoon we went to 'Ayn Minjid, where there is a well-like structure built down into the ground. The little trickling stream of the spring at that time was about as thick as the tendril of a grape-vine. In winter the water rises high up in the well-like reservoir. A child of the neighborhood was once drowned by falling into it over the unprotected edge in the time of full water. Thence we went to the spring of 'Ayn Mizrâb, where there is a similar well-like place, built up of hewn stone and cemented on the inside, making a shaft, with the spring at the bottom. This spring was even weaker than 'Ayn Minjid. There was a tiny depression in one side of the bottom which held a little water. Some girls were trying to scrape up some of it with their skin-buckets. The well was fully twelve feet deep. The leather bucket was let down by a rope. The top of the bucket was held open by a stick stretched across its mouth. There was hardly a basin of water in the bottom of the well, and the most skilful casting of the bucket could gather very little. From one side of the well at the bottom was a canal leading out into some vineyards. To 'Ayn Mizrâb the women are said sometimes to bring their jars at midnight and set them about the fountain, the first one placing a jar thus claiming the right to draw first when it becomes light enough. If the moon is out they can draw water in the moonlight.

When we first reached Râm Allâh the country was suffering an unusual drought. For the preceding thirty days, during which there ought to have fallen some of the heaviest showers of the season, there had been no rain. The natives were praying for it. The country looked parched and brown at the time when it is usually beautifully decked with flowers. Food prices were high and the outlook for the poor was unpromising. Shortly after we arrived a short, sharp shower fell, but no more came until the middle of May, when the unusual again happened and a heavy downpour shut us in a day or two. We had some cool, blustering weather at a time when the hot days are expected and the dry season well begun. In times of such strange climatic anomalies the natives think they see portents of heavenly significance, that possibly the Messiah may be returning. Rain is the great blessing of nature, as fondly looked for as sunny weather is with us.[1]

Slight earthquakes are experienced now and then in Palestine. A severer one than usual came in the early morning of March 30, 1903, about ten minutes before one o'clock. On awakening my first thought was that people outside were trying our door and then shaking it violently. Then the movement seemed to possess the whole room, as if some mighty force were rocking it strongly and persistently. The bed was jostled. It was this persistent shaking, with the continual and uniform rattling of the

[1] In the Palestine Exploration Fund Quarterly for July, 1906, page 163, Dr. E. W. G. Masterman, of Jerusalem, writes of unusual weather in May preceding. Speaking of a severe hail-storm in Urṭâs and Bethlehem, he quotes the local report among the peasantry which was that "each hailstone was the size of a pigeon's egg and had St. George's image pictured on it."

articles on the wash-stand, that soon brought me to my senses with the exclamation, "It's an earthquake." Mrs. Grant was first awakened by the shaking bedstead. Her next thought was that the house walls were falling. We both felt a sense of nausea. I rose and lighted the candle. The floor was well sprinkled with fallen whitewash that had cracked off from the plastering. A few bottles were tipped over in the room. At first I said that it lasted a minute, but shortly after I reduced my estimate to ten seconds, and now I suppose that it must have been but a third of that duration. The rattling on our wash-stand was as uniform as if the things were on a railroad-train. It was a weird and unpleasant though tuneful jar. Mrs. Grant ran into the far part of the house, where were the dormitories of the Girls' School, and found the girls a little excited but not much frightened. Some of the smaller girls wanted to know what made their beds shake so. One girl said that she thought that Jesus had come. After we had been up a while we heard a wall falling in the vineyards to the south-west of us. In the Boys' School one boy tumbled out of bed. The teacher had taken a strong dose of quinine the night before and accounted thus for the fact that he slept pretty soundly and was awakened only when the flakes of whitewash from the ceiling fell on his face. One or two boys at the Boys' School and one girl at the Girls' School slept right through it all. The woman cook at the Boys' School was much startled and began to cry out and pray, "My Lord, my Lord, there is no other but thee" (Yâ rubby, yâ rubby, mâfîsh ghayrak).[1] Niḳola, the man on the place, who slept in a little house in the yard, went back and forth to his family who lived in the village to assure himself that they were well. One stone in the gable end of the house where he slept was tumbled to the ground. The well-con-

[1] Compare with the exclamation of this Christian, the Moslem attribution of uniqueness to God in the well-known formula.

structed Girls' Training Home showed cracks, while in the poorly built Boys' House, the roof, flooring and walls on the long south side were cracked the entire length. Our neighbor Nyland's house suffered somewhat, so that afterwards he felt it necessary to bind the walls with iron girders, which were run through the house and clamped on the outside walls at the ends. Other effects were noticed in a morning walk through the village. In the western part of the village the damage seemed greater than in the central or eastern. One small house on the east and several on the west side had lost a wall apiece. These were the so-called *sḳîfeh* dwellings, or loosely constructed stone huts. In each case the front wall had fallen outward. Quite a number of larger, stronger houses were slightly cracked along a side or on top. One house wall bowed out threateningly. In one fine new house, not quite completed, there were laterally running cracks on the two longer sides of the roof. Word was brought to us that a man in Baytîn was killed by a falling stone from a house.

A large party of Russian pilgrims on their way up through the country, who had been quartered in the village the night of the earthquake, took up the customary march to Nâblus soon after. They always start northward from Râm Allâh before light.

The dominant religious influence in Râm Allâh is the Greek (Orthodox) Church. It is customary all through the near East, the field of the Greek Church, to admit to the chief ecclesiastical positions priests of Greek blood only. The head priest of the Râm Allâh Church was a Cretan who had come to this village in 1899. He spoke the Arabic language but lamely. He was very affable and rather good looking. All Greek priests wear the hair long though they knot it up for convenience. The ordinary dress is a long black gown and rimless, cylindrical black hat. When we called on the priest he conversed courteously and treated us to preserves and coffee. His attendant was a lad from the Greek islands

THE VILLAGE OF RÂM ALLÂH AND OUTLYING VINEYARDS

whom he also used as his censer boy at church functions. This head priest goes by the title *raîs*, that is, head-one among the people. He is unmarried, as are all the superior clergy. There are four other priests for the church, who are natives of the place, speak the Arabic language, of course, and are married. The title for such a priest is Khûry. Whenever there is such a one in a family of Syrians the entire family is apt to adopt the word Khûry as a family name. The names of the four khûrys of the Râm Allâh Greek Church during my acquaintance with the village were Ḥanna, Ayûb, Ḳustandy and Salîm. These under priests have most of the intercourse with the people, intermeddle with all sorts of affairs, like any native villager, and are a visible bond between the common and the ecclesiastical life of the village. One of these four, who is reputed to be wealthy, acts as a sort of private banker in his parish, lending money about at the enormous rates which obtain among the peasants. The government rate is nine per cent, but this legal percentage is often more than doubled in practise, while for small, short-time loans the charges mount to huge proportions. One day as I walked out into the village I saw this khûry sitting in front of the dispensary. He had been consulting the physician about some ailment and had received the advice to take a sitz bath, but he lacked the very important aid of a bath-tub. He applied to me, as he saw me, to lend him a bath-tub, but I had nothing of the kind that was portable. He next heard that I was buying some articles for a new boarding-school for boys and suggested that if I bought some of the large copper vessels called ṭunjerehs, one of the variety used for washing clothes would suit his purpose. But again I had to disappoint him, as I told him I was just then short of money and decided to buy only the smaller cooking ṭunjerehs at present. He looked surprised at my confession of temporary poverty, but followed up his lead affably by declaring that I was very welcome to come to his bank. It was some minutes before I saw the line of thought the thrifty fellow was following, that I should borrow money of him (the rate was then about twenty per cent) to buy bathing facilities which he might borrow of me. This will help to illustrate the unembarrassed egotism with which some of the people deal with one after the " heads-I-win, tails-you-lose " order. They are as unimaginative as children in setting your interests at naught and complacently securing all for themselves. And they will do it with all the dramatical touches of idealism and an unselfish air.

The village tradition of the founding of Râm Allâh is told by the peasants as follows: A certain Christian shaykh living in Shôbek, down towards Wâdy Mûsâ, became the father of a little girl. A Moslem shaykh, visiting the father, spoke in a complimentary way of the little child and was courteously answered, as in all cases where praise is bestowed on any possession, whether a new article or a new child, the owner or father usually replying, " It is for you." So in this case the father replied, " She is for you," meaning, of course, nothing by it except the usual courtesies. Years passed by and the little baby girl became an attractive maiden, when the Moslem shaykh came and claimed her for his bride. The father protested, but was reminded of the visit of years before and the reply of the father, which had been taken in real earnest by his visitor. Consternation fell on the Christian family at the impending fate of the little daughter claimed by a Moslem. They would rather that the girl should die than marry thus, but they were in no condition to resist the demand. During the night the Christian shaykh took the only course possible, the desperate one of flight to other parts. Accompanied by his four brothers and their families he fled. No members of the large family could be left behind lest vengeance should be executed on them for the disappointment. They journeyed northward and were joined by certain Moslems who also had reasons for seeking a change of home. The two parties traveled together, probably for greater safety. They all came into the country north of Jerusalem and the Christians, being blacksmiths, chose what were then wooded hills, the present site of Râm Allâh, though now there is no growth to evidence the early conditions. The Moslems settled about el-Bîreh. To-day when the Bîreh people laugh at Râm Allâh people and say, "Your fathers must have been foolish not to choose lands near the good Bîreh spring, but over there in that thirsty country," some of the Râm Allâh people answer, "Our fathers were blacksmiths, and in their days the hills here were covered with woods which supplied them with charcoal." To-day, as has been noted elsewhere, the largest section of Râm Allâh's people is called the *Ḥadadeh*, that is, "the blacksmiths."

Another version of the story has it that the Christians settled at el-Bîreh and the Moslems at Râm Allâh, but because the Christians were blacksmiths they arranged with the Moslems to exchange sites since there was so much material for charcoal around Râm Allâh. If this version could be credited it might help to account for the old mosk in Râm Allâh.[1]

The villagers of Râm Allâh are often hard workers. Their hours of labor are from sunup to sunset. They often sing happily while they are digging the vineyards in lieu of plowing them where the vines are close. Twenty-five cents a day is fair pay for unskilled labor of this sort, though for skilled labor, such as that of a first-class mason and builder, the price may run to a dollar, or a little over. Women and boys work hard for from twelve to fifteen cents a day. From four to eight dollars a month secures a man servant who, if he is a clever one, will do countless services and become almost indispensable. He will try hard to meet the foreigners'

[1] See page 115.

ideas and wishes and improve in his ability to anticipate them.

It does not do to nag and annoy the native helper by too close and nervous application of Western ideals of work, accuracy and punctuality, for one gets oneself into a very unlovely state of nervous irritability and often wears out a really valuable servant by unnecessary trifles of supervision. The peasant is used to a certain ease and generosity of judgment and if wisely watched will accomplish a good deal of work in a very fair way.

One fresh from Europe or America is tempted to supercilious airs, as if everything native to the country were inferior and vastly so. But a longer acquaintance emphasizes the fact that, the world over, our virtues, superiorities and so forth are put on in spots rather than in a consistent through and through grain. And one soon finds plenty of occasion in Palestine to blush for occurrences which must make a sensible native think us a very unlikely set of people to be receiving so many gifts from a kind Providence. The conditions under which they see most foreigners persuade them that lack of money does not exist in America and possibly that it is not very common in Europe. Then, too, they see so many childless married couples, these naturally being the freest to travel, or to undertake missions, that the contradiction of this apparent curse upon us mystifies them. And as to sanity of mind and clearness of religious doctrine or practise, foreigners in Jerusalem must often be on the defensive in order to keep even self-respect.

El-Bîreh, with its eight hundred inhabitants, lies on the southeast side of a curve in the carriage road, fifteen kilometers almost due north from Jerusalem. From it Jerusalem may be seen. North of it on the opposite side of the carriage road is an unusually prominent watch-tower by which el-Bîreh can be located from afar. Local tradition says that Ibrahîm Basha (Pasha) camped near here. The people of el-Bîreh are all Moslems, except one family named Rafîdya, who number about eighty and are related to a household of the same name in Râm Allâh. These Rafîdyas take their name from a town near Nâblus, whence they migrated some years ago when their lot there become unbearable. They are now among the most prosperous dwellers in the village, managing the large new khân, the little store in it and the carriage business that runs a service between el-Bîreh and Jerusalem daily. They worship in the Greek Church in Râm Allâh. One member of the family is being trained in the Greek school in Jerusalem. One goes by the complimentary business epithet of *esh-Shayṭân* (Satan), equivalent to *clever.* This family, or tribe, dwell in the northern part of the village, not far from the carriage road. Their khân is a typical country caravanserâi. Thousands of people pass it: messengers going up and down the country, village priests or teachers going to Jerusalem to get their monthly pay, sellers and buyers, caravans of wheat carriers from the Haurân, tourists, pilgrims, missionaries, mokaries, camping outfits, mounted Turkish soldiers sent to some village to bring in offenders wanted by the Jerusalem government or to collect taxes.

The chief pride of el-Bîreh is the copious spring of excellent water at the southwest of the village, where the carriage road begins to ascend the hill. The new mudîr of the district in 1903 caused some improvements in masonry to be constructed over the Bîreh fountain. A busy scene can often be observed there. Women and girls come and go, chattering and scolding, eager for the first turn to put a jar under the flow. The women are seen washing on the smooth stones near the spring, pounding with a short stout club the well-soaked garments. The water from the spring at its flood and the rains have gullied the paths hereabouts and left the pebbles like hobnails, so that to walk about the place is like using the stepping-stones of a dry brook.

From a point a little to the east of the fountain a path to the right (south) leads in a few steps under a picturesque little ruin in stone, the inner rim of an arch which spans the path with airy grace. Just beyond it on the right there is a long, low stone building, an old khân in good preservation. There are ruins all about under the trees. Continuing on the left after a turn one comes to an immense old khân in ruin, of which four sections or rooms still remain. It has a quadruple arched roof and fine columns. Masons' marks are to be seen on some of the heavy old stones and Arab graffiti on others. Some of these scratchings are very good. A horseman lifting a long spear is one of the best. This great khân would still shelter several scores of camels and their loads if inclement weather necessitated a resort to it.

South of the fountain are some old reservoirs built of heavy stone and meant to treasure up the overflowings of the brook in its downward course through the valley from the spring. Further southward of these reservoirs, which are now out of repair, one goes through fig-orchards towards the little Moslem shrine of Shaykh Sâliḥ, around about which one often sees numerous little piles of stones on the tops of the stone walls, reminders of the pious and their petitions to the departed shaykh or wily. The course of the brook from the spring continues down the valley to Wâd es-Suwaynîṭ and thence, by the way of the Wâdy Ḳelt, to the Jordan.

Along the sides of Jebel Ṭawîl, the long ridge to the southeast of el-Bîreh, one sees the walls of a quarry, whence huge blocks must have been taken long ago, as the smooth, unbroken surface remaining measures many yards. Northeast of el-Bîreh the hillsides show similar quarrying.

In the northern part of the village is the ruin of a Crusaders' Church, one of the better preserved specimens of that kind of building in Palestine. A considerable part of the east end, with its triple apse and most of the north wall, though this latter bulges ominously, are still standing. The south wall, too, is pretty well preserved. A low passage through it leads to the site where the old convent used to be, now the home of a Moslem boys' school taught by a white turbaned urbane khaṭîb. Several visitors of late years searched in vain for an inscription that M. Clermont Ganneau mentions as having seen. Among the ruins of the church several masons' marks of the crusading style may be seen on the building stone. The church is some eight centuries old. The cement in these old structures is exceedingly strong. Though the north wall seems in such imminent danger of falling, the earthquake of 1903 did not accomplish its overthrow. Cows and donkeys wander about the weedy interior, and the neighbors spread out there heaps of gathered dung to dry for fuel.

There are many signs of squalor in el-Bîreh. The level of the floor in many of the huts is below the threshold. In fact, a large number of the houses, excluding those of the shaykhs and the Christian tribe of Rafîdya, are of the very old style of sḳîfeh dwellings, a few of which were mentioned in describing Râm Allâh, the style of buildings made with stones bedded in earth, or at best held together by poor mortar and having dirt roofs supported upon heavy boughs. The village, though possessed of wide lands, a good situation on the traffic route of the country and the best spring for many miles around, compares very poorly with Râm Allâh, just twenty minutes away and possessed of none of these advantages. The very marked superiority of the Christian village and its rapid development in the last century is a matter of significant observation. A study of the house structure already suggested in the two villages shows the typical development of village building. There are in Râm Allâh some of the sḳîfeh-huts of the same style and age apparently as the larger number of that kind proportionately in el-Bîreh. Others of this same order were pulled down long ago in Râm Allâh and replaced by houses made with dressed stone and mortar and having rolled dirt roofs, similar to some of the better grade of houses in el-Bîreh to-day. But this kind is already counted inferior in Râm Allâh, where the larger number of dwellings have the heavy, arched, dome roofs of stone, of which there are but few in el-Bîreh. An improvement even upon these is gaining ground in Râm Allâh, and much better houses, having several rooms, modern window openings and paved floors and provided in some cases with cisterns for oil or water, are being constructed by the wealthier villagers. The development of several centuries in highland peasant homes may thus be traced. A significant change in the interior structure is the doing away of the elevated living platform in the room reached by stairs that command the doorway.

EL-BIREH (FROM THE SOUTH)

CHAPTER X

OTHER VILLAGES AND ENVIRONS

About a mile northwest of Râm Allâh on the Jânyeh road is a region which goes by the name of eṭ-Ṭîreh, a name commonly met in Syria. There is a question as to what it may mean. If the localities thus named were always, as they more usually are, lofty places, the suggestion has been made that eṭ-Ṭîreh might be derived from the root meaning *to fly*, and so such a place might be dubbed *The Flyer*, in the sense of a *high place*, but Prof. E. H. Palmer derives the name from a root meaning *fort*.[1] At this eṭ-Ṭîreh there are many remains of former buildings, the central one being the Ṣalâ't eṭ-Ṭîreh, the ruin of a Christian church. A large tract of ground including it has been walled in by the ecclesiastical owners. The oil of the olive-trees in the enclosure is said to be used for church purposes. The remains of the old church are very scanty compared with those at el-Bîreh, Burj Baytîn, eṭ-Ṭayyibeh or even at Khurbet el-Moḳâṭir. Some of the remaining stones have been reset in an attempt to restore the line of the wall, and the result is a smaller space enclosed than originally. At present the main enclosure is roughly fifty-two feet long by twenty-six feet wide. The line of the apse is marked by one course of stones standing loosely together. Plenty of tiny white cubes, remains of tessellated pavement, are scattered around. There are bases of four columns, many blocks and some pieces of columns.

Northeast of the ruin is a little inclined path that leads underground, where there is a fine old olive-press. It is of

[1] טירה, see preface to Arabic and English Name List in Palestine Exploration Fund Memoirs.

the kind generally used, though recently some screw-presses have been introduced into Râm Allâh.

There are two sorry-looking fig-trees in the grounds, the fruit of which is said to be free to all comers. Here and there in the country these traditionally free fruit-trees are seen. I remember one on the valley road to Bayt 'Ur et-Taḥtâ. The whole property, otherwise, is *ḥarâm*, that is, sacrosanct. The dwellers in Palestine have a very vivid sense of that ecclesiastical or religious quality that attaches to a place once acknowledged as devoted to religious purposes. Despite all encroachments, persecutions of hostile governments or religions, the mind of the people persists in returning again and again to the subject of the sacred nature of any such spot, and this obstinate tradition sooner or later gets that piece of property back under the care of the church. The Râm Allâh people tell a story which illustrates how the *powers* assist in preserving devoted things. " One day a man was digging in the ground when his pickaxe (*fass*) struck against the lid of a copper vessel (ṭunjereh) containing treasure,[1] but as he began to clear away the soil so as to come at the find, his hands became, as it were, bound together with cords and his feet were likewise powerless."

Out beyond the enclosing walls of the Greek property are fine olive-trees and many heaps of old building stone, with other evidences of a former habitation of men. The land and olives west of the Ṣalâ't eṭ-Ṭîreh are owned by a well-to-do Râm Allâh family, Dâr Abu Firmand. The view of Râm Allâh from this place is very good, impressing one with the fact that it is indeed situated on a rise of ground, which effect one does not get in coming to it from the higher ground to the south and east of the village. A vague story is told of a former prosperous settlement of Christians at eṭ-Ṭîreh and of their massacre.

The road from Râm Allâh toward the northwest runs just

[1] Matt. 13: 44.

under one of the walls of the enclosure at Ṣalâ't eṭ-Ṭîreh, having that wall for its left-hand boundary. After passing the walled grounds thus on the left a little valley begins, branching off from the main path and running down to the right. It is called the Khullet el-'Adas and in the late winter is well filled with varicolored anemones. On the right side of the valley, up in the terraces, are tombs, five or six of which I have seen and three of which I have measured. The first one is the farthest from the path that runs down into the Khulleh, but it is not more than two stones'-throw from the nearest corner of eṭ-Ṭîreh enclosure. About the entrance to the tomb the rock has been scarped to a width of eight feet two inches and to a height of five feet. There is the usual low entrance to the tomb-chamber. In this case the doorway is about two feet high. It is eighteen inches wide and is bordered with a cut facing five inches wide. The inner chamber, ten feet wide and eight feet eight inches deep, has five vaulted niches, one opposite the chamber entrance and two on each side. Just within the chamber, at the right of the entrance, in the corner, is a tiny niche, like those in a columbarium, probably for a lamp. The second of these tombs is nearer the path, a little way down the valley. Its door measurements are similar to those given for number one, except that the width is one inch more. The inner chamber has but three niches, each one with rounded top as before, but with a squared facing at the entrance. The third tomb is yet nearer the path. The facing, cut about the entrance to the chamber, is seven inches on each side. The width of the entrance is eighteen inches. In the chamber, as in those mentioned above, there are three vaulted niches, but they are very high and considerably deeper than in tombs numbers one and two. The remaining tombs mentioned are higher up the hillside and still farther away. Numbers two and three of those described are easily seen from the valley path.

The little village of 'Ayn 'Arîk, about an hour and a quarter north-of-west of Râm Allâh, is occupied by a mixed population of Greek Christians and Moslems. The situation is on the side of a very fertile valley amply supplied with water. Pomegranate orchards in abundance, gardens and a few olive, fig and lemon-trees make a running patch of green for about a mile down the valley. Our first visit to the village was on September 26 in 1901. We passed on the way the ruined village called Kefr Shiyân or Kefr Shiyâl. Probably the older form is the one with *l*, the later usage favoring the ending in *n*. This place is mentioned by Dr. J. P. Peters in the *Journal of Biblical Literature* as a Byzantine ruin. Some of the 'Ayn 'Arîk people have sufficient antiquarian interest to try to make out that this ruin represents ancient Shiloh. One path to 'Ayn 'Arîk goes to the right of Kefr Shiyân and keeps to the left of the venerable tree called Abu 'Aynayn (father of two fountains), which is perched on a hilltop. Another path to 'Ayn 'Arîk goes to the left of Kefr Shiyân, between that ruin and another smaller ruin on an opposite hillside, the ruin of 'Ayn Ṣôba. Down this path we have seen camels, loaded with boxes of raisins from Râm Allâh, making their way towards Jaffa via 'Ayn 'Arîk. The more usual route to Jaffa, however, leaves the 'Ayn Ṣôba ruin on the right instead of on the left, as we do now in going on down to 'Ayn 'Arîk. Before reaching this latter place we pass a spring with a reservoir to catch its overflow. It is about fifteen minutes this side of the village, in the valley, near the beginning of the olive-grove. The spring and place about are called Umm el-Khuruḳ (the mother of rags). From here to the village the path runs through olive orchards. The pomegranate orchards begin below the village. The other springs which may be said to be at or near 'Ayn 'Arîk are:

'Ayn el-Jâmi' (The Spring of the Mosk), in the village;

'Ayn Râs el-Bîr (The Spring, the Head of the Well), near the village;

Ayn esh-Shaykh (The Spring of the Shaykh), near the village;

'Ayn eṭ-Ṭoreh, near the village;

'Ayn el-'Azâb, ten minutes away from the village;

'Ayn el-'Aṣfûr (The Spring of the Bird), fifteen minutes' distance.

The people of 'Ayn 'Arîk are greatly favored with the natural conditions of prosperity and ought to develop considerably. The most helpful influence exerted in the village is that of the day-school for children maintained as an out-station of the Râm Allâh Friends' Mission and taught by one of their trained native women.

From el-Bîreh to Baytîn (Bethel) the distance is about two miles. The path leaves the carriage road a little north of the former village and strikes off to the right through a small patch of boulders, stirrup high, to a level stretch of ground that rises a little as one comes to an interesting group of remains clustered about a spring, 'Ayn el-Kusa'.[1] Some well-worn rock-cut steps lead up to a rock-platform seven or eight feet above and alongside the bridle-path. The spring starts from the hillside, a little distance away, the outlet being artificially improved and a connection made with a system of trenches and pan-shaped hollows cut in different places over the top of the rock platform. Down by the path-side, under this platform, is a rock-cut chamber or cave with two heavy supporting columns hewn from the rock. The water system above is connected with it. All around the interior walls and clustering at the foot of the columns are beautiful maidenhair ferns growing out of the ooze in the bottom of the cave. A few yards farther on is another smaller cavelike room or reservoir which was never finished or connected with the spring and chamber above.

[1] See page 17.

Between these two caves there is a connection by a sort of trough cut in the wall-side. The intention may have been to connect the two caves as catch-reservoirs with a lower cistern or pool. This latter is suggested by a circular-shaped line of dressed stone in the very path. Many have asked what it was, whether a former pool, the top of a cistern or a shallow basin trough. The path must once have avoided it, though it now stumbles over it. Below the path little gardens catch the drainings of the spring.

A few rods beyond this the bridle-path to Dayr Dîwân and Jericho diverges to the right (east) from the main caravan road to Baytîn and Nâblus. This main road continues to the 'Ayn el-'Aḳabeh (The Spring of the Descent, or, of the Steep Place) and on up the steep path to the top of the hill before Baytîn (Bethel). There are small gardens near the spring and a few old tombs in the vicinity. The people of Baytîn are Moslems. They are apt to be rude to small parties of foreigners. Though few, about half as many as in el-Bîreh, they have a name among the near-by villages for strength and fearlessness. In going into the village one passes the cemetery and the large ancient pool. North of the village is a field of large rocks that have never lacked notice since the records of history began. Shortly beyond the big rocks, which lie in the road to Nâblus, a branching path takes one towards eṭ-Ṭayyibeh, seen at good advantage from this fork in the paths on a prominent hill a little north of east. Due east from Baytîn is Burj Baytîn, five minutes away, a picturesque ruin among some fig-trees.

From Burj Baytîn we may bear to the right to Dayr Dîwân, going through the extensive fig-orchards of the latter or take a straighter road which leads one by a very rocky hill Tell el-Ḥajar (right) and another (left) that looks like a rampart of pebble with flattened top, called et-Tell and identified by some with ancient Ai. West of Dayr Dîwân are a lot of boulders with flat table tops that would be the delight of picnickers desirous of a place to spread a cloth. The distinguishing thing about the appearance of Dayr Dîwân is that the houses stand quite apart from each other, one story high, each with its own little space about it. The entrance to the village from the west is a little precarious for horses because of the slippery rock surface that abounds. The people of the place are Moslems. They are quiet folk. A while ago a Râm Allâh man (Christian) kept a grocery shop in the village.

From Jifnâ to eṭ-Ṭayyibeh the way leads by Dûrah and through 'Ayn Yebrûd. Part of the route is low and hot, so that the natives have dubbed it the Ghôr. Dûrah is a small, healthfully located Moslem village. Its inhabitants have a good reputation for peaceful relations with the Jifnâ Christians. The Dûrah people raise many vegetables. A little beyond Dûrah the path goes by the sacred oak-trees, Umm Barakât. Here one turns to the left (north),— in the distance are the brown cliffs and cave holes of the Wâdy Khulleh; also the village of 'Ayn Sînyâ, — then up a steep hill path to 'Ayn Yebrûd (a Moslem village) and past the little mosk and more big ballûṭ (oak) trees to the Nâblus-Jerusalem road.

From the south side of the village 'Ayn Yebrûd, near its spring, there is a way through the Wâdy 'Arâḳ el-Kharûf (Valley of the Sheep Rocks) which comes out on the Bîreh-Baytîn path just a little southwest of the pillared cave mentioned on page 217. The end of the valley nearer 'Ayn Yebrûd has ancient tombs. The deepest part of the valley is bordered with pinnacled cliffs. Where the way broadens out toward the south we once saw a mile of dhurah (millet) under cultivation. Thence the path leads over a little tableland to the road from el-Bîreh.

As we proceed easterly from 'Ayn Yebrûd across the Nâblus road we go through a very stony, sunken, basin-like piece of ground called Wastîyeh, between the stones of which some rich soil seems to lie. The path through here may be easily lost. There are some old cisterns along the way. Into the big one north of the path they say that a murdered man was once thrown, and so a fear has been cast over the neighborhood. Beyond the Wastîyeh the road goes across the Wâdy Sha'b el-Ḳassîs. Thereafter one is soon at eṭ-Ṭayyibeh.

The path from Dayr Dîwân to eṭ-Ṭayyibeh takes one out through the northeast part of the former village and then in about ten minutes to one of the sheerest descents attempted by a Palestinian bridle-path. It zigzags down into a deep valley, faced by Wâdy el-'Ayn, which leads up towards eṭ-Ṭayyibeh, and is crossed (left to right) by the long wâdy that comes down from the north of Baytîn and extends towards the Ghôr (Jordan and Dead Sea region). Going up or down this steep hill one usually prefers to walk, seeing to it that one's animal takes no unnecessary risks, for there are many little deviations from the plainer path which a donkey may attempt but a horse had better leave untried. The natives sometimes help a loaded donkey going down such paths as this by holding on to the animal's tail and allowing it to balance itself by the help of the caudal tug. But beware of offering such help to Palestine mules. I believe they could kick at any angle.

Once at the bottom of this hill one goes right on up the valley facing northward, past the little spring, crossing the brook bed again and again to keep the path. There is one corner where one had better walk if on a horse which is afraid of smooth rock. Sometimes this part of the valley is called Wâd eḍ-Ḍab'a (the valley of the hyena). Half-way up the valley there joins it on the left (west) another valley, with a path which is the more usual one from Râm Allâh or Baytîn to eṭ-Ṭayyibeh, and which may be used in returning. Just at the junction of these valleys we saw once on the hillside four gazels together. On up the valley to its head one goes

VINEYARDS AND STONE WATCH TOWERS

PEASANT PLOWING

under some sheer straight cliffs. Arrived at the head of the valley, eṭ-Ṭayyibeh is at the right.

The Christian village of eṭ-Ṭayyibeh, three hours northeast of Râm Allâh, is perhaps a little less than half the size of Râm Allâh but exhibits similar marks of advantage over its Moslem neighbors. The village is on the back (east) of the central ridge of Palestine and its lands slope, in consequence, towards the warm regions of the Ghôr. This situation also tends to place it on the frontier between the hill villages and the Bedawîn tribes. The people are a jaunty, fine-looking set. The men wear the Bedawîn head-dress and, in general, the population seems to combine some characteristics and manners of both the nomads and villagers. Robinson visited eṭ-Ṭayyibeh in 1838. The population was then between three and four hundred souls belonging to the Greek Orthodox Church. It has probably increased fourfold since his day and the allegiance of part of the people is now given to the Roman Catholic faith. The English Church Mission holds Sunday services and maintains a day-school for boys. The Râm Allâh Friends' Mission sustains a day-school for girls.

After Dr. Robinson's visit to the village he met some of the inhabitants with their wives and children and their priest down in the Ghôr near Jericho, where they were gathering in the wheat-harvest on shares with the inhabitants of the low country. The Ṭayyibeh people had sown the crop as partners of the Jericho folk. The custom then mentioned continues to this day. Every year large numbers of the villagers of eṭ-Ṭayyibeh go down into the Ghôr and work the fertile lands on shares with the lowlanders. Some of them even penetrate the east-Jordan country and make similar arrangements with the nearer Bedawîn. I have in mind one family from eṭ-Ṭayyibeh that goes on this business as far as ʿAmmân, Jerash and es-Salṭ.

The views from eṭ-Ṭayyibeh are extensive. The east-

Jordan hills confront one there. On the south is the little Moslem hamlet Rammûn (Rimmon) and, far away, Frank Mountain. A sweep of olive-trees to the southeast leads the eye on down to the Dead Sea, which shines, when the air is clear, like silver. Often a haze disguises it. Hard desert hills, hot and bare, fall away to the east towards the Jordan.

The tendency to perch villages on hills had full effect in the placing of eṭ-Ṭayyibeh, for it has one of the most picturesque of the many hill sites. It is easily seen from the roads north of Jerusalem. In times of country feuds an enemy would have to fight the entire village at once, so compactly are the houses coned over the hilltop and so narrow are the streets. The finest possible watch-tower is provided by the old castle on the summit. The village has its cisterns within itself, where the rain-water from the roofs is caught. Of course, whenever feasible, spring-water is brought from a distance for drinking. The winds are sometimes very strong in this region and in summer there is very little defense against the beating rays of the sun.

Jifnâ (Gophna), about an hour and a half north of Râm Allâh, is a Christian village of about six hundred people. The place is full of evidences of ancient structures, old dressed stones, columns, rosettes and carving. The locality is fertile and orchards and vineyards are cultivated. The vinedressers here stake up the grape-vines, contrary to the general fashion in Palestine. There are day-school privileges provided by the Friends for girls, and by the English Church Mission for boys.

The path from Râm Allâh to Jifnâ goes near the wily *Shaykh Yûsuf* and past the little Moslem village of Ṣurdeh (Zereda), where there is a large sacred tree. In the hill south of Shaykh Yûsuf, within a few feet of the path through the olive-trees, is a large ancient tomb, the vestibule being thirteen and a half feet wide by nine and three-quarters deep and six feet high. The door leading from the back of the vestibule into the tomb-chamber measures five feet six inches in width and, so far as visible, measures five feet high. It is choked with earth. The view of the valley filled with olive-trees as it falls toward the Mediterranean is very pleasant.

The tiny Moslem village of 'Ayn Sînyâ is about a mile due north from Jifnâ. It will be well served by the new carriage road, which sweeps around here in one of the prettiest stretches on the route. Indeed, the section from the hills above Jifnâ to 'Ayn Sînyâ is one of the pleasantest which the new Jerusalem-Nâblus road provides. The village of 'Ayn Sînyâ is practically the property of an influential native official in Jerusalem. It is said that his influence prevailed to have the carriage road constructed this way, north from el-Bîreh, instead of by the more usual tourist route via Bethel and 'Ayn Yebrûd. There is consolation in the thought that the ancient Bethel country is left to be reached by the ancient paths and its modernizing may be delayed a century more, so far as roads are concerned. 'Ayn Sînyâ is a natural garden spot. Mulberry and walnut-trees are plentiful about it. Its natural advantages, reenforced by the government road, may now be more fully developed than in the past.

In the country near Jifnâ and Bîr ez-Zayt are quite a number of old tombs. One leaves Jifnâ on the right in going to Bîr ez-Zayt. The two places are near, and in plain sight of each other. There is a small community of Moslems in Bîr ez-Zayt, but most of its people are Christians. The English Church Mission is represented by a good work, a boarding-school for girls and a church whose congregation has a native Protestant pastor. The ruins on top of a high hill to the west of the modern village are supposed to be those of old Bîr ez-Zayt. The olive-trees of the village are very fine and, what is more rare, pear trees of considerable size, in the season so loaded with blossoms as to look like huge bouquets, are to be seen north of the place.

Two hours and a half northwest of Bîr ez-Zayt is the little village of 'Âbûd, with four hundred Christians and three hundred Moslems. The English Church Mission sustains work there. The road thither passes the tiny hamlet of Umm Ṣuffah, the houses of which seem to be made with a core of tiny stones and cement, faced with larger stones. The ruin Khurbet Jîbya is near by. The road then passes near Neby Ṣâliḥ, where it enters the little Wâdy Rayyâ, following which one comes to the tombs of Tibneh within forty minutes of 'Âbûd.

Northwest of 'Âbûd is a place called Muḳâṭ'a, evidently an old quarry, the working of which had disturbed a still older cemetery of rock-cut tombs, some of them painted. The carving in some of these is elaborate. One tomb, with a vestibule twenty-one and three-quarters feet wide and ten feet deep is ornamented at the top with a grape cluster suspended between two wreaths. Another vestibule twenty-six feet two inches wide shows gate sockets on each side. This vestibule served two tomb-chambers, one directly in front as one enters and the other in the right wall. The entrance to the former has been crushed open, leaving a large irregular hole. Within are nine full-sized *kokim* with smaller, shallow cuttings in the tier above them which looked like embryo kokim. The right-hand tomb-chamber has three kokim on the left side and three opposite the entrance, one of the latter having been broken or cut through to the daylight, probably in the process of quarrying from the other side. This smaller tomb shows a fresco in black and red and perhaps yellow paint. The design is in large, diamond-shaped figures, with a rope border over it. There are many scratchings on the walls.

CHAPTER XI

THE VILLAGE AND THE OUTSIDE WORLD

As one becomes acquainted with Palestine life to-day one is impressed with the submissive attitude of the villagers towards the city dwellers, especially towards the Moslem official class, *the effendîyeh*. But we are assured by those within whose lifetime the period falls, that half a century or more ago things were not so well ordered as now. For some years before that time, according to veracious writers, there was a state of internal turbulence in which the fellaḥîn were often in the ascendency and the city people glad to treat with them. In those days the walls of Jerusalem were of practical use in resisting the power of the country folk. Two great parties divided the allegiance of the villages. They were called Yemen and Ḳays. Headed by shaykhs and aided by Bedawîn, these partisan villages waged feuds and rendered commerce and travel precarious or impossible. Abu Ghôsh and his sons from their vantage of Ḳuryet el-'Anab held much of the country in terror of his raids.[1] He levied toll on travelers and was too powerful to be curbed by the government, such as it was, at Jerusalem. 'Abd er-Raḥman and other shaykhs held certain districts. The troops were few and the Turkish hold on the country weak. The province came near to a condition of anarchy. Every man did that which was right in his own eyes.[2] To this day any intelligent peasant will tell the inquirer which of the villages are of the Yemeny and which of the Ḳaysy party. The lines of division are still plain though the feuds are dormant. The Turkish government has strengthened its position in the interior affairs of Palestine steadily for forty or fifty years

[1] *Cf.* Judges 5: 6, 7. [2] *Cf.* Judges 21: 25.

back. To-day there is not a murmur that avails nor the disposition to antagonize the centralizing authority of the ruler. Even the east-Jordan country appears to be growing tame. Within a few years a firmer hold on the village situation has been taken by the establishment of extra mudîrships, so that instead of governing the village districts from Jerusalem and other large centers by a squad of soldiers sent out occasionally to do police duty or to bring in taxes, now a local official called a mudîr is placed in the most important village of a small district. He is a subordinate of the governor, *muteṣarrif*, of Jerusalem. By the appointment of such as he a closer observation and administration are secured. At Râm Allâh in 1903 a mudîr was appointed to have charge in that and a score of other villages in a district thereabouts. Jerusalem is still the head of those villages, but a compacter administration is effected.

To the country peasant the chief functions of the government seem to be those of restriction and oppression. The fear of imprisonment, fines and confiscations keeps the peasants down. The imprisonment of a peasant leaves no taint of dishonor, having as purely unfortunate an aspect as confinement in a hospital. There is no such thing as successful complaint unless it can assume such influence as would procure the removal of the official involved. The peasants look suspiciously on every movement of every officer, refusing to believe that any government representative can have good intentions or do worthy actions. Government provisions or improvements are looked upon as gloves for the hand that is stretched out for more of the means of the villager. The taxes are farmed out to tax-collectors whose approach is dreaded extremely.[1] Every dozen years or so a new schedule of valuation is made by the assessors, who travel about the country revaluing businesses and properties. Their progress from village to village is the signal for

[1] *Cf.* Luke 19: 2, 8.

feasting, treating and bribing. The cost of the many attempts to persuade these assessors to reduce valuations or readjust them in favor of the briber must be considerable. There is a possibility that all such attempts may be defeated by the revision of the entire list at headquarters. The visits of the soldiers to a village are always occasions of dread, and much relief is felt when they leave. On the frontiers and in out-of-the-way places, where the task of the government is less easy, a more conciliatory spirit is shown. In the Ghôr, for instance, the tax may be paid in kind, and this always makes it easier than the practise into which the collectors have fallen with the villages. They drop in upon the villagers at odd times through the year, long after the crop is out of the way, and demand money payment in cash. This helps to make the fortunes of the local money lenders, but it causes a double damage to the peasants, who are forced to sacrifice their stores for low prices in ready money, or to mortgage their crop expectations for the coming season.[1] At Bîr es-Seba' and all such places where the government is seeking to strengthen its hold upon a district, the early steps are taken courteously and softly and the later with a nailed heel. At points east of the Jordan, where the problem of every government that ever sought to control the country has been to withstand, and finally to render impossible, the raids of the desert tribes of nomads, the present government is slowly reclaiming the country to authority. In some places colonies of Circassians have been introduced as buffers on the frontiers.

The tendency among the villagers is to settle their disputes so far as possible without resort to the government. If quarreling arises and the government gets information of it, soldiers are sent out to investigate and compel order, and incidentally to secure as much money as possible. To avoid these dreaded quarterings of soldiers on themselves, and to

[1] Neh. 5: 4.

escape the money-making ingenuity of city officials, who seem to welcome quarrels and litigation for the profit ensuing, the disagreements and even bitterer issues may be submitted to councils of neighbors. Sometimes eight or ten men from a village will be asked to act as arbitrators in the quarrel of another village. We know of one such case where a quarrel of some years' standing was settled by the assistance of men from another village. The case had been complicated by the heavy claim for damages put in by a man whose finger had been shot off by his enemy. Very often, even after the government has apparently settled a case, the parties concerned will come to an additional settlement, through their representatives and friends, to wipe out all old scores and the sense of personal resentment. Sheep, rice, semen, garments and such country articles are used as presents back and forth until good-will and satisfaction seem established by mutual consent.

The attitude of the local government to the people may be gathered from the following incident. A Râm Allâh man, going back to his village from Jerusalem, was entrusted by a friend in the city with the sum of four napoleons, partly in gold and partly in change, to be taken to Râm Allâh. The man put the money in a handkerchief, knotted it up and tucked it into the bosom of his dress. It slipped out and fell to the ground without his knowledge. A woman from Silwân picked it up, but was noticed by a Jew, who demanded it, asserting that it was his. Then a third, who was passing, put in a claim for the money. An officer coming upon the party, seized the handkerchief with the money, saying that he would have the public crier announce the find. The man who had lost the money did not notice his loss until the afternoon. He went to the Serâi to claim it. He described the handkerchief, the gold pieces and the small change, but the officer denied the accuracy of the description. The man begged to be allowed to see the find, declaring that if everything did not agree with the description already offered the money was not his. The officer, thus pressed, said, " Look here, no money goes out of the Serâi when it once gets in," and turned the peasant away. The loser made an outcry and sought the help of one of his village's shaykhs who happened to be in the city. The poor have very scanty legal resources, but they have an almost preternatural persistence and a genius for making themselves disagreeable. Witnesses of the finding were brought and other measures taken, despite repeated rebuffs. Finally the officer of the Serâi acknowledged having the man's money and gave him a receipt for four napoleons which could be presented in lieu of payment of future taxes to that amount. Further satisfaction it was impossible to obtain.

Those who ought to know claim that the body of Turkish law is excellent and that impartial administration of it would be all that could be asked. But administration is lamed by the refusal of the courts to recognize in any practical way the testimony of those who are not Moslems and, among the Moslems, of those who are not rich. The court performs merely a formal function, the cases being determined in most illegal ways. No case is taken to court when there is any possible way of keeping it out and settling it. If a case must come up in court one seeks out among the influential official class of the city the most powerful help he can afford to pay for and forestalls his opponent, if possible, the court being a mere incident in the problem. Does a squabble take place in a village and is some one injured with an ever-ready stone? The families of the participants would fain patch up the matter themselves, but they know very well that the news will soon reach the city and that soldiers will be sent out to investigate. The result will be arrests and heavy fines all around. To anticipate this, representatives of either side may be seen hastening along the road to Jerusalem. The first one in tells his story and buys up friends among the officials. The most money counts, but the officials take care that each side of the matter is made profitable to themselves. The case may drag on for months, scores of dollars being reaped by the officials, who may then consent to an amicable agreement among the principals. And yet, the fear of such pecuniary consequences acts as a restraining influence in many villages in which there is not a single official representative of the government. Such villages are controlled through an abundance of talebearing. On the other hand, who can blame an underpaid class of influentials for welcoming lucrative disturbances? Those who hold office have to pay largely for the privilege, and the salary being merely nominal, they have to reimburse themselves and live in the only way that Turkish practise encourages.

The officials in charge of the important posts are usually sent from Constantinople and are not generally citizens of Palestine.

The levies of troops are sent for service to parts of the empire distant from their homes, so that the local soldiery in Palestine has little in common with the people.

One will be pained to miss the spirit of public weal, the commiseration of the unfortunate or the willingness to undertake enterprises that would be for the general good. Absolutism means individualism only relieved by the wonderful tie of kinship and family among the common people.

There is a local Turkish postal service, with offices at all the large centers and in some of the inland villages of importance. Mail destined to points without the empire must bear postage stamps of a different issue from those affixed to domestic matter. The readiest way to distinguish these two issues is to notice that the stamps allowed to go out of the country are provided with the emblem of the crescent at each of the upper corners, while the stamps restricted to domestic use have but one crescent at the top, and that in the middle of the top line.

Besides the Turkish postal facilities there are also, by special rights of extraterritoriality, offices and services by the posts of other countries. At Jerusalem and Jaffa there are Austrian, French, German and Russian post-offices. The Germans have one at Ramleh also. The telegraph service is in charge of the government and connects a number of towns east and west of the Jordan with each other and the outside world. The service is reasonable in price, but precarious in results. I once telegraphed from Beirut to Jerusalem and asked the operator if the message would reach its destination by noon, then several hours away, and was answered, "If God wills." During the unquiet times in Beirut in the summer of 1903 some one in Jerusalem, anxious concerning friends in the disturbed city, essayed to send the simple inquiry, "Are you well?" but the message was refused at the office. No reference, inquiry or information is ever allowed, officially, concerning any troubles in any part of the empire. Nevertheless, news has a remarkable way of sifting into the country and passing from lip to lip very rapidly. When the Ottoman Bank was dynamited in Salonika the news quickly reached the ports on the Syrian coasts and went as a rumor all through the country. For some reason or other, messages by telegraph and cable for European and American destinations, and messages from those places, often take three or four days in transmission, and sometimes longer, if, indeed, they "come through" at all.

Travel to and from Palestine is often impeded by the imposition of quarantines against certain ports. Very much of the time a quarantine of from five to ten days is ordered against vessels from Egyptian ports, and sometimes from other directions. The excuse for the discrimination against Egypt is usually the bubonic plague, sometimes cholera. All vessels from Egypt must proceed to Beirut, or some other port provided with a quarantine station, and pass the required time. If, in returning to Jaffa after the quarantine, severe storms should hinder a landing, and the vessel should proceed southward to touch an Egyptian port again, the quarantine would again be enforced on the ship and passengers, and the same procedure as before be necessary. Passengers have thus been carried by Jaffa more times than once and greatly hampered, even though they had joined the ship at Beirut only, with Jaffa as their destination. These inconveniences are overshadowed by the crippling effect on trade and travel when a state of panic has resulted in the enforcement of quarantine back and forth between different ports, and even different towns and villages within the country itself.

The coastwise traffic is carried on by means of several lines of steamships: the Khedevieh Line, under English control; the Russian, the Austrian Lloyd, the French, " Messageries," and sometimes the German Lloyd. Some of these touch at Haifa as well as at Jaffa and Beirut. There is a little coasting steamboat that plies between Haifa and Beirut, touching at Acre, Tyre and Sidon. This is called the Jolly Boat, but unless one is an extraordinarily good sailor I should advise him not to be beguiled by that name. On the other lines mentioned there are generally three classes of passage tickets. The deck passage is taken by many Orientals, who travel with ample equipment of bedding, food and bottle-pipes, and camp out on the decks day and night. Much of their time is spent in the routine of family duties and religious observances. The rest is devoted to music, stories and games. Mohammedans, Jews, Greeks, Copts, Abyssinians and Armenians are seen at their devotions. Their object may be trade, migration, military service or a religious mission. Many are pilgrims, saving long and tedious land travel by the swifter, safer and healthier journey on sea.

The railway service actually working in Syria consists of the line between Jaffa and Jerusalem, the service between Beirut and Damascus, the extension from Reyâḳ on the

Damascus line through Ba'albek, and the line from Damascus southward to Mezayrîb and the east-Jordan country, destined ultimately to reach Mekka. A line from Haifa to connect with this latter line is under way. Two classes of passage are provided. The cars generally have compartments, though some, as the second class on the Jaffa-Jerusalem line, have one-room cars with seats running along both sides and a bench through the middle. Even in the second-class cars a separate section is often provided for the use of women. This section is known as the *ḥarîm.* In the seclusion of the ḥarîm apartment the women may put off their veils and have the freedom of the place. When the conductor comes for the tickets he raps sharply on the door of the ḥarîm to give the women warning. After sufficient time has been allowed them for veiling their faces the conductor may step inside if necessary for the collection of fares. The word *ḥarîm* signifies any place reserved for the exclusive use of women. It may be in a dwelling, a mosk or a railway-train, or it may apply to the group of women sitting under a tree or on the roadside or in the cemetery. This term, generally spelled *harem* in English, has no polygamous connotation in itself whatever. A man's wife, mother, sisters and daughters, as we should say collectively, *the women of the family,* are denoted by the analogous expression ḥarîm.

The great majority of travelers go afoot or astride the backs of animals. Pilgrimage opens connection with the outside world and makes the road travel take on a cosmopolitan look. The largest contingent of foreign pilgrims is that from Russia, made up of peasants, who number sometimes as high as ten thousand in one season. These are, of course, members of the Greek Orthodox Church. They are assisted by a pilgrimage society in Russia and by a system of escort and hospices within the country of Palestine. Montenegrin kawasses (cavasses) and other officers guide the parties. Arrived at Jaffa by Russian steamships, they undertake long marches afoot and show every sign of religious ecstasy at beholding the land of their desire. A few asses are provided for the infirm. Young people, particularly very young women, are not usually allowed to come. The pilgrims are for the most part middle-aged or old peasants. They live very humbly and visit the holy places with great zeal. They often march through the country singing, picking flowers and decorating with them their pilgrim staffs. The observance of Easter at the shrine in Jerusalem is the climax of such a pilgrim's errand, but additional journeys of devotion are undertaken to Nazareth, Bethlehem; also the Jordan, where the pilgrims bathe in the waters. At the Church of the Holy Sepulcher in Jerusalem all the traditions are observed and many objects of piety, as they are called, pictures, crosses and souvenirs of the Holy City, are purchased to be taken back to Russia. Some of these are carried within the tomb and laid on the venerated slab, where, for a few cents, an attendant of the church sprinkles the articles with holy water, thus giving them a permanent value as sacred treasures.

These Russian pilgrims often suffer severely when caught on the road in raw, inclement weather. Such as die in the land are counted as favored, especially if they die at Jerusalem. They thus secure burial near its sacred shrines. A large caravanserâi is provided at Jerusalem, where they set up housekeeping while in the city. On the road, hospices and the Greek churches are open to them. One's general impression is that they are well protected. They usually change their money into metliks, small Turkish coins valued at a little over a cent. In Jerusalem a number of shops cater especially for their trade. These are arranged in the sides of the street leading to the gates of the Russian Compound, within which the lodging quarters, a fine church and the administration buildings are found. They are thus enabled to hear their own language and buy tea, bread and other articles of food somewhat familiar to them.

The pilgrim business brings Russian interests to the notice of the country people. The result has generally been a favorable attitude on the part of Palestinians towards Russians. This has been helped by a generous expenditure of money for courtesies as well as in the purchase of land and the construction of buildings. Churches, schools and hospices have been erected and much land has been transferred to the Russian agents.

Other pilgrim parties arrive from different countries of Europe. The Roman Catholics from France and Austria are most numerous after the Russians. For a quarter of a century past, a large French party of tourist pilgrims has been made up each year to start from Marseilles and make the Palestine visit. The round trip costs about two hundred fifty dollars. We saw the party in May, 1901, when it numbered one hundred ninety-four. They entered the country at Haifa, drove by carriage to Nazareth and to the Sea of Galilee. Thence they rode to the top of Mount Tabor, where there is a Roman Catholic as well as a Greek monastery, and so on down through the country via Dôtân (Dothan), Samaria, Shechem, etc., to Jerusalem. The Franciscan monasteries and the hospices of other foundations give ample accommodations. The Armenians, Copts and Abyssinians, also, as well as the Greeks other than Russians, make ample provision for the entertainment of the religious pilgrims. Whenever the rightful claimants on the hospitality of these various houses do not take all the accommodations, any foreign traveler may find shelter and assistance at them. In some cases letters of introduction from the Jerusalem patriarchates are required, but these are not difficult to secure. The German hotels in the country are excellent providers for the wants of tourists.

The companies of tourists, if they are to be distinguished

from the pilgrim parties, are generally made up of Americans, English and Germans, the first mentioned being the more numerous. Tourists go in parties under the care of a director and his corps of assistants, or sometimes singly or in very small parties with a native guide. Sometimes the travelers depend on the shelter of hotels, monasteries and native houses by the way; sometimes they take a complete outfit for a tenting party. Horses are provided for the travelers, and mules for carrying baggage and equipment. Supplies are usually purchased at such starting-points as Jerusalem, Damascus, Beirut and Haifa. The peasants along the route are on the alert to sell services or beg favors.

For any extensive travel through the country an official certificate is required. Foreigners and natives must have these official papers, called *teskerehs*, which describe the bearer's person, residence and destination. They must be produced, when required, and at the destination must be stamped as a sort of permit for the return journey. Without this authorization delays are apt to occur and fines may be imposed before the defect can be remedied.

The Turkish coinage alone is sure of general acceptability in the back districts.

The different posts register parcels and sell money-orders at very reasonable rates. For sending small sums to and from the country the money-orders on the Austrian, French or German post-offices have proved the safest and cheapest way. There are forwarders whose business it is to assist in the passage of goods through the ports, and to see to customs, freights and insurance on the same. Mr. K. U. L. Breisch and the Messrs. Singer, of Jaffa and Jerusalem, do a great deal of this business for Europeans and Americans. Baggage should always be in trunks; never, if it is avoidable, cased up in boxes, as it is then very difficult to explain to the officials the difference between personal effects and merchandise. Most of the leading tourist agents, forwarders and dragomans have an understanding by which trunks are passed through the customs without opening, on payment of a small fee, especially if a considerable number of people are traveling together.

The Credit Lyonnaise and the Deutsche Palestina Bank are very much used by foreigners. Drafts on London and letters of credit are in constant use.

The consulates are retreats of great comfort in Asiatic Turkey. The complaints that are so often heard against such service in other countries are changed to praise in Syria. One may expect intelligence and consideration on the part of the official of one's own race and tongue, but one should not make unreasonable demands upon even a countryman. The United States of America and Great Britain are nobly represented by men who understand both the Western and Eastern points of view.

One traveling in the country and getting at all familiar with the people will be sought pretty surely by persons who wish to be helped to emigrate to America or some other Western country. The first impulse will be the generous one to assist such in their ambitions. But on second thought one will often reflect that it would be a doubtful kindness. The Syrian peasant, especially the Christian, who is most apt to wish to go, is surrounded by family interests and a respect that he could seldom, if ever, enjoy anywhere else. If he emigrates he usually goes alone and has chiefly in mind the earning of money. While in America he acquires little culture, being a sort of exile here, endeavoring to make and save money to take him back to live comfortably where he was born, or immersing himself for life in one of the foreign colonies of our great cities. A visit to the Syrian colonies in the American cities will convince many that the Syrian there is less attractive than in his proper and unique setting in the Holy Land. That land is to be redeemed by the vigor of its own people, not by their absence. One will notice that many of the would-be emigrants are of the best stock of Syria, very often skilful, wide-awake people, who are very valuable at home in the development of the country and among their families, but are of negligible quality and importance in another country, where foreigners are at a discount. I have in mind a strong, capable young man whose desire for emigration to America has been very earnest. He gave up a good position and made ready to start, but his wife interposed firmly. She said that she had been widowed once, having lost her first husband. According to the custom of the country, when she married again her children by the first husband had to be separated from her. She objected to losing her second husband and being left with his children, helpless to provide for them except by giving them up. So she said that if her husband would take their children along with him she would submit, but she objected to his going off on a venture of so uncertain issue and leaving his family in such a precarious condition. She prevailed, and the man remained, being fortunate enough to secure his old position. He is a respected, capable young man of large and fond family connections. His wife is industrious and skilful, his children young, healthy and favored. He has the advantage of being a somebody in his village and tribe and of setting an excellent example. Anywhere else he would be cut off from all his advantages and introduced to an appalling list of disadvantages and limitations. He would be homesick, for he loves his family. Money alone would explain his absence from them, and that would not be a sufficient cause for the unnatural condition which would be brought about. It is these good people whom their country cannot spare and whom no Western country especially needs who are most apt to have the emigration fever. Those who do not come up to this high standard are of questionable value anywhere.

APPENDIX

THE CALENDAR

In 1904, January 1, according to our Gregorian calendar, came on Friday. The Julian calendar, the one used by the Greek Orthodox Church, made this same day the nineteenth of December. According to the Moslem calendar it was the thirteenth day of the month Shawwâl, and by the Hebrew calendar, as it is read in Arabic by the Jews in Palestine, it was the thirteenth day of the month Ṭebet. For the year 1904 the correspondences of the four calendars were as given on the next page.

The following list shows the names of the months, as used by the native Arabic-speaking Christians (first column), by the Moslems (second column), and by the Jews (third column):

Kânûn ith-thâny	Shawwâl	Ṭebet
Shibâṭ	Dhû il-ḳa'dat	Shabâṭ
Âdhâr	Dhû il-ḥajjat	Âdâr
Nîsân	Muḥarram	Nîsân
Âyyâr	Ṣafar	Âyyâr
Ḥazîrân	Rabî'a il-âwwal	Sîwân
Tammûz	Rabî'a il-âkhir	Tammûz
Âb	Jumâdâ il-ûlâ	Âb
Aylûl	Jumâdâ il-âkhirat	Aylûl
Tishrîn il-âwwal	Rajab	Tishry
Tishrîn ith-thâny	Sha'bân	Ḥishwân
Kânûn il-âwwal	Ramaḍân	Kislû

The Oriental churches use the Julian calendar, while Protestants and Roman Catholics use the Gregorian. The Moslem year is a lunar year. Thus it can be understood readily that the variety of designations for any given day is considerable. Moreover, the Copts and the Armenians have methods peculiar to themselves.

		Gregorian		Julian		Moslem		Hebrew	
January	1	Kânûn ith-thâny	1	Kânûn il-âwwal	19	Shawwâl	13	Ṭebet	13
	14		14	Kânûn ith-thâny	1		26		26
	18		18		5	Dhû il-ḳa'dat	1	Shabâṭ	1
February	1	Shibâṭ	1		19		15		15
	14		14	Shibâṭ	1		28		28
	17		17		4	Dhû il-ḥajjat	1	Âdâr	1
March	1	Âdhâr	1		17		14		14
	14		14	Âdhâr	1		27		27
	17		17		4		30	Nîsân	1
	18		18		5	Muḥarram	1		2
April	1	Nîsân	1		19		15		16
	14		14	Nîsân	1		28		29
	16		16		3		30	Âyyâr	1
	17		17		4	Ṣafar	1		2
May	1	Âyyâr	1		18		15		16
	14		14	Âyyâr	1		28		29
	15		15		2		29	Sîwân	1
	16		16		3	Rabî'a il-âwwal	1		2
June	1	Ḥazîrân	1		19		17		18
	14		14	Ḥazîrân	1		30	Tammûz	1
	15		15		2	Rabî'a il-âkhir	1		2
July	1	Tammûz	1		18		17		18
	13		13		30		29	Âb	1
	14		14	Tammûz	1	Jumâdâ il-ûlâ	1		2
August	1	Âb	1		19		19		20
	12		12		30		30	Aylûl	1
	13		13		31	Jumâdâ il-âkhirat	1		2
	14		14	Âb	1		2		3
September	1	Aylûl	1		19		20		21
	10		10		28		29	Tishry	1
	11		11		29	Rajab	1		2
	14		14	Aylûl	1		4		5
October	1	Tishrîn il-âwwal	1		18		21		22
	10		10		27		30	Ḥishwân	1
	11		11		28	Sha'bân	1		2
	14		14	Tishrîn il-âwwal	1		4		5
November	1	Tishrîn ith-thâny	1		19		22		23
	9		9		27	Ramaḍân	1	Kislû	1
	14		14	Tishrîn ith-thâny	1		6		6
December	1	Kânûn il-âwwal	1		18		23		23
	9		9		26	Shawwâl	1	Ṭebet	1
	14		14	Kânûn il-âwwal	1		6		6

TIME

In Palestine villages the time of day is reckoned with reference to sunset, which is called twelve o'clock. If the sun should set at six o'clock, European time, then seven o'clock in the evening, as we should say, would be called the first hour of the night by the Arabs, and seven o'clock the next morning by our watches would be the first hour of the day according to Arab time. The two methods of keeping the time are termed, respectively, Arabi and Franji.

CHAPTER XII

FURTHER CONSIDERATIONS

DURING fifteen years, Syrian migration to western countries grew apace. Whereas the Lebanon district had been the chief loser before, Palestine now sent large quotas. Among these latter were many men from the Ramallah region. There was no freedom at home. The political, religious and economic pressure became heavier. Release in foreign countries proved enticing to thousands. Besides the itinerating venders of dry goods and the operatives in mills, there were a number of students and graduates in arts, sciences, theology, law, medicine and engineering. Syrian artists and poets as well as prosperous merchants were known. From the time that Joseph went to Egypt, Syrians of ability have prospered in foreign countries.

When the Turkish revolutions promised enfranchisement, numbers of Syrians returned to the home land only to find, after the first enthusiasm and manifestations of brotherhood, the old oppressions in new forms and an increased feeling of suspicion. The army service now became compulsory upon Christians as well as upon Moslems and certain of its conditions were odious to the newly drafted men. The government required that all schools should introduce Turkish into the course of study, but it was very difficult to find suitable teachers and to introduce them into the lower schools.

When the War came on and Turkey disallowed the capitulations matters grew worse. The Arab, always hostile to the Turk, had the sympathy of those Syrians who had any trace of Arab blood and others of more mixed race. A Syrian was loyal to his country but found it difficult to be loyal to the course of his government. He felt drawn to the Allies but was often drafted against them. After the Arab revolt there followed in due course, the deliverance of Palestine and much of Syria from thraldom to the Turk. The Turkish genius is not appropriate for Syria. The culture suitable there is one sincerely tolerant, yes better than tolerant, appreciative of the various faiths represented in the land. This culture, so far as it is schooled, should be based upon classical and scientific preparations. Syrian education has for a long time been under the guidance of western thought, whether at home or abroad, and the Syrian mind is of the character to fellowship with the West. Those who think otherwise, recalling the peculiar conditions of tyranny and corruption that have been forced on the country for a thousand years, should remember that the larger part of all the educational enterprise in Syria and Palestine, for nearly a century, has been the work of missionaries from the West. It is Syria's destiny to be practically a western country, or better, to absorb the best intellectual inheritance of the modern world. It has the physique and the brains. Has it the humility and teachableness requisite for this destiny? Has it the courage to be idealistic in the midst of the solid realistic achievements to be gained? One thing within them the past has crushed. Magnanimity must be restored in them before they can become great. If they can learn to lose themselves they will find themselves forever.

Syrians are often clever with their hands in mechanical work. Such schools as the old Schneller's orphanage for boys did a great deal of good along much needed lines. They are keen in literary and philosophical pursuits. Born linguists, excellent in such studies as law and economics, they could adorn an era of peace when once they are persuaded of a generous spirit of fair play.

Schools of all grades are needed and there is no reason,

except the slender resources of the people, why they may not be gradually established. Such schools as the Men's Training College in Jerusalem among the newer and the Ramallah Friends' (Quakers) Schools among the long established have a great opportunity. They know the problems and have good methods. But the poverty of the people would keep the vast majority of the children of the country from such institutions. Scholarships and more substantial aid is needed to help such schools accept a larger proportion of those applying for entrance. It has long been the writer's thought that such fine finishing schools as those at Ramallah, for example, should be supplemented by many elementary schools which would keep close to native customs, dress, food, etc., in the numerous small villages and which could send their choicer pupils to the advanced schools. A two or three branched scheme of education and training should take the children at twelve into classical, scientific, and technical or trade lines of development. The temptation to hasten expansion faster than the supply of good Syrian teachers can be provided, should be resisted. The teachers should be more than formally trained. They should be picked with a view to their personal character, loyalty, common sense and vision.

The British civil administration in Palestine may be said to have been fairly launched by the arrival and pronouncements of Sir Herbert Samuel in July, 1920. The first six months of his official presence have given a good impression among citizens, villagers and Arab tribes. His Excellency outlined his plans and hopes in an address on July 6. The policy of the British government in Palestine "safeguards the rights of all sections of the inhabitants of Palestine in relation to the Holy Places, to the ownership and cultivation of lands, and to all other matters in accordance with the dictates of justice." An Administrative Council with advisory functions met on October 6. Various sections of the population are represented as will be seen from this list taken from *The Palestine Weekly*.

Mr. J. B. Barron, Mr. Ben Zwi, M. Norman Bentwich, Michel Effendy Berouti, Mr. W. H. Deedes, Mr. R. A. Harari, Ismail Bey El Husseini, Colonel G. W. Heron, Colonel R. Holmes, Abdel Haj Effendy El Khatib, Mr. K. M. Kalvaresky, Mr. R. J. Legge, Sheikh Ferieh Abu Middein, Suleiman Bey Nassif, Colonel F. J. Postlethwaite, Dr. Habib Yateen Salim, Mr. E. R. Sawer, Suleiman Abdul Razzak Effendy Toukan, Mr. R. Storrs, Mr. David Yellin. All but three of this list were present and their substitutes were provided. The list was made in an effort to represent the various interests of the land, regional, religious, and economic by the best persons available for the service.

The railways are under the administration of the government. Duties connected with education, banking, land transfer, health, post-office, customs, courts, town planning, afforestation and antiquities have already been attempted by the new régime. The government schools are, so far, attended by Moslem children chiefly, since the Christians seek to safeguard religious instruction and the Jews wish to cultivate their ancient language and the national ideals. But even as things stand the government schools reach but ten or twelve thousand Moslem children out of an estimated total of over a hundred thousand. Probably the proportion of Christians and Jews in school is much better, but it will be seen how serious a problem the educational need presents.

A plan for loaning money will probably be adopted which will provide for loans on real property by the government banks. A new ordinance for land transfers has been made which is explained as follows:

"The general principle of the Ordinance is that all transactions, other than leases for a term of not more than three years, must be carried out through the Land Registry, and must receive the consent of the administration; otherwise they will be null and void, and persons disposing of, or acquiring land illegally, will be liable to fine and forfeiture of the property. The restrictions on transfers have been introduced purely in the interests of the people. The principle reason for requiring the consent of the Administration is to prevent speculation in land which will cause an excessive rise of prices and prevent development. Transactions will only be allowed if the person requiring the land will cultivate it, supposing it is agricultural land, or develop it immediately supposing it is urban land.

"Another object of the control of the Administration is to protect the small farmer in his holding. If he is the owner of land he will be unable to sell such part as is necessary for the maintenance of himself and his family; and if he is the tenant the landlord will be unable to sell without leaving sufficient land for him. The amount to be left for the small landowner will differ in various parts in the country, and will be determined according to the quality of the land by the District Governor.

"Every disposition of land will be commenced by a petition to the Governor which will be presented through the Land Registry of the District, setting out the proposed transactions. A disposition includes a sale, a mortgage, a gift, a constitution of wakf, and any lease for more than three years. The petition will be accompanied by a certificate from the Mukhtars as to the title of the transferer and by his documents of title.

"The Registrars in the district registries will give all persons desiring to dispose of their land full details as to what is required, and will furnish them with the necessary forms. If the application for the transaction is made by an agent or by nominee, the proposed purchaser must be disclosed and registration must take place in his name. Registration in the name of other persons will be invalid and will make the parties liable to penalties. The Registrar will see if the conditions of the Ordinance are satisfied and will examine the title of the transferer. If the transaction is found to be in order, it will be referred to the District Governor for his consent.

"The District Governor will give his consent only if the person acquiring the land fulfils the following conditions: (1) He must be a resident of Palestine; (2) he must not acquire land exceeding either L.E. 3000 in value or a certain area; (3) he must prove that he intends to cultivate or develop the land immediately.

"These restrictions are introduced to prevent the land being bought by speculators from outside the country and also to prevent the increase of large areas of land in a few hands. In order to prevent speculation, a further restriction is introduced, that if the land has been disposed of within a year the Governor shall not give his consent to a further disposition unless the transferer gives a satisfactory reason for wishing to dispose of it again. It would be a satisfactory reason if the original purchaser had died during the year and his heirs had to sell the property. But the restriction will prevent people from buying land simply in order to sell to others at a profit.

"The High Commissioner can consent to land transactions without any restriction, provided that he is satisfied that they will be for the public benefit. And all transactions which cannot be passed by the District Governor either because of the value and area of the land to be disposed of, or because the person acquiring is not a resident will be referred to him." Taken from *The Palestine Weekly* for October 1, 1920.

Within a few months of its inauguration the civil administration was able to report fifteen government hospitals with 293 beds, twenty-one dispensaries, eight clinics, five epidemic-posts and plans projected for combating malaria scientifically.

The new plans drawn for the suitable preservation and adornment of Jerusalem, provide that the walled city shall be safeguarded, that a parked space outside the walls shall be assured and that the most sacred spots beyond that space shall be protected in a region largely open. This last region will include Scopus, Olivet and Bethany. Expansion of suburbs beyond those preserves will be allowed in an attractive system of streets and dwellings to the north, west and south.

A new broad guage railroad has been constructed between Jaffa and Lydda. A few tractors have been introduced for use on the better agricultural land. Strikes have not been unknown. In one reported from Jaffa the government told its officers to preserve a neutral attitude in time of labor disputes, to preserve order and not to interfere with peaceful picketing.

The difficulties of the telephone service in a polyglot town may be suggested by this caricature from the "*Weekly.*"

"Our office boy has just repeated to us the kind of conversation he hears when our telephone bell happens to ring. 'Hello; that The Palestine Weekly?—Bukra subeh? Tayeb! —Ken, gevereth, ani rotzeh—Hello! Exchange! Exchange! I say, miss—aywa, aywa—buzz—aywa—Have you got them yet?—Have I the—Je vous prie, mademoiselle, tachez—shalom, mayesh = Righto, kiddie, but I don't leave till five—La, la, moush awez. Enta—alors, monsieur, demain matin, mais vous savez bien que—Oh, ring off, Please! I'm not asking for—m'a salaami—Finished yet?—I say miss, do give them another—Sapristi, mais cet instrument —Y'allah—What the—click!'

"At present we find it quicker and more private to send a postcard."

Palestine is like a sealed museum of historical lore. In the hills are stored many antiquities. It is hoped that systematic excavation will bring many of them to the surface. The Palestine Exploration Fund of London, England, is the veteran society for digging and publishing the many treasures still lying beneath the soil of the Holy Land. British and American supporters have in spite of their small number made a brave and continuous effort to gather the archæological materials which will illuminate the Bible.

The Quarterly periodical of the Fund and its annual volume keep subscribers informed of the discoveries and discussions. Since 1900, The American School of Oriental Research in Jerusalem has endeavored to make the most of opportunities to explore, study and teach the interesting data for biblical and Semitic research. It has experts in residence at Jerusalem and offers a fellowship to graduate students. It needs a budget of from twenty to twenty-five thousand dollars to make the best use of its rare opportunity to advance religious and scientific research. The new government has taken the matter of antiquities in hand in a way which will probably insure a better treatment of those who conduct research and a better disposition of the treasures as they are unearthed.

The test offered the new order by neighboring Arabia and the Arabs will be a critical one. Let us take a quick survey of this field of interest and consider some of those conditions past and present which make the Arab.

Arabia, the great south-central part of which is unknown to civilized man, is an immense peninsula hanging between the mass of the Asian continent and Africa, two spheres which have been greatly influenced by the forces issuing from the land of the Arab. The huge rectangular mass of sand and rock and tropical coasts, larger than India, slants easterly and south from the Mediterranean to the Indian Ocean and is bounded on the sides by the Red Sea and the Persian Gulf. The country has never been easily accessible to any but Arabs and it is even now a question how much of the inland territory is easily traversible by them. The desert region of North Arabia receives some rain, after which a succulent growth appears which lasts but a short time, say from a few weeks to a few months. This is probably true of some other less well known parts of Arabia. We know that oases exist, where palm-trees, wells and a settled population contrast with life on the freer steppe-land.

Broadly speaking, the people fall into two great groups, the Northern and Southern Arabs whose struggles through the centuries are based upon the two incompatibles, rapid increase and scanty sustenance. The pastures and springs do not suffice for them all. Certain tribes pay chief attention to camel breeding, others to sheep and goats, others who live near the agricultural lands even go so far as to strike bargains with the peasants to protect the crops which the latter have prepared. Certain tribes are in the transport business, using camels as carriers. Still others, not so highly regarded, are skilled in the cruder work in metal and leather, as smiths and tanners. Of all these, the camel-breeding Arab is considered the type of the true sons of the desert.

Petty war (raiding) is the ideal occupation of the best young manhood of the desert. This follows upon the mode of nomadic life. The property of a bedawy tribe is all movable and with subsistence too scanty for growing populations the nomads crowd upon each other insistently for the use of the springs and pastures. In the springtime of a good year there may be enough for all, but for most of the year the supplies of food would not go around if the population grew unchecked. No such multiplication of resources is possible as in agricultural and manufacturing countries. The produce of the herds and flocks, milk, butter, cheese, hair, and wool and a few simple fabrics made from them are used by the tribes or exchanged for the products of the oases and the towns, dates, grain, implements, ammunition, cloth and garments.

The basis of family prosperity is found in those qualities of a vigorous stock which insure success in war and the accumulation of wealth. To have many sons is, therefore, an ideal and to have them leagued together in the interest of family strength is in some degree a necessity. The simple government required is exercised by the patriarch of the family. Such a strong, growing family will be joined by other families in self-defence and will rapidly develop into a strong tribe if no untoward accident befalls it. These different families are only theoretically of one blood, though by marriage the original differences may be minimized. They are known by some common tribal name and brand their camels with a common tribal mark, or "wasm." Their greatest need, practically their religion, is the existence for which they strive. A kind of morale ensues which is the tribal convention. According to it the women have their work, often very hard, the men their duties of brotherhood, raid and revenge. Even the children have their sphere into which they fit according to sex and into which the stranger may not come at all except by the fiction of relationship. It will be readily seen that, in a land of wastes where groups only can exist and no mere individual, to be excluded by the judgment of the tribe from its membership would mean death. Such outlawing is the ultimate treatment of the serious offender. Patriotism is that higher form of self-interest which makes an Arab the devotee of his tribe's welfare. The successes, failures, quarrels and fate of the tribe are his own. The results of the raid, whether gain or loss, are shared.

The shaykh of the tribe is its leading man, not a legislator. He exerts authority by personal influence and moral suasion and cannot constrain otherwise, in theory at least, any member of his tribe. The preëminence is likely to remain in his family if it continues noble and well-to-do, a useful object of pride to the tribe. If a higher organization of the tribal life should follow upon extension of power, the leading man may become a prince or emir or even a conqueror and ruler, as on several occasions in history.

The passions of the Arab are intense. His hungry life for so large a part of the year, his picturesque imagination, and simple demands join with a chivalry born of the tribal manners to make him cultivate at once ideals of generosity and vengeful hate. To be a noble host of the wayfarer and the implacable foe of the one who has harmed him are equally demanded by his code. ʻAbd al-Malik the son of ʻAbd ar-Rahim, a poet of the Sons of Dayyan, sang:

"Like rain of the heaven are we; there is not in all our line
One blunt of heart, nor among us is counted a niggard.
We say nay whenso we will to the words of other men:
But no man to us says nay when we give sentence.
When passes a lord of our line, in his stead there rises
straight
A lord to say the say and do the deeds of the noble.
Our beacon is never quenched to the wanderer of the night
Nor has ever a guest blamed us where men meet together."
(Lyall's trans.)

In a poem by Al-Fadl (Lyall XIII) occurs the following:

"Each of us has his ground for the loathing his fellow
moves,
A grace it is from the Lord that we hate you, ye us."

Kurait, son of Unaif, poured scorn upon the people who weakly fail to avenge wrongdoing and holds up to contempt their softness in the words:

"They requite with forgiveness the wrong of those that do
them wrong,
And the evil deeds of the evil they meet with kindness and
love." (Lyall I.)

Poets form the most renowned class of men among the Arabs. Great enterprises were led by the word of the poet. To him they looked for stimulus and guidance in their raids, encampments, aspirations, disputes, loves and hates. The Arab is exceedingly sensitive to the spoken word of praise or blame. There is in him also a primitive response to the oracular, the mysterious and the magical. Speech is probably the most pretentious and commanding gift of man in early stages of culture. Even among highly civilized people it is the vehicle of the profoundest intellectual possessions and abilities. Human nature is impatient for the goods of the world. The slow process of causes has been brushed aside and resort has been had to magical means. Besides this there is the human hunger for the fairy-tale. We slip the leash of the real that we may run riot in the delights of a care-free world of the imagination. In that world the old time non-democratic spirit prevails and princes and powers and gorgeous effects are barbarously indulged. The poet is one of those who minister to us of this world of imagination.

A strong reason for the veneration which was felt for the spoken word in Arabia, as elsewhere in Semitic lands, is the innate conviction that the burden or message of the word is an entity for good or ill, independent of the human personality which serves as a medium. For it is thought that in the utterance of blessings or cursings supernatural powers seize upon the mind or the organs of speech of possessed personalities and speak effectively through them. Thus if a curse can be held back, or a blessing restrained, there is a non-existence of that fact instead of its existence to be reckoned with. The sting of satire set free by a poet's eloquence is a veritable wound more serious than a physical stab. The humiliation and despair of an early Arab who fell under the shafts of a real poet were without remedy unless there was a superior poet to wreak adequate revenge. Certain of the old poets were warriors as well and represented the complete ideal. They were hardy rangers of the desert wastes, patient, chivalrous, vindictive, devotees of the claims of blood-kinship. The flourishing period of classical Arabian poetry was during the century and a half preceding the death of Muhammad.

Muhammad was born in Mecca and spent the last ten years of his life at Medina. Both cities are in the rough highland, between the district of Nejd and the coast. This highland ridge goes by the name of the Hijaz or Barrier and is near the route of the traders' caravans from South Arabia to Syria and the Mediterranean. Mecca and Yathrib (original name of Medina) on account of this caravan route rose to be cities of prominence. Mecca was specially important because it was also a place of resort for pilgrims long before the rise of Islam. At first this may have been because of the presence there of a remarkable meteoric stone, which still remains, sheltered by the Ka'ba and venerated by the whole Moslem world. Moslem tradition began early to elaborate the traditions of Mecca and has put them beyond the disentanglement of criticism. To the Moslem, Mecca was the city of Abraham who, with all the good saints of old, was a Moslem. The Moslems claim that the Jews and Christians have so perverted the original sacred scriptures of the Old Testament and the original faith, which was the Moslem faith, that not until Muhammad's time were things seen in their true light. However, there were in Arabia in the period a little earlier than Muhammad forerunners, who were essentially monotheists, the so-called haneefs. Muhammad was, therefore, the renewer, not the inventor of Islam, the prophet to destroy the idolatries of Arabia which had accumulated in the jahiliyya, or uncivilized period. Certain members of Muhammad's own household and tribe were among his earliest converts. His wife may have been the first. He seemed, to many of his own kinsfolk and townspeople, to be a dangerous innovator. They must have feared the effect of his iconoclastic teaching on the preëminent position of their city and on the incomes derived from the pilgrimages to its shrines.

The Ka'ba itself, within which were ranged many idols, was in the special care of the prophet's tribe, the Kuraysh, which was the leading tribe of Mecca. Before the birth of the prophet a city to the south of Mecca, called Sana, had been a competing shrine but had lost prestige in favor of Mecca. All Arabs had felt a thrill of triumph in the defeat inflicted on the forces of Persia at the battle of Dhu Qar in 610 A.D. Just as the ancient Greeks had felt an increased sense of solidarity when they discovered the decline of the supposedly powerful Persia of their day through the campaign of the younger Cyrus, so now the Arabs felt relief and gathered encouragement from the revelation of Persia's weakness. Thus in the early lifetime of the prophet a number of forces, linguistic, religious and political, had joined with his sense of revelation and mission to make him an invincible leader. He was a thoroughly representative Arab, superior in mental power and religious fervor, sincere, of the order of Semitic prophets, the man for the hour in Arabia. He shrank at first from his call but was encouraged by his wife and by the devotion of a few friends and converts to go forward. He summoned the Meccans to renounce idols and to worship the one god. He was persecuted severely and would doubtless have lost his life except for his powerful family connections, which made it unsafe for his enemies to risk a blood feud. At last he took the step that made him the non-partisan apostle to Arabia and in 622 A.D., accepting the invitation of the citizens of Yathrib, he fled from his own house, where he was enduring a state of siege, and made his way to the town that was henceforth to be known as Medinet en-Neby, the Prophet's City, or in its shorter form, Medina, The City. There he waxed prosperous and used the sword of vengeance as well as of conquest. Converts came individually and in groups. He campaigned against his own home city, Mecca, conquered it and purged it of many of its grosser abuses, including the idols. He sent letters to the sovereigns of Persia and Constantinople demanding submission. In 632 A.D. he died and was buried in Medina, where his tomb is the principle treasure of the great mosk. Within seventy years of Muhammad's death his Arabs had conquered the whole of Egypt, North Africa to the Atlantic, the Spanish peninsula, and parts of India. Surely this was no ordinary man or influence that could thus turn the desert ranger into a citizen of Europe, Africa, and Asia, and turn so many provinces and kingdoms to the speech and doctrine of the Arab. Native populations in the conquered countries secured exemptions and brotherhood if they accepted the faith of Islam. Otherwise they paid tribute or were harried by the sword.

Four caliphs (successors) followed Muhammad at Medina. They kept close to the primitive ideal of the warring prophet of Islam. They were Abu Bakr, 'Umar, 'Uthman and 'Ali. They fall within the thirty years after the death of the prophet. They were followed by a dynasty of rulers of less Muhammadan characteristics which established the government at Damascus. (661–750 A.D.) They were succeeded by still a different type of rulers, the princes of the House of Abbas at Bagdad. The Damascus House, known as the Umayyads, had wrested the power from 'Ali and the Prophet's family, but their success was always resented by the more southerly Arabs and fought especially by Iraq (Mesopotamia) and the Arabs near Persia. Thus the political unity of Islam was early broken up and is less and less likely to be restored. The real strength of Islam was abroad where Arabian soldiers were quartered in camp cities or were engaged in victorious armies and where their fateful fighting qualities and intense loyalty to the missionary idea of Islam made a distinctly contrasted class as against the populations they overcame by the sword or by conversion.

In all historic times desert Arabia has been a political hollow between the great powers. It was empty of the things for which civilization fought, but it was the home of a virile stock of nomads who possessed comparative freedom at least. In the deserts the type of life has not changed for thousands of years. Such a life is free because the outsider does not covet it. The native will relinquish it only gradually. The roaming Arab is bound by the inexorable natural conditions of his world and the social conventions which those conditions impose. His treasures are his family, his horse, and his instruments of petty warfare. Before Muhammad's time, there were on the Eastern borders of Arabia princes who were practically subsidized by the Persian emperors. On the Western side were other princes under the protection of the Byzantine rulers, while in the far South were still other kingdoms and loyalties to political patrons, influenced at times by the kingdom of Abyssinia. Muhammad and his four successors gave this divided Arabia the completest unity it has ever known. At present it is reaching vaguely for something approaching that same unity. During the World War the Shereef of Mecca, with his sons, threw off the control of Turkey and made the Hijaz, which includes the sacred cities of Mecca and Medina, a free kingdom. Into this sacred land no Christian or other non-Moslem is supposed to step. Lawrence the intrepid went there to counsel with Emir Faysal, third son of the shereef, by special and dangerous arrangement. He found the Arabs resting after their initial campaign and stirred them to aggressive action, northward, to destroy the Turkish communications and to stir the more northerly Arabs to combine and to furnish support on the East and right of the operations under Allenby who was working up from Egypt through Palestine.

READING LIST

THE ENCYCLOPÆDIA OF ISLAM.

NICHOLSON: "A Literary History of the Arabs."

BROWNE: "The Literary History of Persia."

FREEMAN, E. A.: "History and Conquests of the Saracens."

MARGOLIOUTH, D. S.: "Mohammed and the Rise of Islam."

WRIGHT, W.: "Early Christianity in Arabia."

TOTAH, KHALIL A.: "Journal of Race Development." Vol. 6, No. 3. Jan., 1916 (pp. 315-323).

ALI, SYED AMEER: "Short History of the Saracens." London, 1899.

INDEX OF SCRIPTURE PASSAGES

PAGE

Gen. 8:22 22
9:6 169
15:2 63
23:11, 15 147
24:3, 4 53
24:25 135
24:60 53
24:65 57
25:34 79
27:5 168
28:2 53
29:22 59
29:26 54
29:34 54
30:14 25
30:20 54
38:18 91
43:23 161
50:3 100
Ex. 20:12 71
Num. 20:29 100
22:6 178
22:24 34
35:21 169
36:8–11 53
Deut. 4:19 123
8:8 144
11:14 25
12:2 111
14:1 100
14:21 52
15:3 52
19:21 169
21:1–9 53
22:8 70

PAGE

Deut. 22:10 136
22:23, 24 55
23:20 52
23:25 134
24:20 140
25:4 136
27:17 132
34:6 119
Josh. 4:3–5, 20 127
5:11 86
15:19 20
21:12 131
Judges 4:19 84
5:6, 7 225
5:16 142
5:25 84
6:2 16
6:11 62
12:6 173
13–15 17
19:5–8 161
21:25 225
Ruth 1:20 74
1:22 136
2:8, 9 135
2:10 163
2:14 86
2:23 136
1 Sam. 1:10, 11 117
2:12 175
7:5 38
13:5, 6 16
14:11, 22 16
16:12 47
17:28 142

INDEX OF SCRIPTURE PASSAGES

	PAGE
1 Sam. 17: 40	142
17: 43	178
19: 24	99
21: 12–15	99
23: 1	136
25: 35	161
26: 20	168
30: 6	38
30: 12	81
2 Sam. 2: 12	73
2: 29	153
3: 27	169
3: 31	100
6: 14	119
12: 16	100
18: 17	116
18: 33	100
21: 9	136
23: 4	23
23: 20	23
1 Kings 6: 23, 31–33	39
12: 18	38
17: 7	15
18: 4	16
18: 28	120
18: 43–45	24
19: 9, 13	16
20: 32	158
21: 3	142
2 Kings 3: 25	38
4: 19	95
4: 39	87
9: 17	44
17: 24–41	125
18: 26	174
20: 7	94
20: 20	22
2 Chron. 20: 7	114
Neh. 5: 4	227
5: 15	180
Job 1: 1–3	43, 131

	PAGE
Job 1: 14	133
2: 11	94
3: 1	178
4: 7	118
6: 15, 17	15
9: 33	150
21: 32	100
29: 23	25
Psalms 1: 4	137
23: 2	142
55: 17	118
55: 23	118
63: 1	133
65: 9–13	25
91	118
104: 10	16
107: 4–7	35
126: 5, 6	135
127: 3–5	53
129: 6	27
131: 2	66
144: 12–15	51
Prov. 11: 22	183
12: 27	168
13: 3	182
15: 17	182
15: 27	180
16: 15	25
18: 23	161
21: 19	182
21: 23	182
25: 16	183
25: 23	26
26: 1	24
26: 2	178
Eccl. 2: 6	21
7: 17	118
12: 5	100
Song 2: 11	22
2: 12	28
2: 15	31

INDEX OF SCRIPTURE PASSAGES

		PAGE
Song	4: 2	20
	5: 10	47
	6: 6	20
	7: 13	25
Isa.	5: 2	34, 38, 139
	5: 5	140
	5: 6	139
	5: 23	180
	9: 3	135
	28: 4	40
	28: 24, 25	133
	32: 2	28
	33: 12	35, 151
	35: 7	19
	40: 11	141
	41: 8	114
	41: 15	136
	41: 18	19
	42: 15	19
	50: 2	180
	59: 1	180
	61: 10	59
Jer.	2: 32	59
	3: 3	25
	4: 3	36, 133
	5: 24	25
	6: 16	35
	6: 26	100
	8: 20	25
	9: 17	100
	18: 17	25
	22: 18	100
Ezek.	17: 10	25
	19: 12	25
	34: 14	35
Hosea	6: 3	25
	10: 11	136
	10: 12	36, 133
	13: 3	12
	13: 15	25
Joel	2: 23	25
Joel	2: 24	136
Amos	4: 7	25
	5: 12	180
	9: 9	137
Jonah	4: 8	25
Micah	4: 12, 13	136
Hab.	1: 13	180
Zech.	8: 5	69
	10: 1	25
Matt.	3: 4	84
	3: 9	114
	4: 5	38
	4: 18	84
	5: 14	34
	5: 38, 39	169
	5: 44–46	52
	5: 47	162
	6: 5	118
	6: 30	79
	7: 19	39
	8: 14	94
	8: 28	99
	9: 15	58
	12: 1	134
	13: 3	133
	13: 25–30	135
	13: 44	157, 214
	21: 33	139
	22: 3, 4	161
	23: 7	161
	23: 27	111
	23: 37	38
	24: 20	23
	24: 41	92
	25: 32	140
	26: 23	89
	26: 73	48
	27: 25	169
	27: 53	38
Mark	4: 29	136
	5: 27	120

INDEX OF SCRIPTURE PASSAGES

	PAGE
Mark 12: 40	180
13: 18	23
Luke 1: 61	73
10: 40	92
15: 16	88
19: 2, 8	226
24: 36	161
John 4: 6	21, 125
4: 9	125
5: 8, 9	76
8: 39	114
8: 59	38
9: 7	22
10: 31	38
John 12: 13	124
12: 20	125
12: 36	175
13: 5	124
15	37
Acts 5: 15	120
19: 12	120
Gal. 3: 19	150
1 Tim. 2: 5	150
Heb. 8: 6	150
9: 15	150
12: 24	150
James 2: 23	114
5: 7	25

GENERAL INDEX

'*Abâyeh*, 142, 144.
Abraham, 114.
Abu 'Aynayn, 216.
'*Âbûd*, 224.
Abu Ghôsh, 225.
Abu Shûsheh, 17.
Alcoholics, 88 f., 98.
American College, 96; Press, 170.
Animals, wild, 31; domestic, 131, 134, 136, 153.
Antiquities, 156 f.
Arabic, 172 ff.
'*Araḳ*, 138.
Architects, 153.
Arrabôn, 154.
'*Aṣfûrîyeh*, 97.
Assessors, 226.
'*Aṭâra*, 20, 190.
'*Aujâ* river, 18.
'*Ayn el-'Aḳabeh*, 218.
„ *'Arîk*, 216.
„ *el-'Aṣfûr*, 217.
„ *el-'Azâb*, 217.
„ *el-Burj*, 200 f.
„ *Fâra*, 16, 20.
„ *el-Jâmi'*, 216.
„ *Jeriyût*, 21.
„ *Ḳânyeh*, 192.
„ *el-Ḳaṣr*, 201.
„ *Kefrîyeh*, 21.
„ *el-Kusa'*, 217.
„ *Minjid*, 201.
„ *Miṣbâḥ*, 196, 201.
„ *Mizrâb*, 201.
„ *en-Nuṣbeh*, 20, 190.
'*Ayn Râs el-Bîr*, 217.
„ *esh-Shaykh*, 217.
„ *Sînyâ*, 223.
„ *Ṣôba*, 216.
„ *eṭ-Ṭoreh*, 217.
„ *Umm el-Kerzam*, 201.
„ *Yebrûd*, 115.

Bâb el-Wâd, 107.
Baggage, 227, 236.
Bairam, 121.
Balû'a, 19, 196.
Bâmyeh, 82.
Banks, 227, 237.
Banners, 119.
Baptism, 66.
Bargaining, 146, 154.
Baṭn el-Hawâ, 200.
Bayt Ḥanînâ, 189.
Baytûnyeh, 199.
Beads, 117.
Bedawîn, 43, 130, 221.
Bethel, or *Baytîn*, 217 f.
Betrothal, 55.
Bigamy, 63.
Birds, 31 f.
el-Bîreh, 191, 207 f.
Birth, 65.
Bîr ez-Zayt, 223.
Blacksmithing, 155.
Blind, 96, 172.
Blood revenge, 169.
Booths, 76.
Boundaries of the village, 192.
Bread, 79.
Bribery, 108, 180, 227, 229.

GENERAL INDEX

Bubonic plague, 231.
Building material, 151 f.
Burghul, 79.
Burj, 44, 200; *Baytîn*, 218.
Business, 130 ff., 209.
Butcher, 146, 195. [See Work.

Cactus, 88.
Calendar, 124, 239.
Calls, 160, 204.
Camels, 12, 136, 155.
Carmel, Mt., 15.
Carob pod, 88.
Carriage service, 154.
Cavasses, 233.
Caves, 16 ff., 217; sanctuary, 196.
Charms, 93.
Children, 64, 66 f., 69; childlessness, 208.
Cholera, 103 ff., 231.
Church influence, 45.
Church law, 59, 63.
Church Missionary Society, 197, 221 ff.
Church, old, at *el-Bîreh*, 113.
Church, old, at *Râm Allâh*, 113.
Church, old, at *eṭ-Ṭayyibeh*, 113.
Circassians, 227.
Cisterns, 21, 75, 222; grain, 137; oil, 195.
City, appearance of a, 33, 43.
Clothing, see Dress.
Coffee, 81 f., 160, 164.
Colloquialisms, 176 ff.
Common dish, 89; cup, 82, 164.
Complexions, 47.
Compliments, 206.
Consular service, 227, 237.
Conversation, 159 f, 165.
Court, house, 76; law, 229.
Crier, public, 149.
Crocodile, 31.
Crusaders' Church, 210.
Culture, 170.
Cup, common, 82, 164.
Curses, 178.
Customs, see Birth, Weddings, Death, etc.
Customs, tariff, 237.

Dabkeh, 168, 186.
Dâfûr, 81.
Daḳḳîḳ, 153.
Dancers, 59; dancing, 168.
Dâr, 51.
Dayr Dîwân, 218.
Deaconesses (*Kaiserswerth*), 83.
Dead Sea, 18.
Death, 99 f., 103, 164 f.
Deeds, land, 192.
Demons, 98.
Dervish, 118.
Dhurah, 133, 219.
Dialectical matters, 173 ff.
Dibbûsy, 142.
Dibs, 81, 138.
Disease, 95, 231.
Dish, common, 89. See Cup.
Dôsh, 167.
Dress, 49, 90 ff.
Drinking customs, 89.
Dry season, 20, 23 ff., 36.
Dumb, 96, 112, 192.
Dûrah, 219.
Dust, 95.

Earthquake, 202.
Easter, 123 f.
Eating customs, 89.
Education, 170.
Effendîyeh, 225.
Elders, 52.

Eli and Sibyl Jones Mission, 197. See Friends.
Emigration, 228 f., 237.
Entertainment, 164, 167.
Esdraelon, 15.
Evening scenery, 12, 190.
Evil-eye, 116.
Exclamatory remarks, 176 ff.; with animals, 134.
Eyes, 47, 94.

Family, 53.
Famine, 107, 109.
Farming, 39, 130, 133.
Fast, *Ramaḍân*, 121; Lenten, 124.
Fatalism, 104, 117.
Feast of St. Barbara, 124; The Cross, 27, 124; St. George, 124.
Feddân, 132.
Fees of priests, 122.
Fellaḥîn, 131.
Ferns, 30.
Feuds, 159, 222.
Fevers, 94.
Figs, 28, 40 f., 81, 139; plaster, 94.
Fines, 229.
Finjân, 82, 160.
Fire-wood, 39.
Flocks, 26, 36, 140.
Flowers, 28 ff.
Foods, 78 ff., 82, 85.
Fountains, 20 f., 190, 196, 200 f., 216 ff., 223.
Foxes, 31.
Friendship, 52.
Friends' Mission and School, 191, 193, 197.
Friends' Mission at 'Ayn 'Arîk, 217.
Friends' Mission at Jifnâ, 222.
Friends' Mission at *eṭ*-Ṭayyibeh, 221.
Frîky, 25, 86.
Fruit, 28, 36, 41, 86.
Fuel, 79, 211.
Furniture, 76 f.

Game, wild, 84.
Games, 70 f., 167.
Gardening, 144, 145, 216.
Garments, wedding, 55.
Gazels, 31.
Geology, 14.
Gerizim, Mt., 126.
Ghôr, 13, 15, 221.
Gipsies, 155, 168.
Girls, 64 f., 67.
Goats, 140 f.; goat-meat, 195.
Go-between, 150.
Gospel and *Ḳurân*, 123.
Gossip, 160.
Government of country from city, 225 f.
Graffiti, 210.
Grain, 133 f.
Grapes, 36 f., 138.
Graves, 18, 99, 103; Samaritan, 126.
Greek Church, 122, 204 f.
Greek fire, 124.
Greetings, 161 ff.
Groceries, 145.
Guest-room or house, 59, 164.

Hail-storm, 202.
Hanauer, Rev. J. G., 176.
Ḥarâm, 214.
Ḥarîm or harem, 120, 233.
Harvest, 25, 135 f.
Head-dress, 91. See Dress.

GENERAL INDEX

Health conditions, 27. See Disease.
Heat, 12, 23.
Ḥelâweh, 87.
Ḥennâ, 59.
Hermon, Mt., 32.
Hills, 14, 39.
Hill sites, 34, 44, 48, 222.
Ḥirdhôn, 31, 179.
Ḥishis, 31.
Ḥiṣrim, 81.
Home affairs, 75 ff.
Honey, 87.
Hospices, 234.
Hospitals, 89, 96.
Hospitality, 160, 165.
Hotels, 235.
Household tasks, 91; utensils, 77 ff.
House structure, 75, 211.
Ḥûleh, 18.
Ḥummus, 137.
Hunting, 168.
Hyenas, 18, 99.

Illness, 27, 94.
Insane, 96 ff., 99, note.
Insects, 31.
Interest, 149, 205.
Invitations, 161.
Irrigation, 22.

Jars, 93.
Jeba', 16.
Jebel Ṭawîl, 32, 210.
Jellies, 86.
Jerîsheh, 79.
Jerusalem, view of, 33.
Jewelry, 54, 59.
Jezreel, 15.
Jiben, 84.
Jifnâ, 222.

Kalîyeh, 86.
Ḳaṣr, 139.
Ḳaṭrawâny, 111.
Ḳays, 225.
Kefrîyeh, 201.
Kefr Shiyân, 216.
el-Khalîl, 113.
Khân, 194, 209.
Kharayṭân, 16.
Khaṭîb, 171, 186.
Khurbet Jîbya, 224.
Kilns, 151.
Kinship, 158, 230.
Khulleh, 196.
Khullet el-'Adas, 200, 215.
Khûry, 122, 205.
Ḳurân and Gospel, 123.
Kursenneh, 135.
Kushân, 192.

Labor, 91.
Lakes, Ḥûleh, Tiberias and the Dead Sea, 18.
Lamps, clay, 111 ff.
Land, holding, 131.
Lane's "Manners and Customs of the Modern Egyptians," 119.
Language, 166, 172 ff.
Learning, 47, 170.
Leaven, 78.
Leben, 84.
Leeches, 95.
Lemons, 28.
Lentils, 79.
Lepers, 99.
Lime, 151; kilns, 35 f.; stone, 15.
Literary work, 170.
Lizards, 31.
Loans, 149.
Locusts, 84.
Looms, 144.

Maḥshy, 85.
Maiden-hair fern, 17, 30.
Maḳâm, 111.
Maḳlûbeh, 85.
Male children, 63.
Ma'lûf, 141.
Mandrake, 25.
Marâmîyeh, 81.
Maritime Plain, 15.
Mâr Jurjus, 114; *Elyâs*, 115.
Markets, 145, 155 f., 194.
Marriage, 49, 53 f.
Masons, 151; marks, 210.
Meals, 89.
Measures and weights, 147.
Meat, 84, 195.
Medical data, 94, 96.
Merchants, 194.
Michmash, 16.
Midwife, 66.
Mikhba, 139.
Miḳlâ', 70.
Mil'ab, 56.
Milk, 26.
Minsaf, 166.
Mîreh, 131.
Mists, 11 f., 24, 135.
Mitchell, Professor H. G., 176.
Molasses, 138.
Monasteries, 125.
Money, 147, 155, 230; changing, 148; lending, 149, 205.
Montenegrins, 233.
Months, Christian, Jew and Moslem, 239.
Mortar and pestle for coffee, 82.
Mosks, 113 f.; Mosk of Omar, view, 189.
Mourners, 100, 103, 164 f.
Mudîr, 226.
Muezzin, 119.
Muḳâṭ'a 'Âbûd, 224.
Mukhtâr, 151.
Mulberry, 28, 223.
Mules, 220.
Mulk, 131.
Mûṣ, 27, 137.
Muzzling animals, 136.

Names, 66, 72 ff.
Nârjîleh, 166.
Nâ'uṣ, 27.
Neby Mûsâ, 119.
Neby Ṣâliḥ, 224.
Neighbors, 159, 198.
News, 231.
Nicknames, 74.
Nights, 23.
Noah's Cave, 17.
Nomads, 130.
Noon heat and rest, 12.
Nuts, 86.

Oak, 28.
Officials, 230.
Oil, 80 f., 140.
Old Testament sites, 117.
Olive press, old, 213.
Olives, 28, 39 f., 80, 140, 223.
Omens, 202.
Oranges, 25, 28, 144.
Orphans, 172.
Ovens, 78.

Palmer, Professor E. H., cited, 213.
Parched wheat, 86.
Parents, titles of, 66.
Parties, 159.
Partnership in crops, 221.
Passes, 15, 226.
Pastures, 36.
Paths, 35, 154.

GENERAL INDEX

Patriarchates, Greek, 122.
Peacemaking, 228 f.
Pear-trees, 223.
Periodical literature, 170.
Peters, Dr. John P., 216.
Philosophy. See Proverbs, Stories, etc.
Phrases, 161 ff.
Pilgrims, 232 f., 235; Moslem, 111, 120; Roman Catholic, 225.
Pine-trees, 28.
Place-names, 174.
Plasters, 94.
Play, 68, 70, 167 f.
Plowing, 39, 133.
Pomegranates, 28, 41.
Ponds, 19.
Population, 43 f., 47.
Portents, 202.
Postal service, 227, 230 f.
Pottery, 93.
Prayer, 203; in sickness, 93; to Abraham, 114; Moslem, 118 f.; for offspring, 117; of women, 114; for rain, 202.
Press, 231; American, 170.
Prices, building materials, 151; food, 146.
Priesthood, Christian, 121 f.
Priests, 204.
Printing, 170.
Proverbs, 52, 83 f., 87, 89, 94, 116, 176, 179 ff.
Pruning, 139.
Public weal, 149 ff., 193, 230.
Punishment, 226.

Quaker Mission. See Friends.
Quarantine, 105, 107, 137, 231 f.
Quarrels, 168 f., 227 ff.
Quarry at *el-Bîreh*, 210.
Quarrying, 151.
Quartering of soldiers, 227.

Rabâb, 164.
Rafîdya, 209.
Railway, 232 f.
Rain, 23 f., 27.
Rainfall, 22.
Rain-water, 222.
Rats, 122.
Raisins, 138 f.
er-Râm, 190.
Ramaḍân, 121.
Râm Allâh, 187, 191 ff.; settlement of, 206; schools, 171.
Reaping, 25, 135.
Refreshments, 86, 160.
Religion, 43 ff., 110 ff., 117; as a social factor, 158.
Remedies, 94.
Reservoirs, 21, 210.
Revenge, 169.
Reverence, 71.
Rice, 80.
Ridicule, fear of, 90.
Rimmon, 220.
Rivers, Jordan, 18; *'Aujâ*, 18.
Roads, 34, 154 f., 189, 223; to Râm Allâh, 187.
Road scenes, 46.
Robinson, Professor Edward, cited, 221.
Rock cuttings, 17, 217.
Rocks, 116, 145.
Roman Catholic Church, 122, 124, 235.
Roman roads, 34, 189.
Roofing-bee, 116.
Roofs, 27, 75.
Rooms, 75.
Rugs, 144.

Ruins, 18, 21, 190f., 210, 213 f., 216, 222.
Rûjib, 127.
Russian influence, 235; pilgrims, 204, 233 f.

Ṣahjeh, 168, 184.
Salâ't eṭ-Ṭîreh, 213.
Salt, 146.
Salutations, 161 ff.
Samaritans, 125 ff.; passover of, 127 ff.
Samson country, 17.
Sanctuary, 113 f. See Shrines.
Scenery, 12, 20, 32.
Schneller's school, 172.
School at el-Bîreh, 211.
Sea, 232.
Seasons, 22.
Sects, 84.
Sha'fât, 189.
Shaykh, 150.
Shaykh Sâliḥ, 210.
Shaykh Yûsuf, 222.
esh-Shayṭân, 209.
Sheep, 57, 59, 140.
Shephelah, 19.
Shepherd, 141 f.
Shipping, 232.
Shôbek, 206.
Shoes, 90.
Shops, 145, 195.
Shrines, 38, 41, 111 ff., 117, 210, 234.
Sickness. See Disease, Medicine, etc.
Sifting, 137.
Sîjeh, 167.
Silk, 144.
Sirocco, 11, 25 f.
Sḳîfeh, 204, 211.
Slings, 70.
Smîd, 79.
Smoking bottles, 76.
Ṣnôber, 80.
Soap, 81.
Sociability, 164.
Society, 158 ff.
Soil, 15, 18.
Soldiers, 126, 149 f., 227, 229 f.
Song, 168, 184 ff.; at weddings, 56, 60 f.; of mourners, 101 ff.
Souvenirs, 234.
Spinning, 143.
Springs, 16, 20, 24; warm, 21. See 'Ayn.
Spring-water, 222.
St. George, 114, 202.
Stones, 18, 38.
Stone trades, 151.
Stores, 145.
Stories, 17 f., 20, 68, 83, 88, 111, 166, 171, 176, 179, 205, 214, 228.
Stranger in village, 132, 164.
Sugar, 146.
Sûḳ, 145.
Summer, 36.
Superstitions, 93 f., 98, 114, 116 f., 202, 213 f., 220.
Ṣurdah, 115.
Sûs, 80.
Swaddling, 66.
Sweetmeats, 86 f.
Syria, future of, 228.
Syrian Protestant College, 96.
Syrians in America, 237.

Talebearing, 230.
Ṭarafîdya, wâdy and *'ayn*, 199.
Tares, 135.
Ṭarîḳ el-Majnûny, 199.
Tattoo, 117.
Taxes, 144, 146, 150, 192, 226 f.

GENERAL INDEX

eṭ-Ṭayyibeh, 221.
Telegraph, 231.
Terrace, 38 f.
Thief, 64.
Thorns, 35.
Threshing, 136 ff.
Tiberias, 18.
Tibn, 137.
Tibneh, 224.
Time of day, 241.
eṭ-Ṭîreh, 213.
Tobacco, 146, 164, 166.
Tomatoes, 82.
Tombs, old, 112, 157, 215, 219, 222 ff.
Tools, stoneworkers', 152 f.
Topographical remarks, 13, 19, 32 f.
Ṭoṭleh, 81.
Tourist agent, 236 f.
Tourists, 225.
Traders, 145 f., 194.
Trade school, 172.
Trades, crafts, etc., 155.
Training of children, 67 f., 71 f.
Transportation, 154, 194, 236.
Travel, 28; afoot, 153; carriage, 154; general, 226, 232, 236.
Treasure, 214.
Trees, 14, 27 f., 41, 223; sacred, 115 f., 219.
Tribes, village, 51.
Turkish Delight, 88.
Typhoid, 95.

'Ûd, 164.
Ukhtiyarîyeh, 135.
Umm Barakât, 116, 219.
Umm el-Khuruḳ, 216.
United Greek Church, 125.
Urṭâs, 41, 145.
Utensils, household, 77 ff.

Valley, 15. See Wâdy.
Vegetables, 82 f.
Vermin, 31.
View from Jebel Ṭawîl, 32.
View from Râm Allâh, 189 f.
View from eṭ-Ṭayyibeh, 221.
View of Jerusalem from Scopus, 188.
View of Râm Allâh, 214.
Views of the Mediterranean, 223.
Village ideals, 51.
Villagers, appearance of, 47.
Villages, appearance of, 33, 43.
Villages, various, 187.
Vine culture, 139, 222.
Vineyards, 13; near Râm Allâh, 200.

Wâdy, 15; those near Râm Allâh, 199.
Wâd Karom Shutâ, 200.
Wâdy 'Arâḳ el-Kharâf, 219.
„ *el-'Ayn*, 220.
„ *eḍ-Ḍaba'*, 220.
„ *Fâra*, 16.
Wâdy el-Kelb, 199.
„ *Rayyâ*, 224.
„ *Sha'b el-Ḳassîs*, 220.
„ *es-Suwaynîṭ*, 16, 210.
Wages, 207.
Wakf, 181.
Walls, 34, 194.
Washing clothes, 92, 209.
Wastîyeh, 116, 219.
Watcher in vineyard, 13; on threshing floor, 136.
Watch-towers, 38, 139.
Water carrying, 68; supply, 20, 22, 222.
Watershed, 19, 191.
Weather, 23, 155.

Weddings, 56 ff.
Wedding songs, 60 ff.
Weeping, 165.
Weights, 147.
Wells, 21.
Wheat and barley, 78, 133, 137.
Widows, 54, 64.
Wilderness, 35.
Wild vegetation, edible, 87 f.
Wily, 111.
Winds, 26, 222.
Winter, 22, 24, 28.
Wives, 54, 58, 63.
Women, 47 ff.
Wool, 142.
Work, 207; woman's, 53, 92.
Writing, 175.

Yâzijy, Shaykh, 170.
Yemen, 159, 225.

Zaghârût, 57.
Zâky, 87.
Zawân, 135.
Zinzilakt, 28.
Zukzâkeh, 27.

www.ingramcontent.com/pod-product-compliance
Lightning Source LLC
Chambersburg PA
CBHW071230230426
43668CB00011B/1376
* 9 7 8 1 5 9 7 5 2 2 7 2 4 *